IMAGES
*of America*

# FRANKLIN

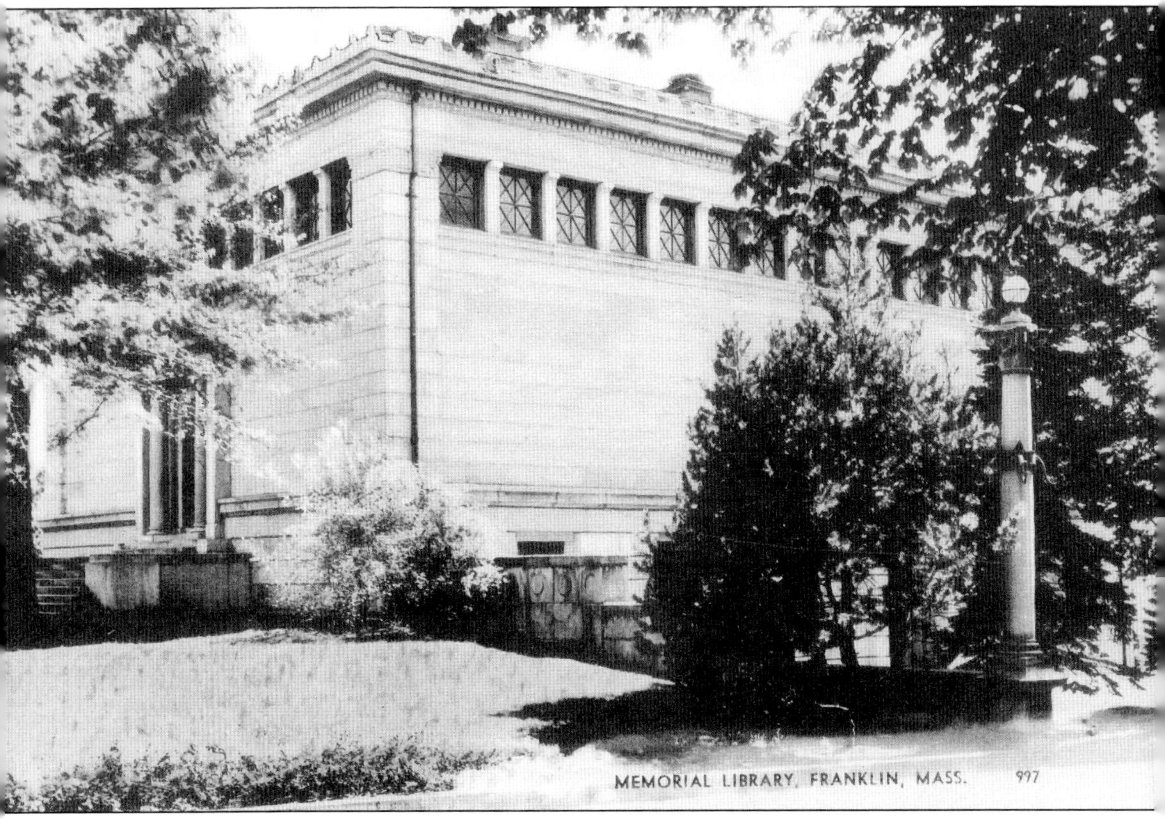


The Ray Memorial Library is a work of art. The interior is lavishly decorated with murals by Tommaso Juglaris, landscapes of heroic size by Henry Hammond Gallison, and tons of marble, red mahogany, and bronze. The building was supervised by Rand and Skinner and was constructed of Milford granite.

IMAGES
*of America*

# FRANKLIN

James C. Johnston Jr.

ARCADIA
PUBLISHING

ISBN 978-0-7385-8848-3

Published by Arcadia Publishing
Charleston, South Carolina

Printed in the United States of America

For all general information contact Arcadia Publishing at:
Telephone 843-853-2070
Fax 843-853-0044
E-mail sales@arcadiapublishing.com
For customer service and orders:
Toll-Free 1-888-313-2665

Visit us on the Internet at www.arcadiapublishing.com

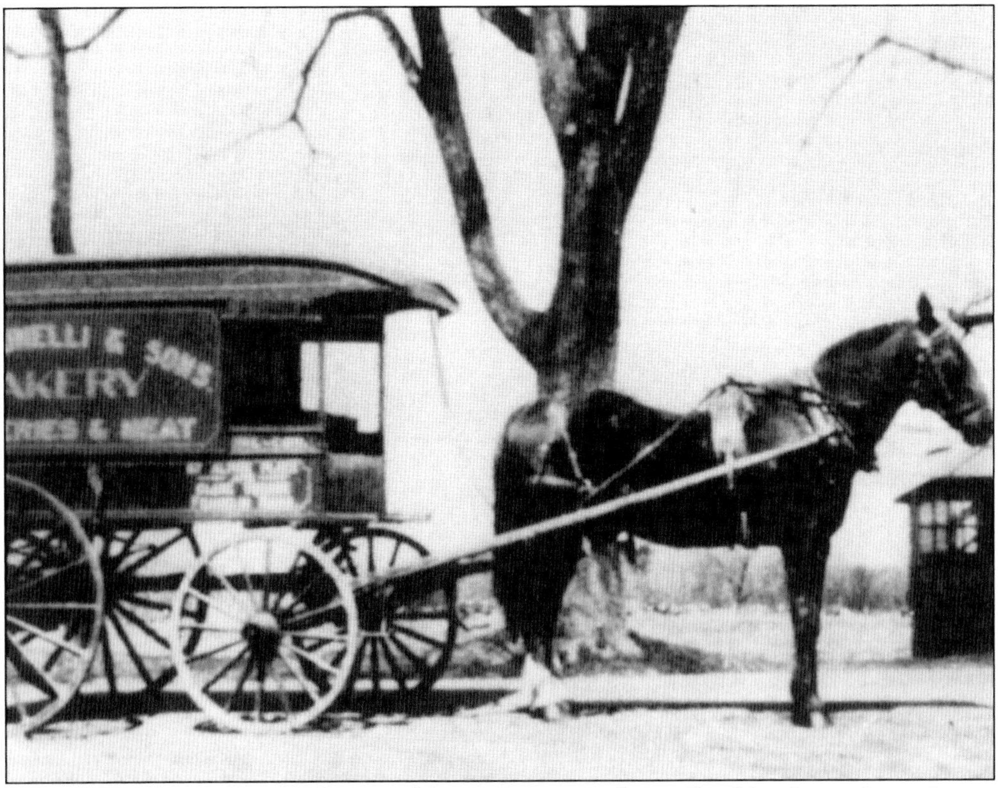

Franceso P. Brunelli's horse and wagon delivered groceries all over Franklin during the early part of the century.

# Contents

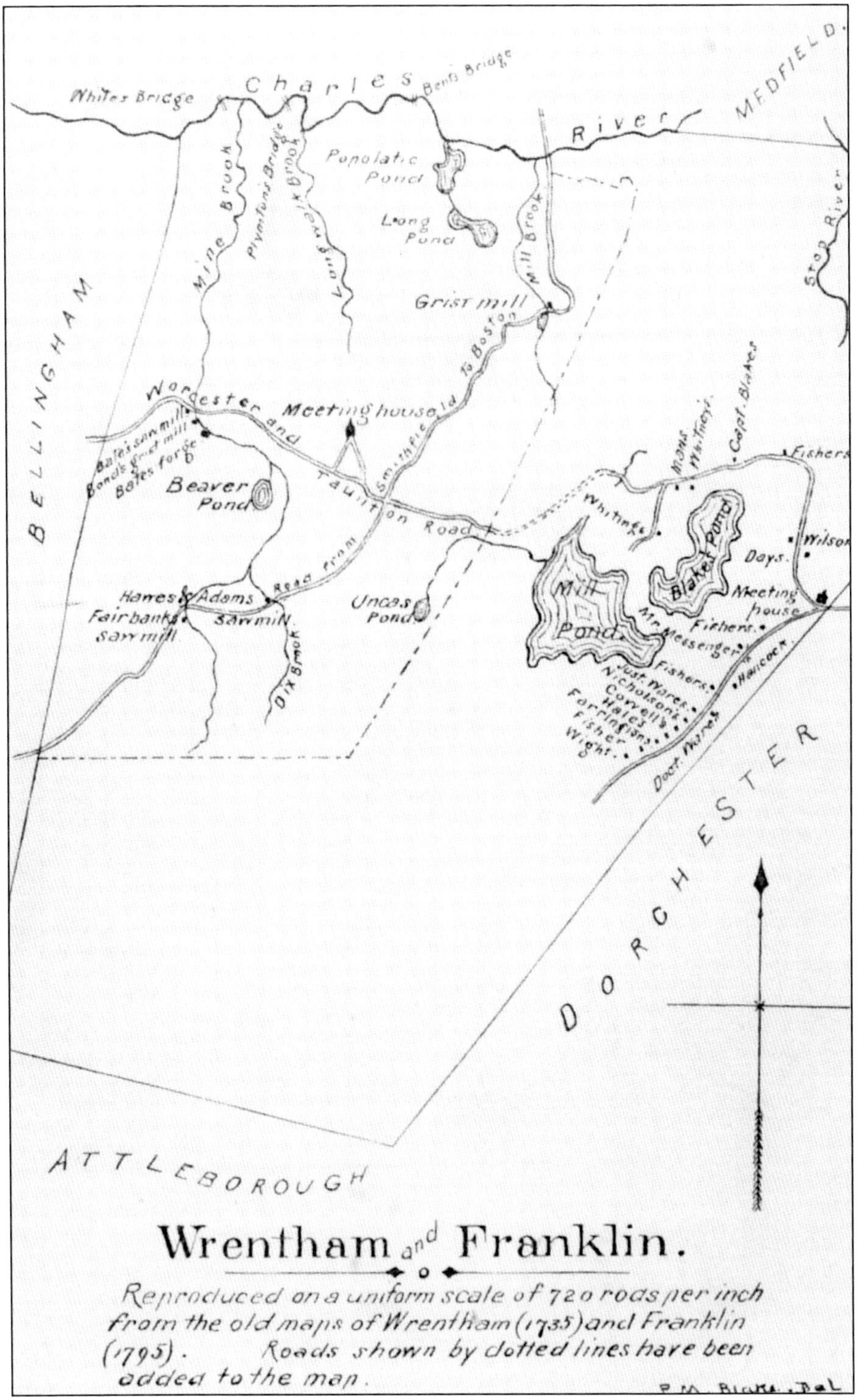


This map was used in Blake's *History of Franklin* (1878). It shows Franklin when it was part of Wrentham from 1673 to 1778. Franklin came into its own as a town on March 2, 1778.

# Introduction

Franklin, Massachusetts, was carved out of the granite face of New England by the great Pleistocene glacier. The rocky soil deposited by the retreating glacier became the land of the Wampanoag, deeply forested and green, dotted by lakes, and framed to the north by the Charles River.

The first European settlers in Franklin were a product of the 1630 Puritan migration to Massachusetts Bay. In 1636, the Puritan town of Dedham was founded. In 1673, Wrentham broke away from Dedham, and Franklin, in turn, broke away from Wrentham on March 2, 1778.

The principal reason new towns grew out of the older communities was the role the Puritan Church played in Massachusetts. Massachusetts was a theocracy, or Bible state, where the law of the church was the law of the land and all were required to attend divine service on Sunday. As populations moved away from a Yankee town center a new Congregational parish would be founded, and a new town would evolve. Such was the case with Franklin. In 1738, a new Congregational church was founded, and during the American Revolution, Franklin was born as a distinct and independent political entity.

Franklin was originally to be called Exeter, but the town fathers thought that they could flatter Benjamin Franklin, the most famous man in America, into giving the town a bell for the new Congregational church by naming the town after him. Franklin was not taken in by this bit of flattery; he remarked in a letter at the time that, "Sense is preferable to sound," and made a gift of books to the town instead. Franklin was the first town named for that great man in America.

Franklin's gift arrived in 1786 and was given into the care of the Congregational minister, Nathaniel Emmons, who became the town's first librarian. Emmons only allowed the books to be used by members of his church, however, until 1791, when the selectmen ordered him to allow all of the town's citizens the use of the "Franklin Books" on an equal basis, thus making Franklin's library the oldest public library in the United States.

The great historic events of the Colonial and post-Revolutionary eras were reflected in Franklin's history. The Battle of Indian Rock, during King Philip's War; Captain Oliver Pond and Captain Jabez Fisher's companies of Minutemen in the American Revolution; and Franklin's contribution in putting down Shay's Rebellion, all impacted Franklin's history.

There was no shortage of great men born in Franklin of national or international reputation. Horace Mann, the "Father of American Education," was born here in 1796. He is considered one of the greatest reformers in a period of great reform movements. James Nason, the inventor of the coffee percolator, was a Franklin man, as was Albert D. Richardson, author and Grant biographer.

George Smalley, along with Richardson, invented the profession of war correspondent during the Civil War. Both men were professionally admired by and worked for Horace Greeley. Smalley became the "Dean of the American Press Corps" and knew everybody from Abraham Lincoln to young Winston Churchill. He was both bureau chief for the *New York Times* in London and the *London Times* in Washington during his long and distinguished career.

Franklin men served in all of the nation's major wars and conflicts. During the Civil War, some were imprisoned in the Andersonville and Libby Prisons. Major Eddie Grant, a son of Franklin, Dean College, and Harvard, became a great baseball hero, playing with the Philadelphia Phillies, the Cincinnati Reds, and the New York Giants; tragically, he was killed in the Argonne Forest while looking for the lost battalion in World War 1. "Harvard Eddie Grant" was the only major league ballplayer killed in the war.

The great western artist Charles Adams was born in Franklin in 1858. He lived a long, full, and creative life, dying in Hollywood in 1942. Franklin is also the home of many living writers, including William Christie, author of *The Warriors of God.*

Franklin enjoyed an industrial revolution that began with hat production in the 1790s and then boomed with the manufacture of textile machinery, pianos, and dozens of other enterprises in the Victorian era. This, in turn, resulted in the creation of an upper class, which built many of the great Victorian mansions in town.

Irish, Italian, and Russian Jewish immigrants of the nineteenth and early twentieth centuries gave great ethnic diversity to the town by 1900. The architecture of the town is also rich in Colonial, Federal, Victorian, Edwardian, Roman, and Spanish Colonial buildings.

The town has boomed from a population of 7,200 in 1928, the year of Franklin's sesquicentennial, to some 26,500 people today. Most of the people who have moved into Franklin over the past few decades live in one of the more than thirty beautiful developments, or in one of the well-kept older neighborhoods. The Horace Mann Museum, the beautiful campus of Dean College, the Franklin Public Ray Memorial Library, and the historic Oliver Pond House are only a very few of the many landmarks of this vital community.

The engravings, photographs, and postcards gathered in this book have been collected by Mrs. Edward M. Wallace, Mrs. Clara J. Johnston, and the author for the purpose of historic preservation. It is our pleasure to share them with you, the reader.

# *One*

# From the Beginning

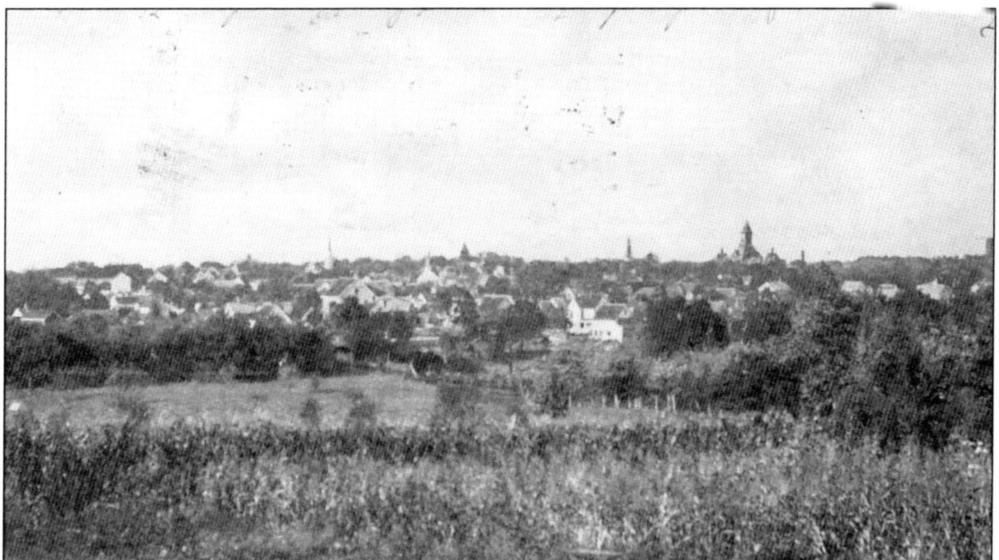

This turn-of-the-century photograph shows a panoramic view of Franklin. Dean Hall is the tallest landmark. The tower on Dean Hall would fall victim to the great Hurricane of 1938.

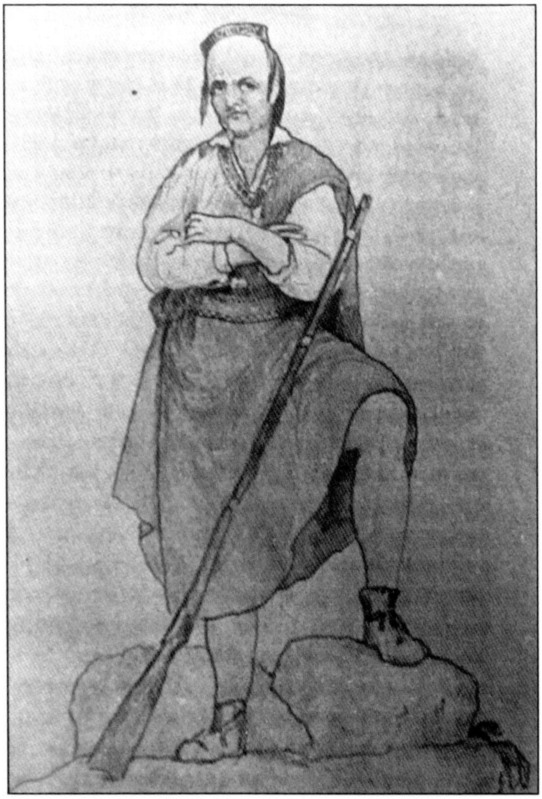

King Philip, whose real name was Metacomet, is pictured in a "Holland Shirt." He made war on the colonists in 1675, and his forces met defeat in Franklin at the Battle of Indian Rock. Philip was killed the following year at Mount Hope.

This old print of King Philip's War caught the spirit of the time. Wrentham, including Franklin, was abandoned during the war.

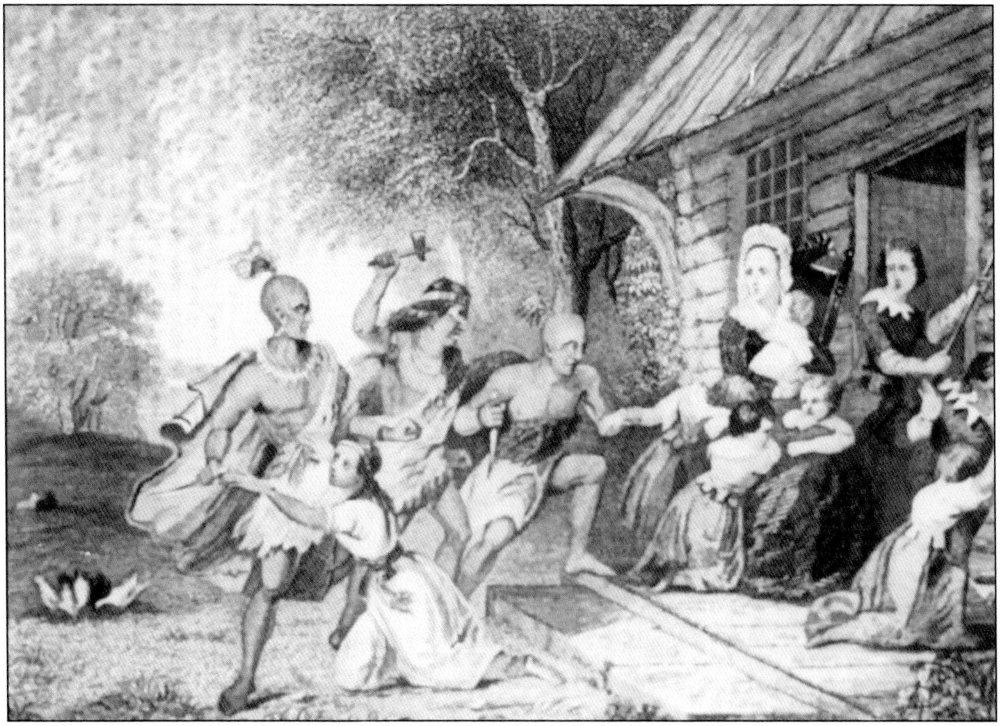

This historic site, Indian Rock, was where Franklin held its 1823 Fourth of July banquet and town celebration. It was here that the Battle of Indian Rock was fought during King Philip's War.

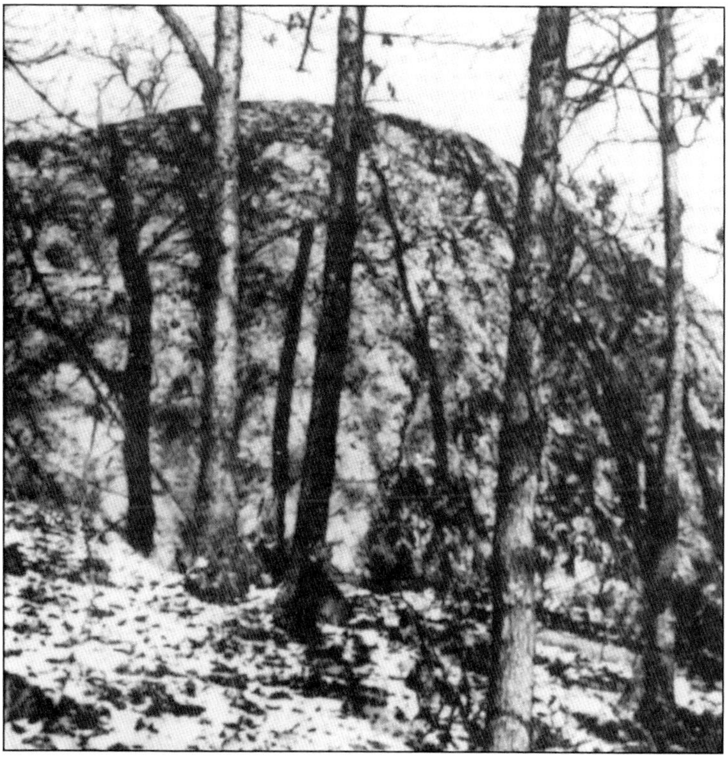

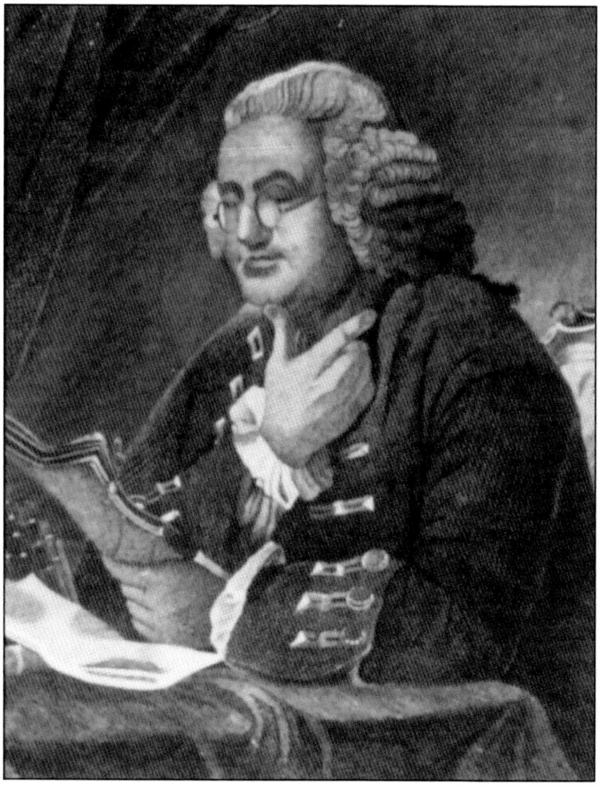

Benjamin Franklin was America's most famous citizen in 1778 and one of the richest as well. The leaders of the new town of Franklin thought that they could flatter the great man into purchasing a new bell for the town. Franklin gave them books instead, with the advice that "Sense is better than sound."

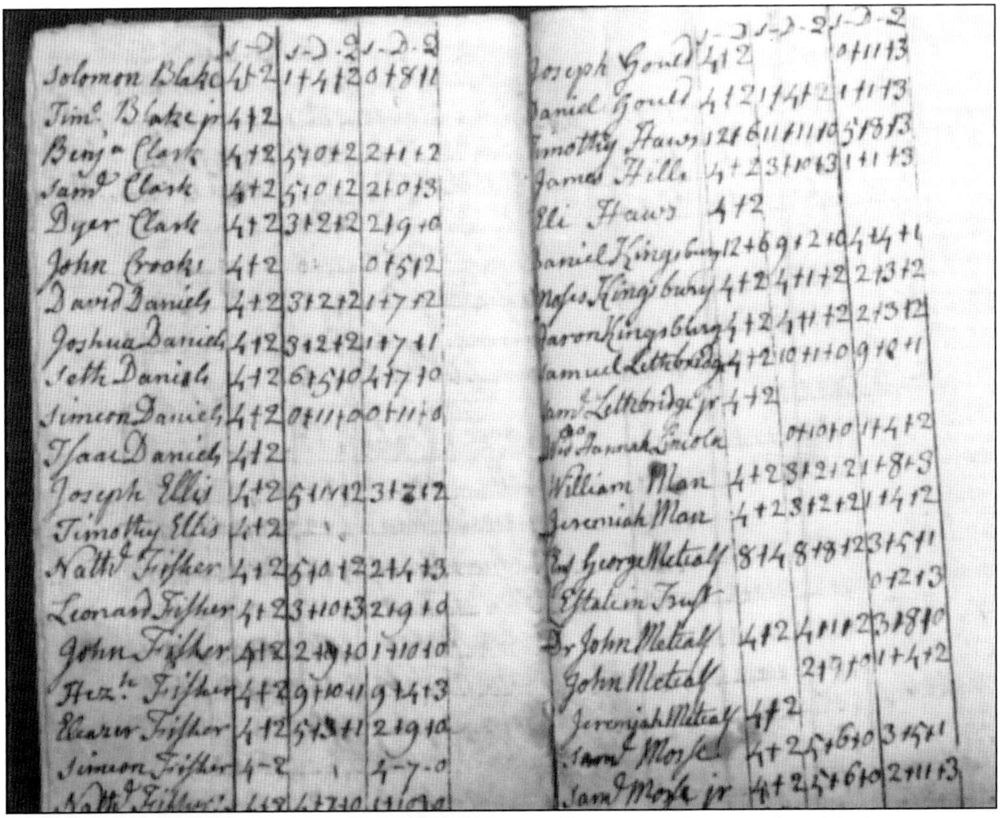

Solomon Blake
Tim. Blake jr
Benj. Clark
Saml. Clark
Dyer Clark
John Crooks
David Daniels
Joshua Daniels
Seth Daniels
Simeon Daniels
Isaac Daniels
Joseph Ellis
Timothy Ellis
Nathl. Fisher
Leonard Fisher
John Fisher
Hezh. Fisher
Eleazer Fisher
Simeon Fisher

Joseph Gould
Daniel Gould
Timothy Haws
James Hills
Eli Haws
Daniel Kingsbury
Moses Kingsbury
Aaron Kingsbury
Samuel Lethbridge
Saml. Lethbridge jr
Wd. Hannah Lincoln
William Man
Jeremiah Man
Revd. George Metcalf
Estate in Trust
Dr. John Metcalf
John Metcalf
Jeremiah Metcalf
Saml. Morse
Saml. Morse jr

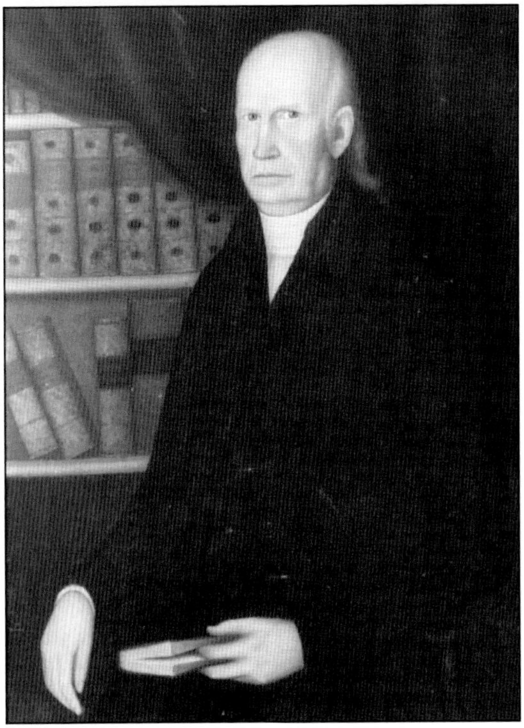

These records not only told what you owed the town for taxes, but they also indicated where you would sit in church. The more money and land you had the closer your pew would be to the front of the meetinghouse. This was a practical application of the Puritan belief in predestination.

Dr. Emmons (1746–1840) dominated the church and intellectual life of Franklin from 1773 until his death in 1840.

These books were given to the town by Benjamin Franklin in 1786. They formed the basis of the Franklin Town Library, which may be the oldest public library in the United States.

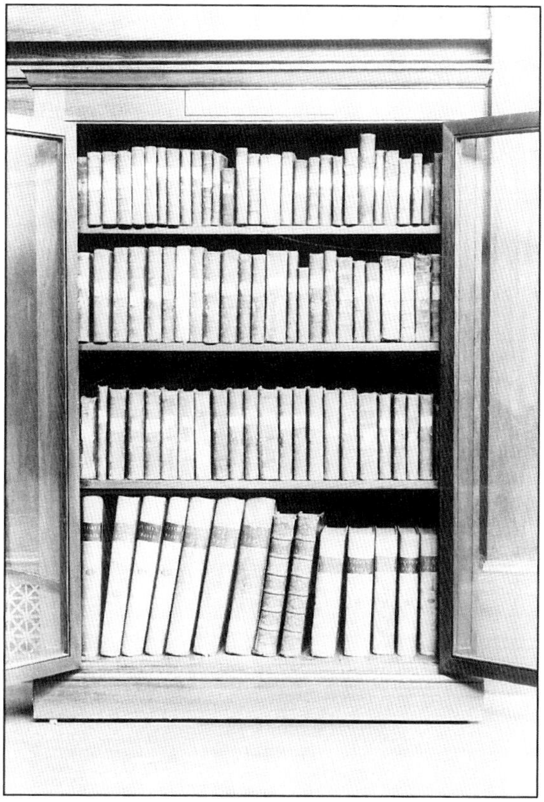

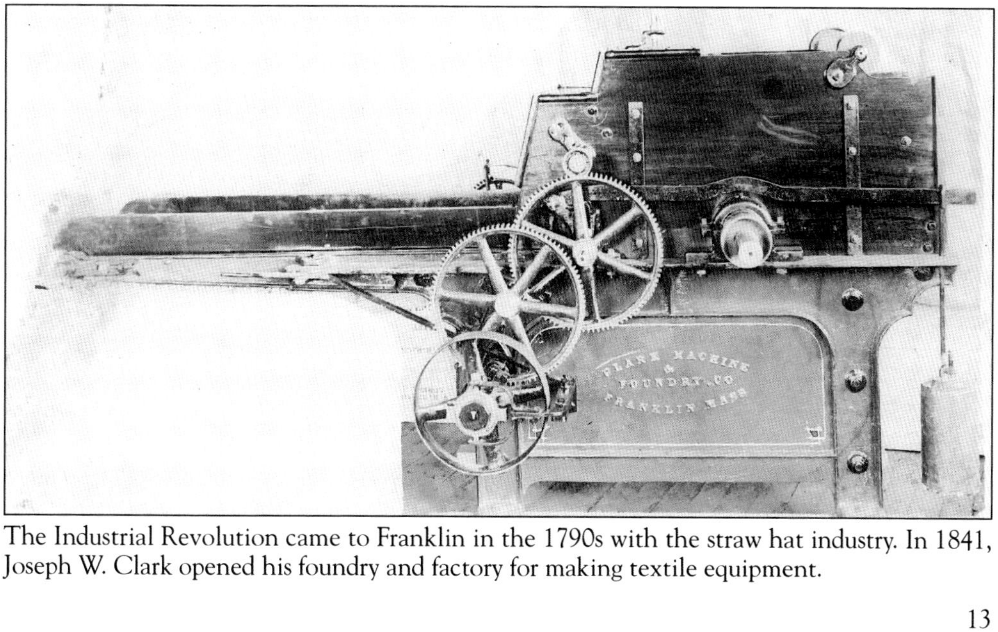


The Industrial Revolution came to Franklin in the 1790s with the straw hat industry. In 1841, Joseph W. Clark opened his foundry and factory for making textile equipment.

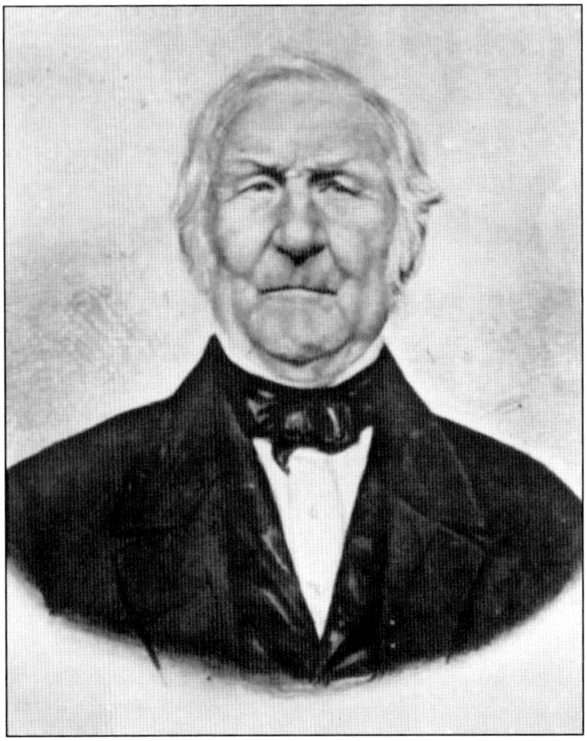

In 1924, the town named its high school after Davis Thayer, an early Franklin merchant-prince and politician.

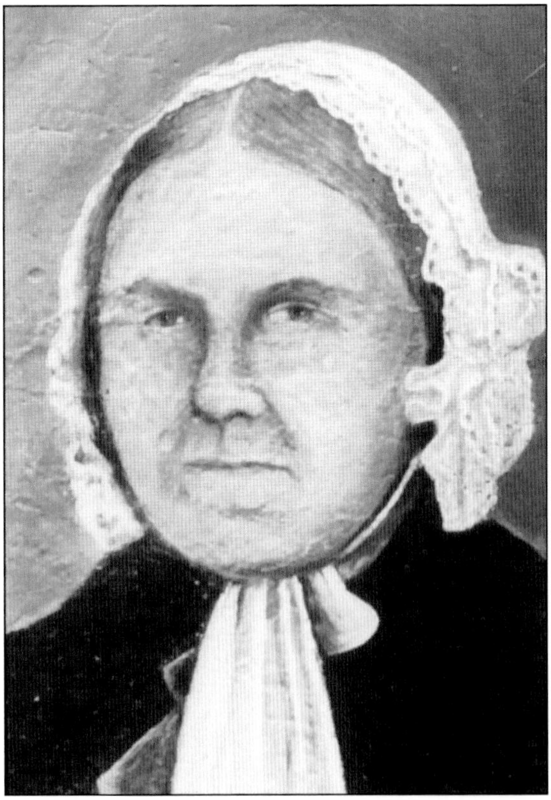

Mrs. Lucretia Metcalf was the mother of Erastus Metcalf, a politician and manufacturing powerhouse. She was painted in 1869.

This reward poster offers $500 for the discovery of the person or persons who attacked Franklin's town treasurer, Joel Daniels, and stole the "Town Trunk," which contained $400 in cash and important town documents, on April 16, 1853.

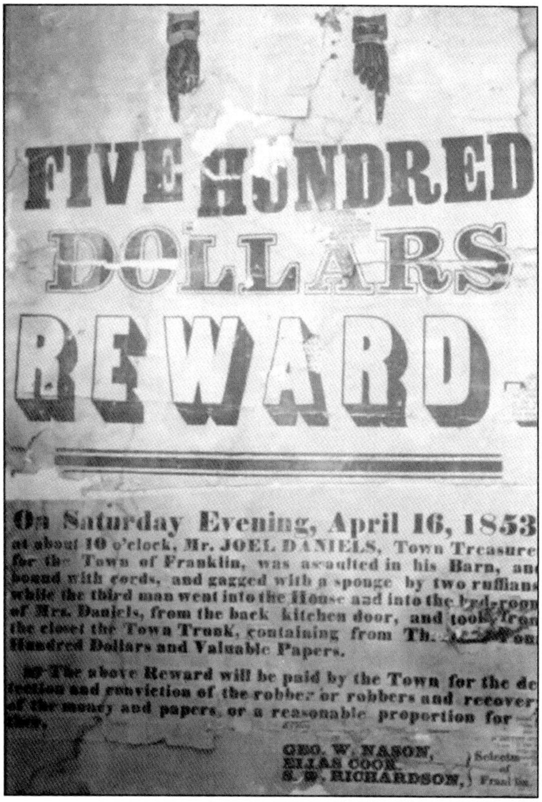


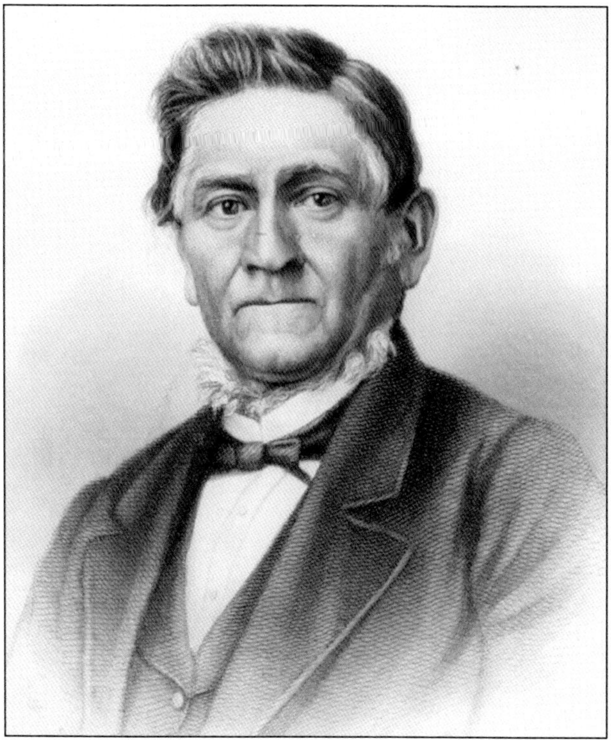

George W. Nason was a town selectman and the father of Colonel George Nason Jr. (of Civil War fame) and James Nason (inventor of the percolator).

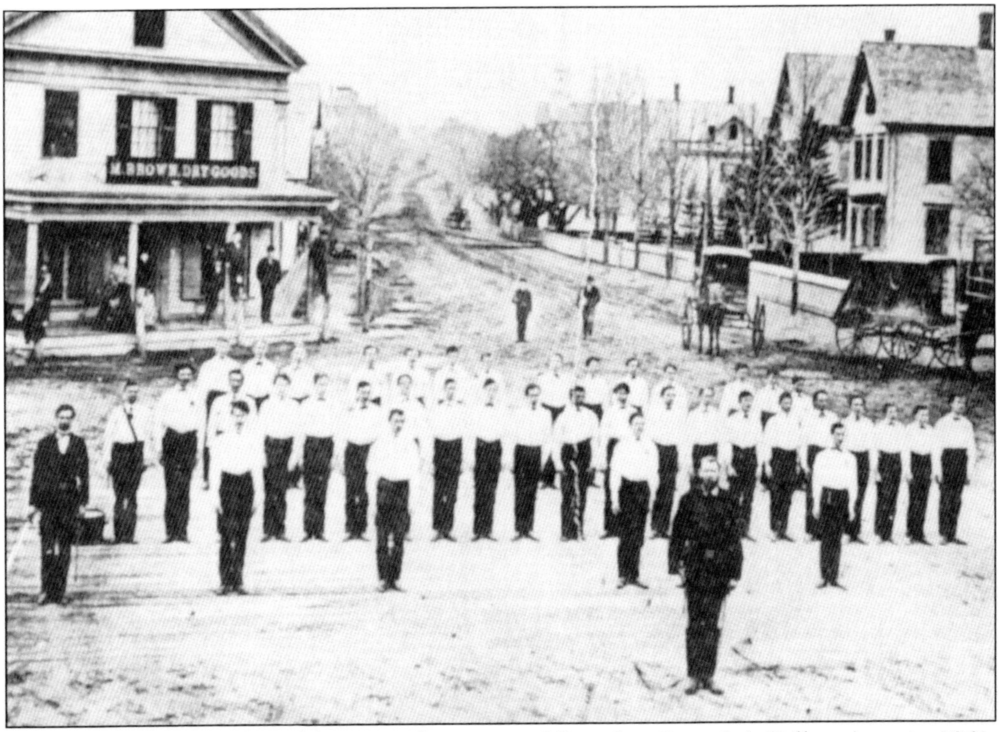

This is a photograph of Franklin men who answered President Lincoln's Call to Arms in 1861. These men served in the Civil War, fought in all major battles, and suffered 9% casualties. Some Franklin men also ended up in the Andersonville and Libby Prisons and lived to tell about it.

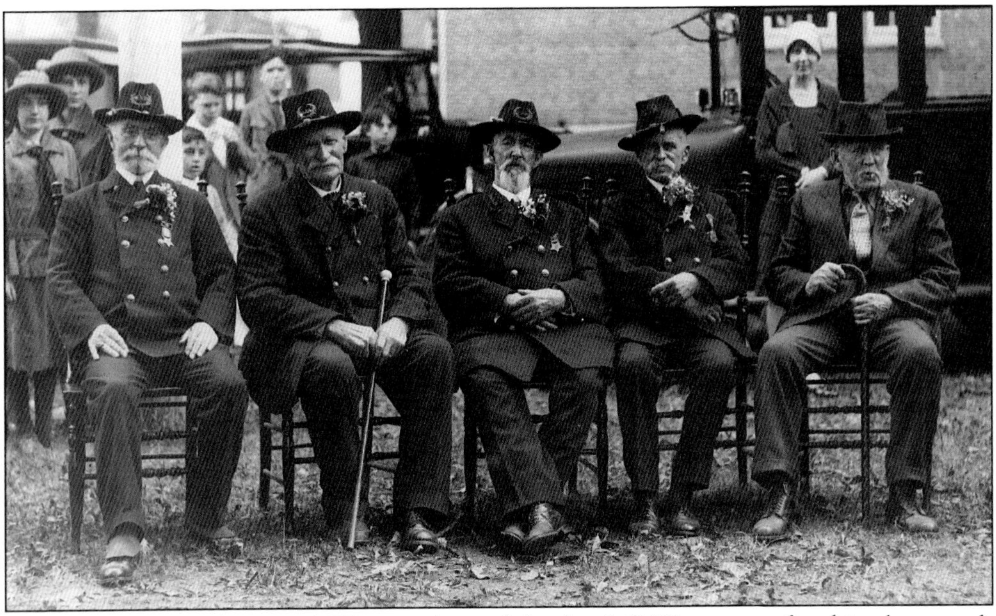

In 1928, Franklin's five Civil War members of the local GAR post sat for this photograph by Stanley G. Chilson. They are, from left to right: Rupert J. Chute, Charles R. Gowen, Albert J. Newell, John C. McWilliams, and Samuel C. Bourne.

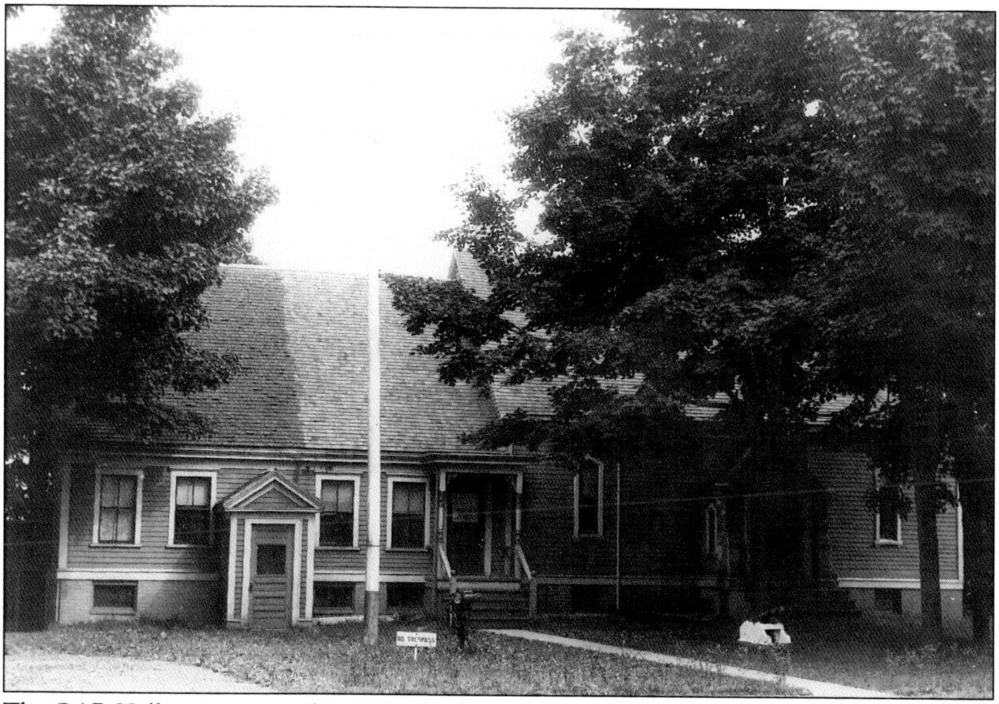

The GAR Hall, as it appeared in 1930, would soon lose its last members.

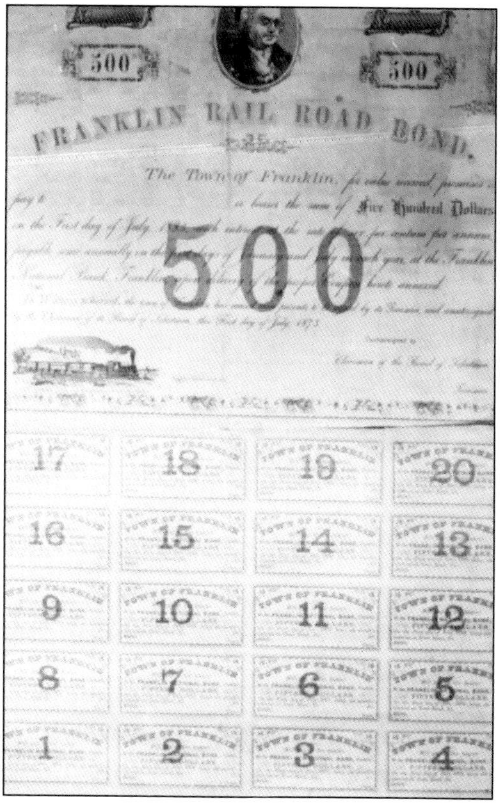


The railroad came to Franklin in the 1870s. It was financed by these bonds.

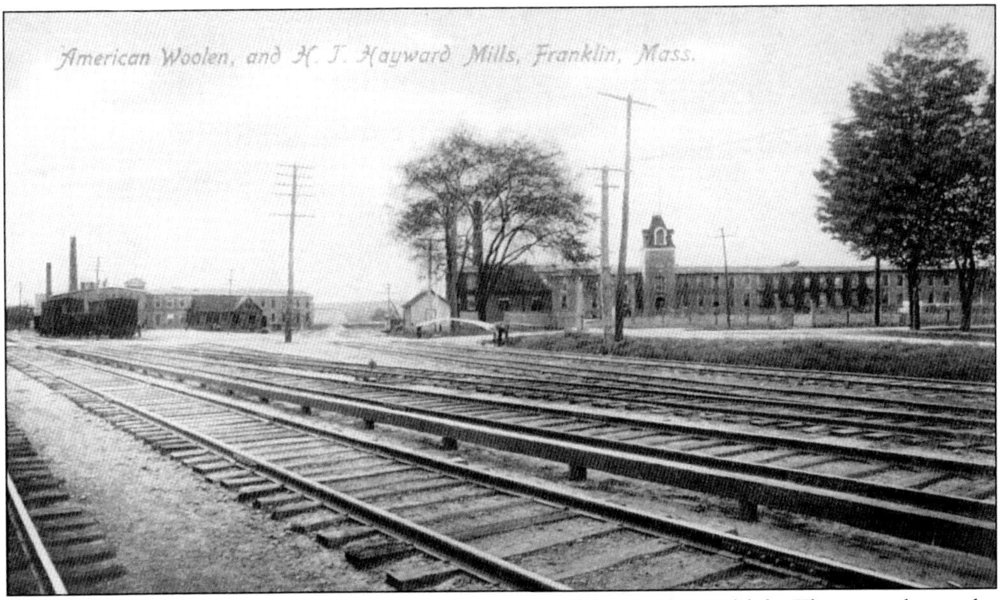


By 1900, the railroad had made a huge impact on Franklin's industrial life. These tracks ran by the American Woolen Mill and the H.J. Hayward Mills.

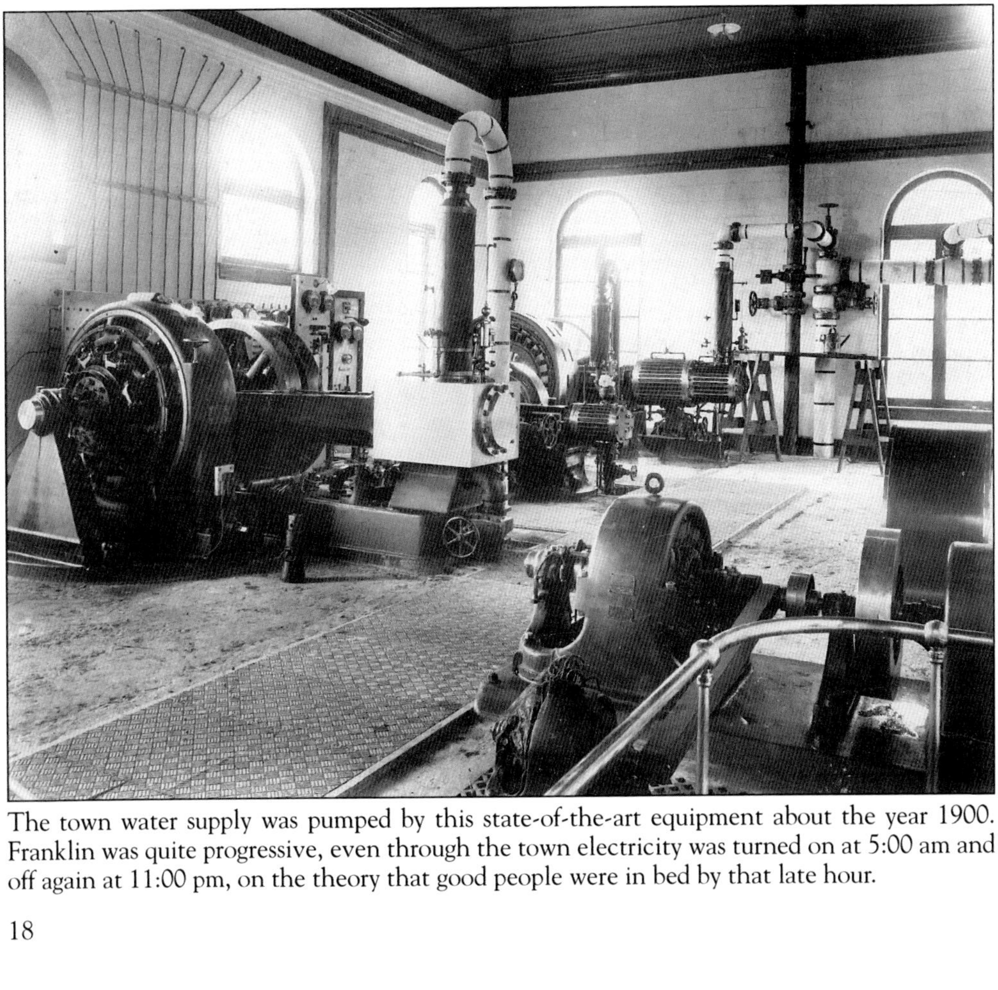

The town water supply was pumped by this state-of-the-art equipment about the year 1900. Franklin was quite progressive, even through the town electricity was turned on at 5:00 am and off again at 11:00 pm, on the theory that good people were in bed by that late hour.

# *Two*

# The Fabulous Rays

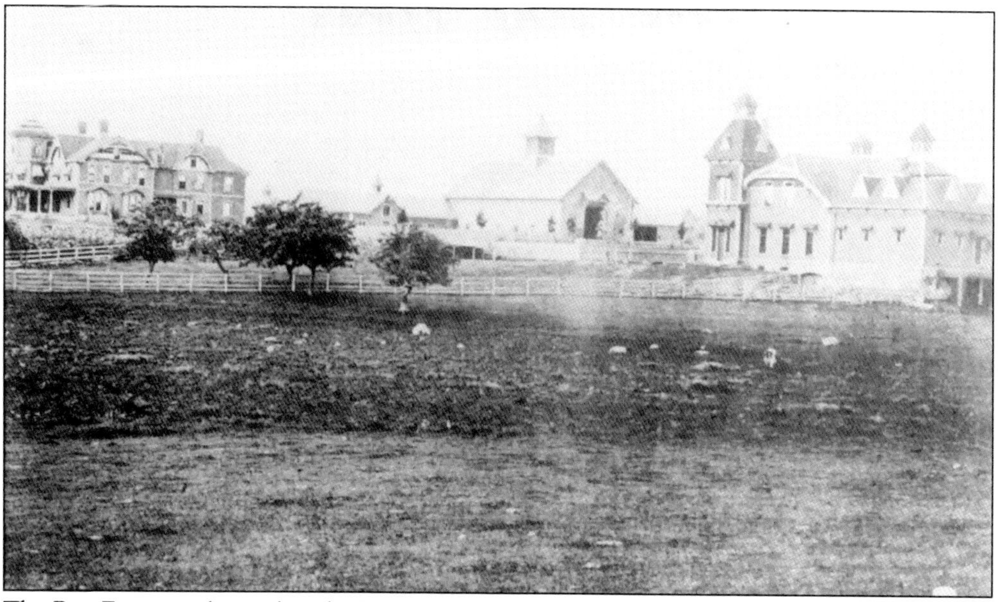

The Ray Farm was located in the Unionville section of Franklin. It is shown here in an 1880s photograph which was later made into a postcard. The Ray family had a profound impact on Franklin life.

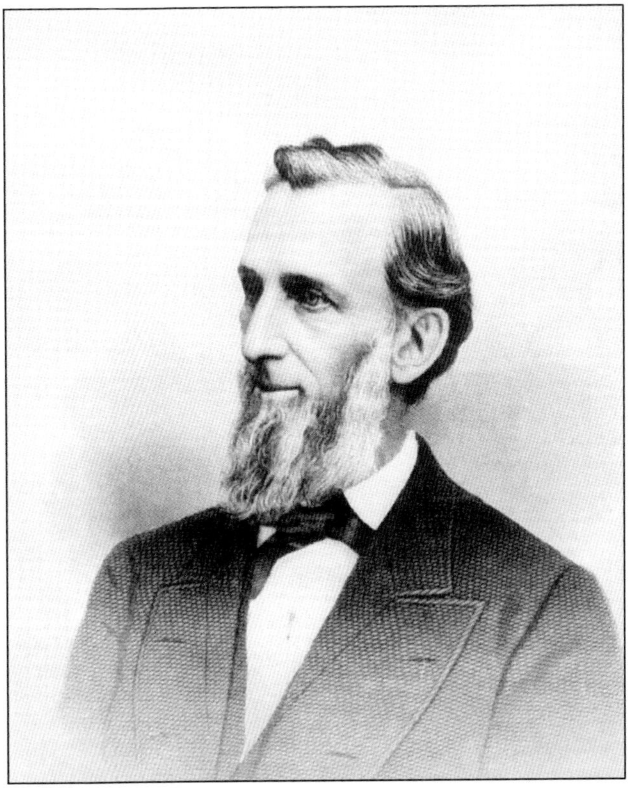

This portrait of Joseph Gordon Ray appeared in Blake's *History of Franklin* (1878). Ray was the magnate who put Franklin on the industrial map in the nineteenth century as a town promoter. He had a deep interest in education and libraries.

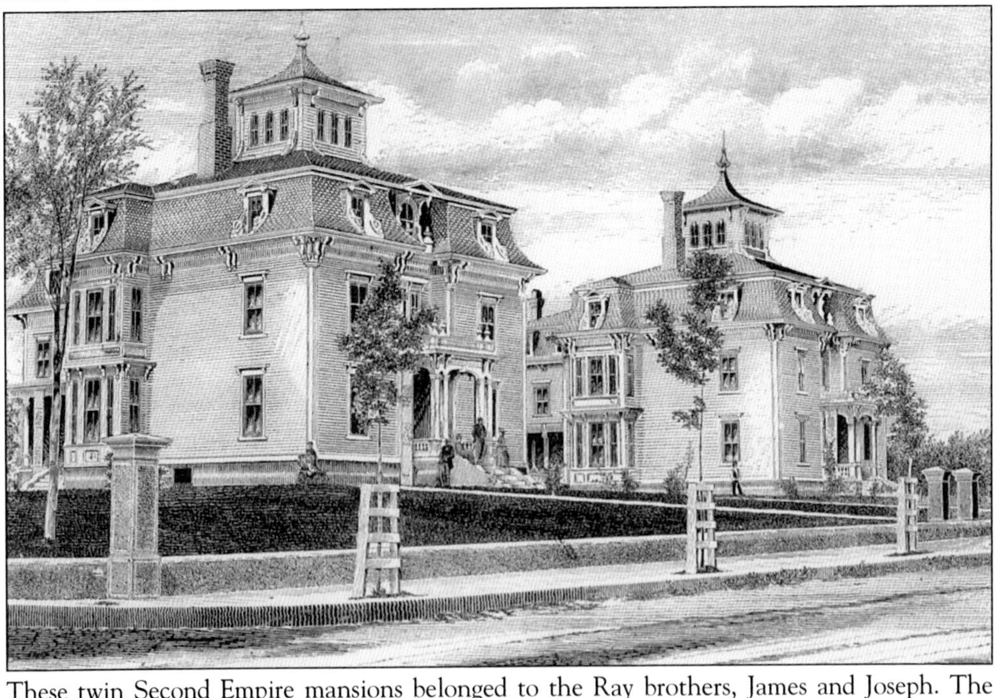

These twin Second Empire mansions belonged to the Ray brothers, James and Joseph. The houses were among the most fashionable homes in Franklin during the "Belle Epoch." This picture also appeared in Blake's *History of Franklin* (1878).

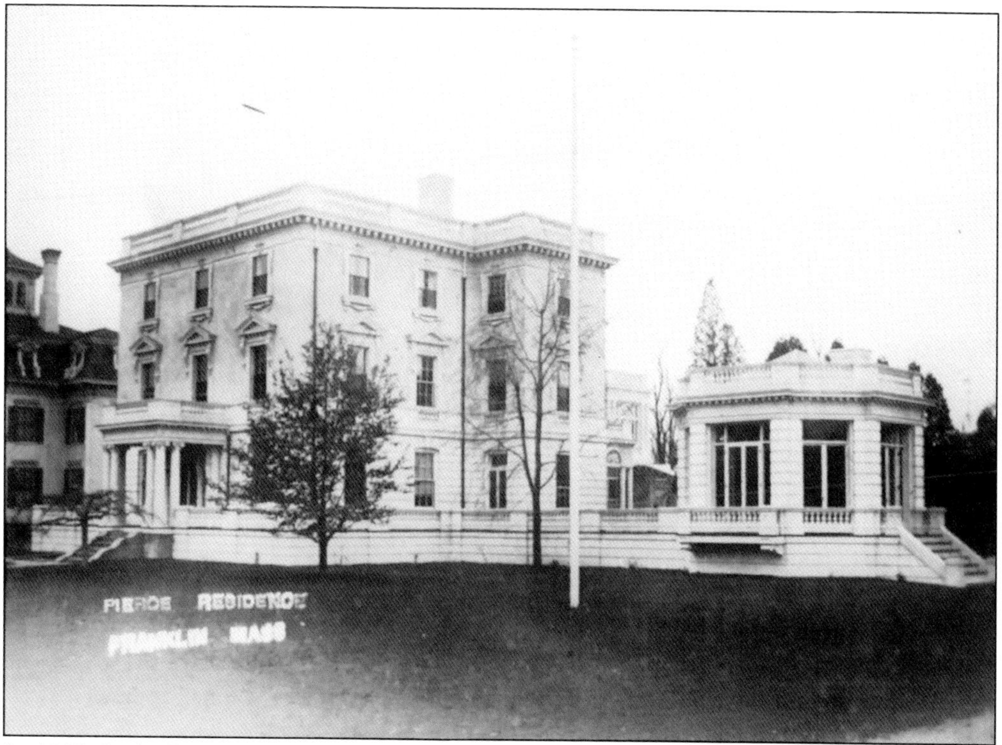


In 1900, Lydia Ray Pierce, Joseph Gordon Ray's daughter, rebuilt the Ray Mansion into an Italian Palace. She and her husband, Arthur Winslow Pierce, had traveled in Italy and fell in love with the architectural style.

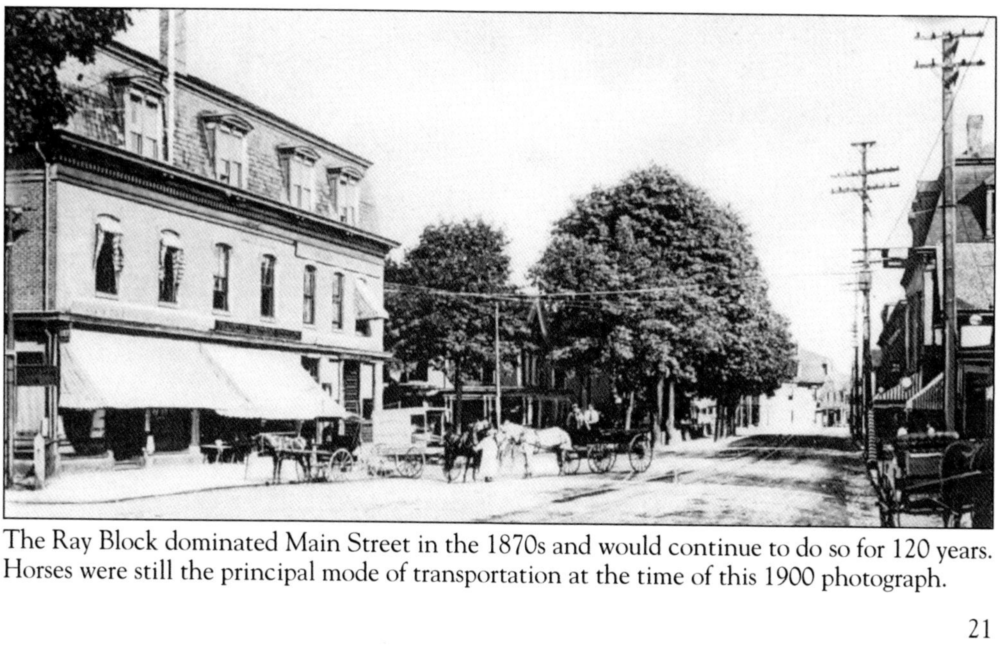

The Ray Block dominated Main Street in the 1870s and would continue to do so for 120 years. Horses were still the principal mode of transportation at the time of this 1900 photograph.

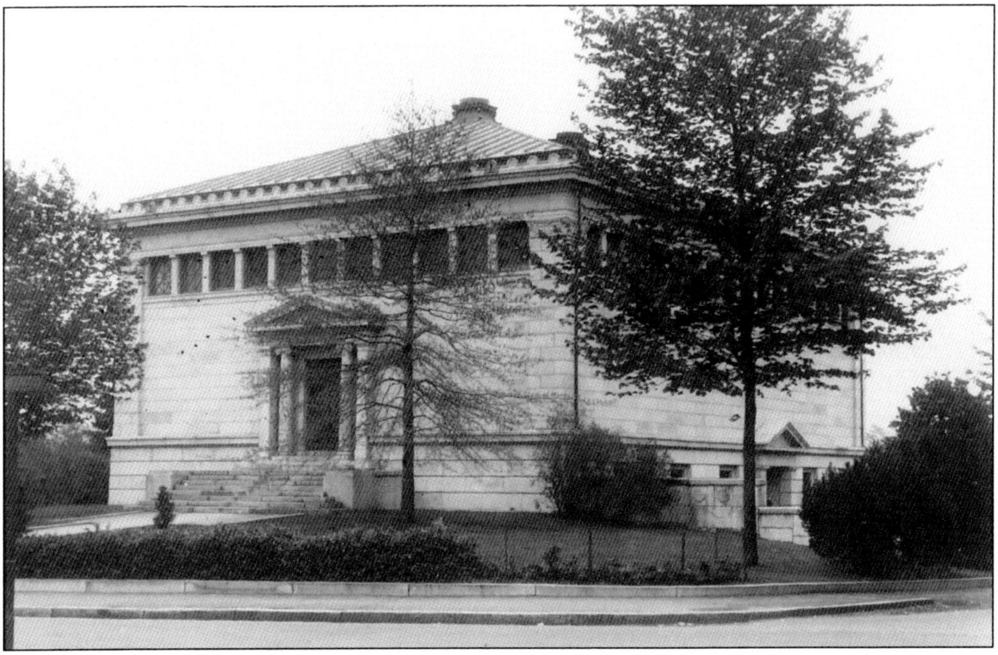

Lydia Ray Pierce and Annie Ray Thayer built the Ray Memorial Library to honor their parents, Mr. and Mrs. Joseph Gordon Ray. The library was dedicated in 1904. The workmen who built it were imported from Italy.

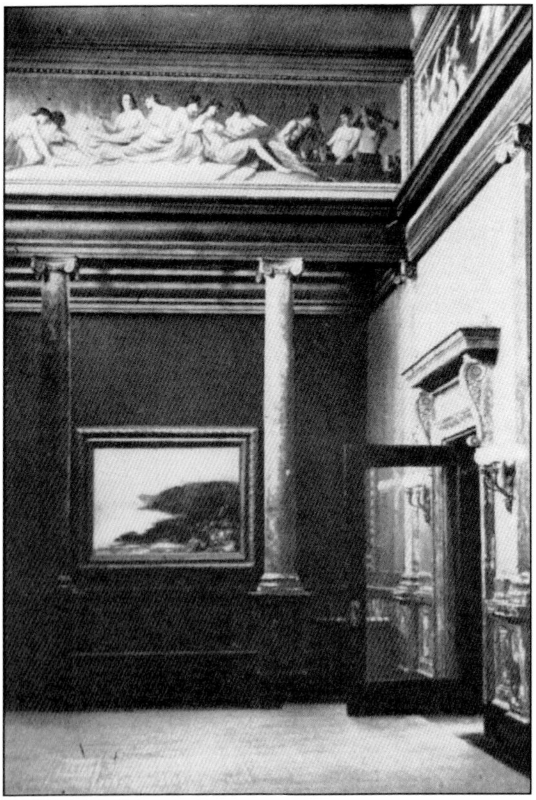

This is Memorial Hall as it appeared in 1904 at time of the library's dedication.

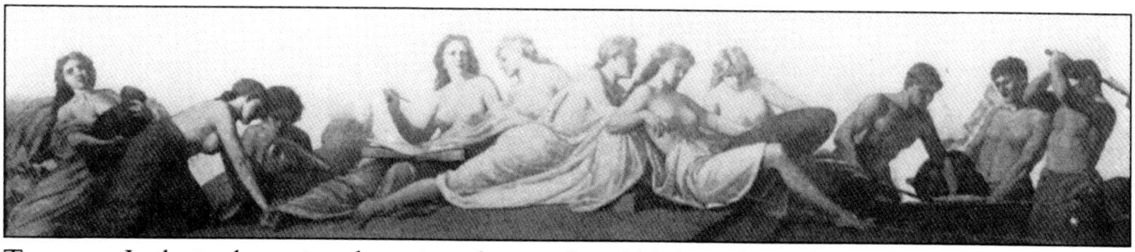

Tommaso Juglaris, the artist who painted more than 150 feet of murals, had to return to Franklin to paint more clothing on his nudes to satisfy the Ray sisters' scruples. The murals were still a culture shock to proper Franklinites, but were a delight to their children.

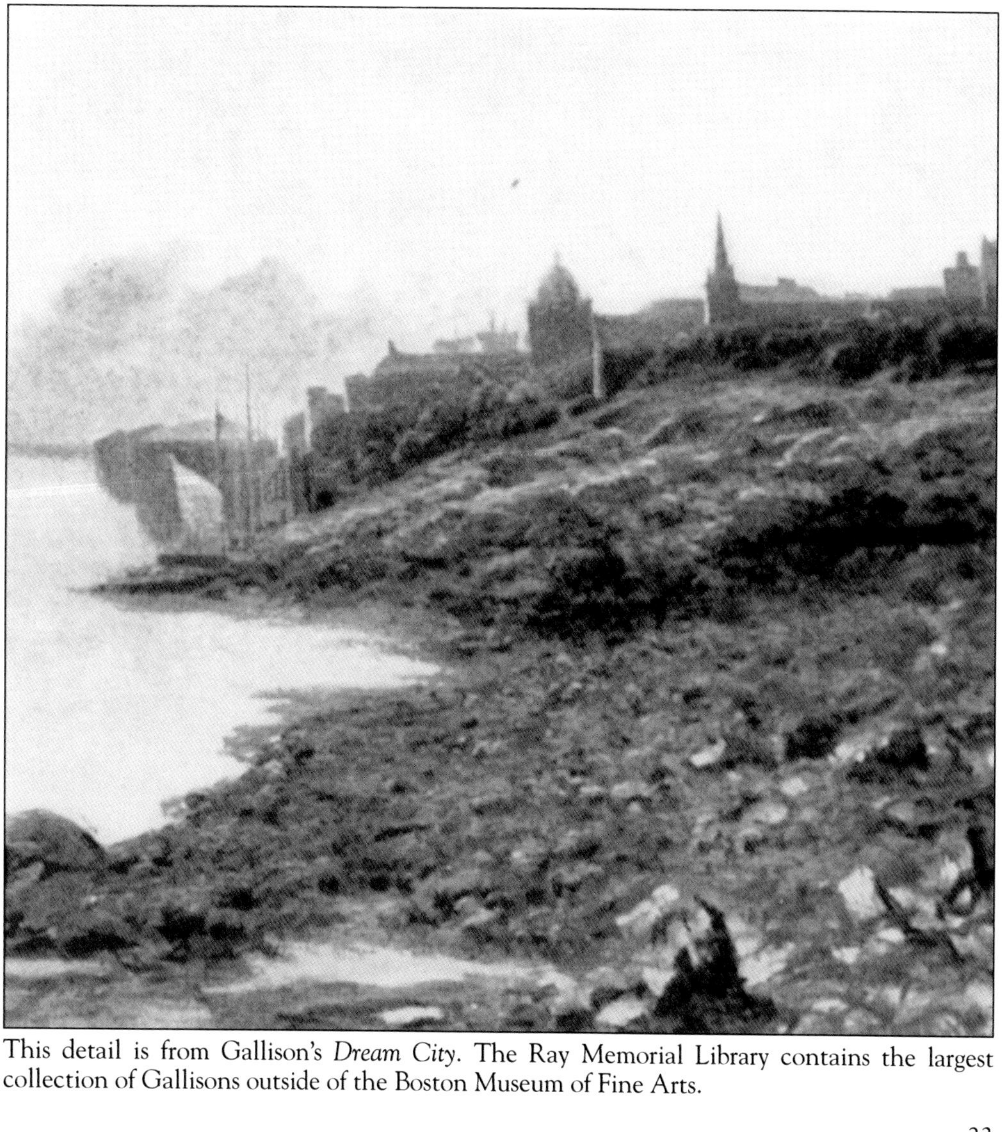

This detail is from Gallison's *Dream City*. The Ray Memorial Library contains the largest collection of Gallisons outside of the Boston Museum of Fine Arts.

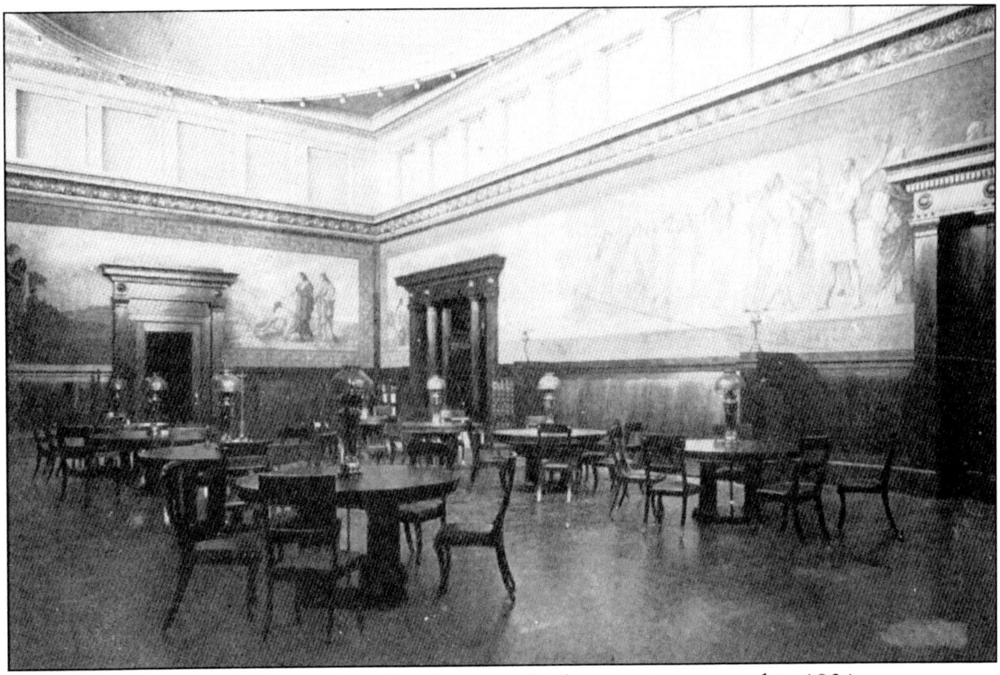

This is the "Reading Gallery" of the Ray Memorial Library as it appeared in 1904.

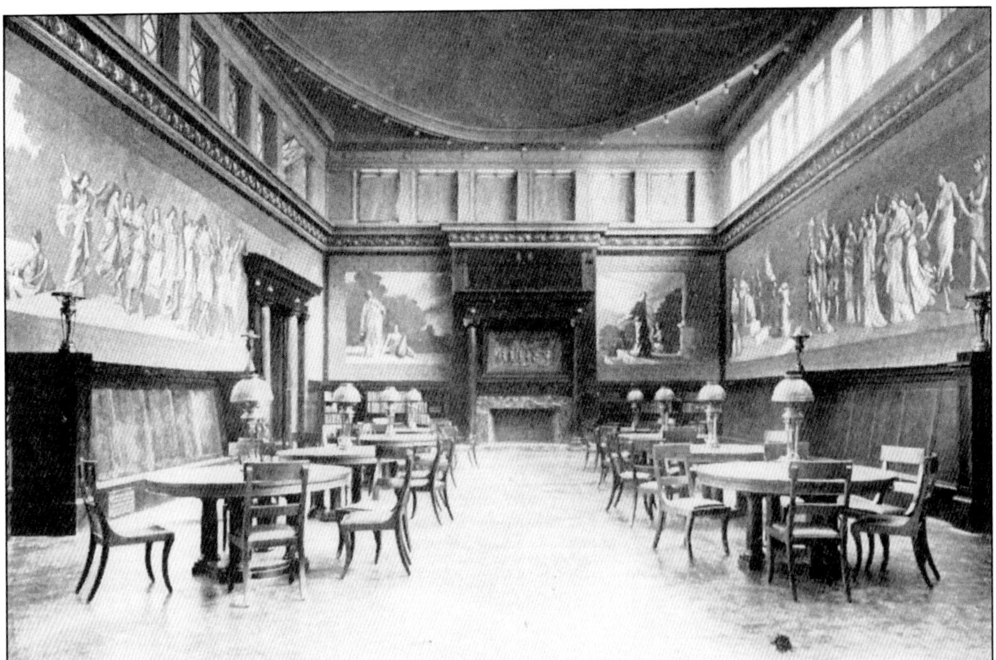

This is another view of the "Reading Gallery," this time facing the beautiful bronze work over the fireplace. Juglaris murals grace the walls.

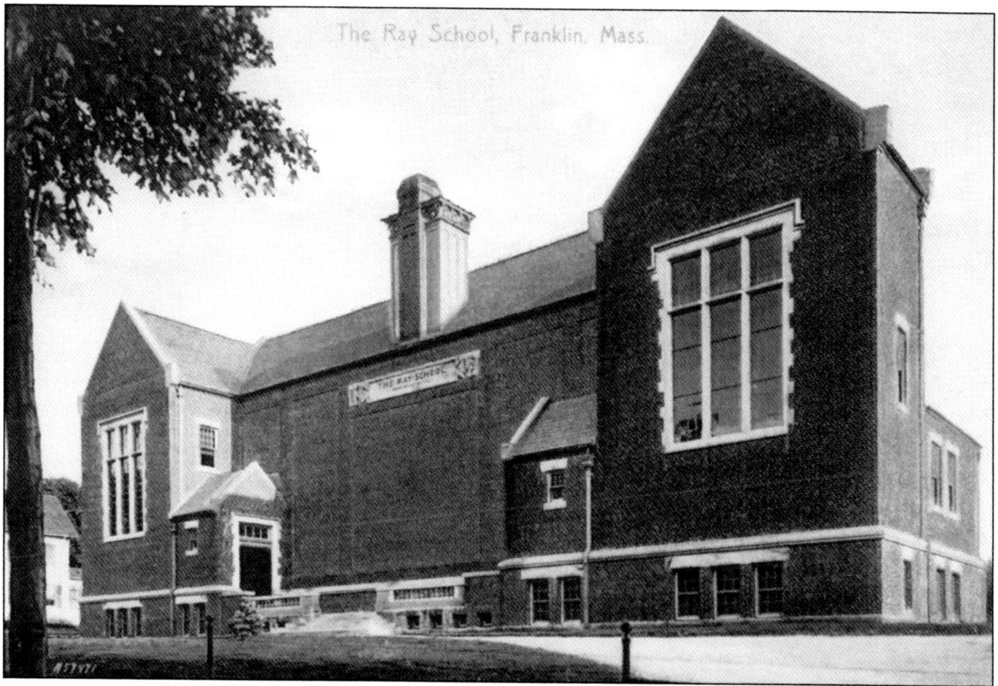


This postcard shows the Ray School. Though it was massive in appearance, it held only four classrooms, and was built to impress passers-by. It was burned by vandals in the late 1970s. This school was another gift of the Ray sisters to the Town of Franklin.

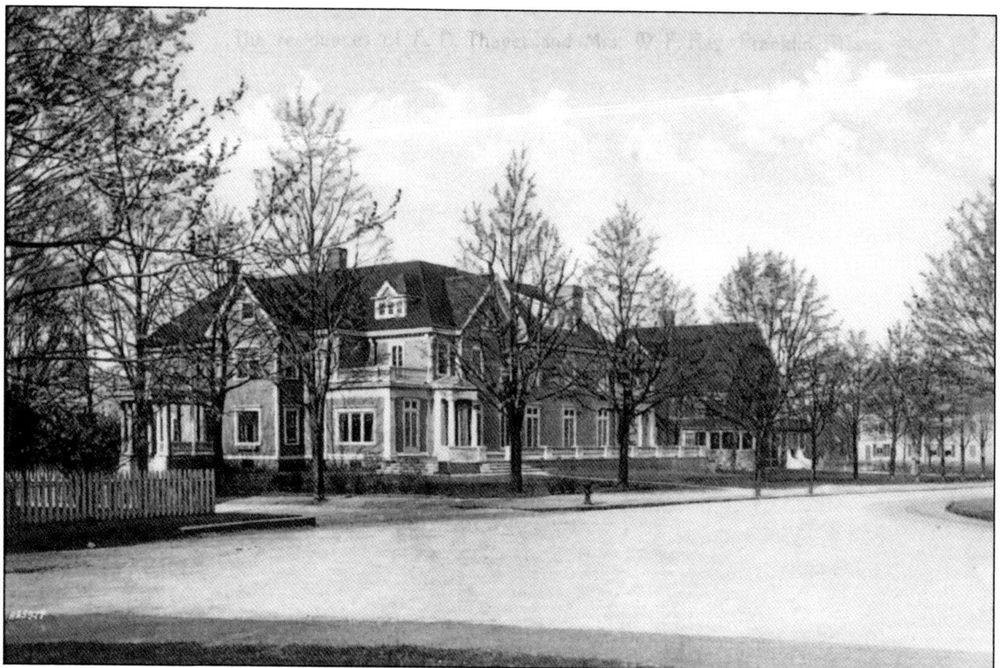

This postcard shows the home of Mrs. Annie Ray Thayer as it appeared about 1907. It was a center of the Franklin social scene and the site of many glittering entertainments. In 1995 it burned, a victim of carelessness.

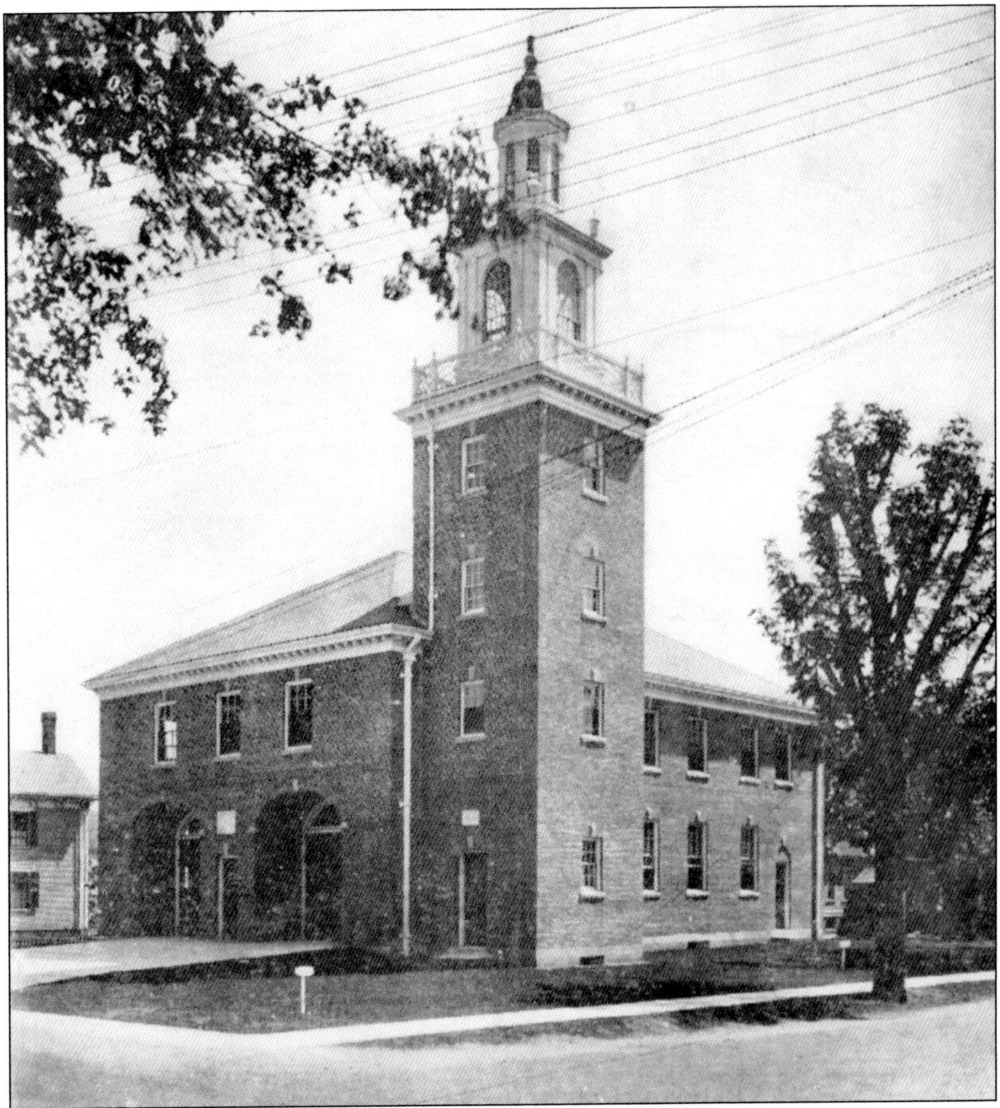

This photograph from a souvenir program shows the Joseph Gordon Ray Fire Station at the time it was dedicated in 1924. As of 1995 it was still Franklin's only fire station. It was donated by Annie Ray Thayer and her husband, Adelbert Thayer. The tower was used in the 1950s by Franklin's Skyway Patrol, which kept watch in case the Soviets attacked during the Cold War. Strange but true.

*Three*

# From Main Street to the Corner

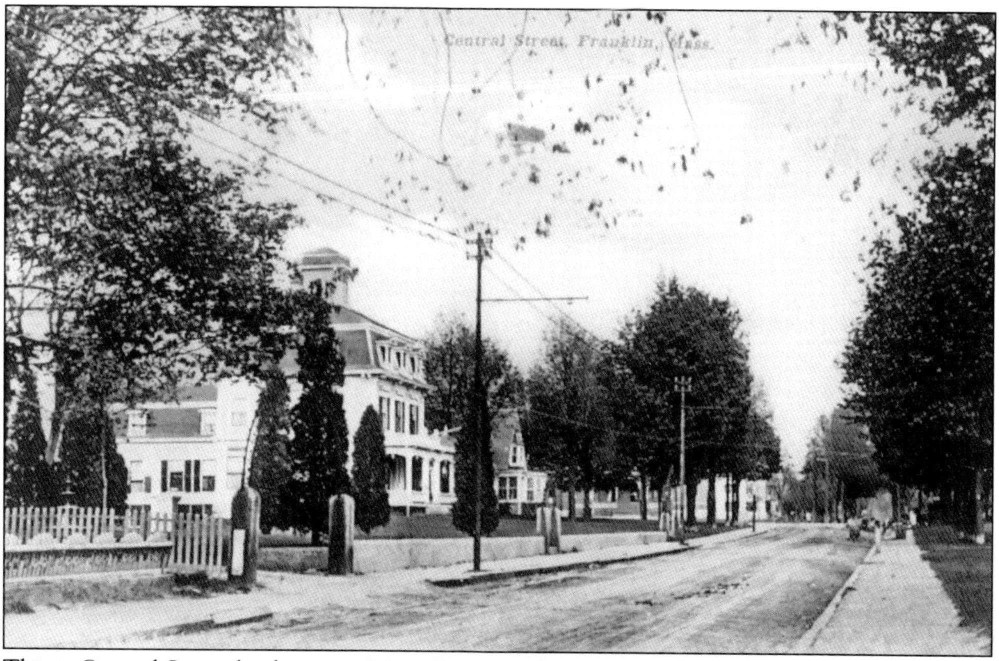


This is Central Street leading into Main Street at the turn of the century. The telephone poles indicate that electricity and telephone service were available even at this early date. Electricity, however, was only available to the town from 5:00 am to 11:00 pm (see p. 18).

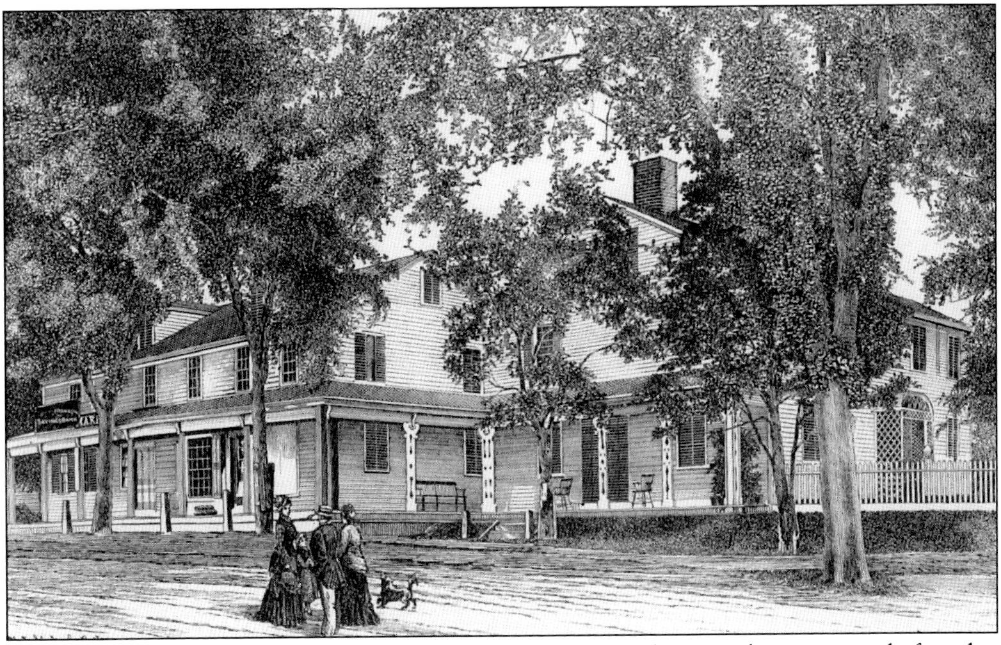

The Davis Thayer home and general store were town fixtures for several generations before this 1878 engraving was made.

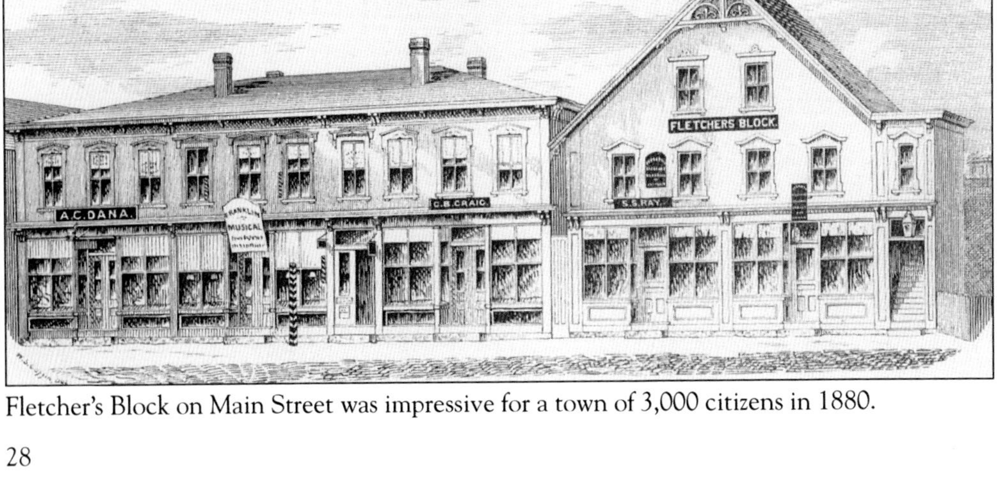


Fletcher's Block on Main Street was impressive for a town of 3,000 citizens in 1880.

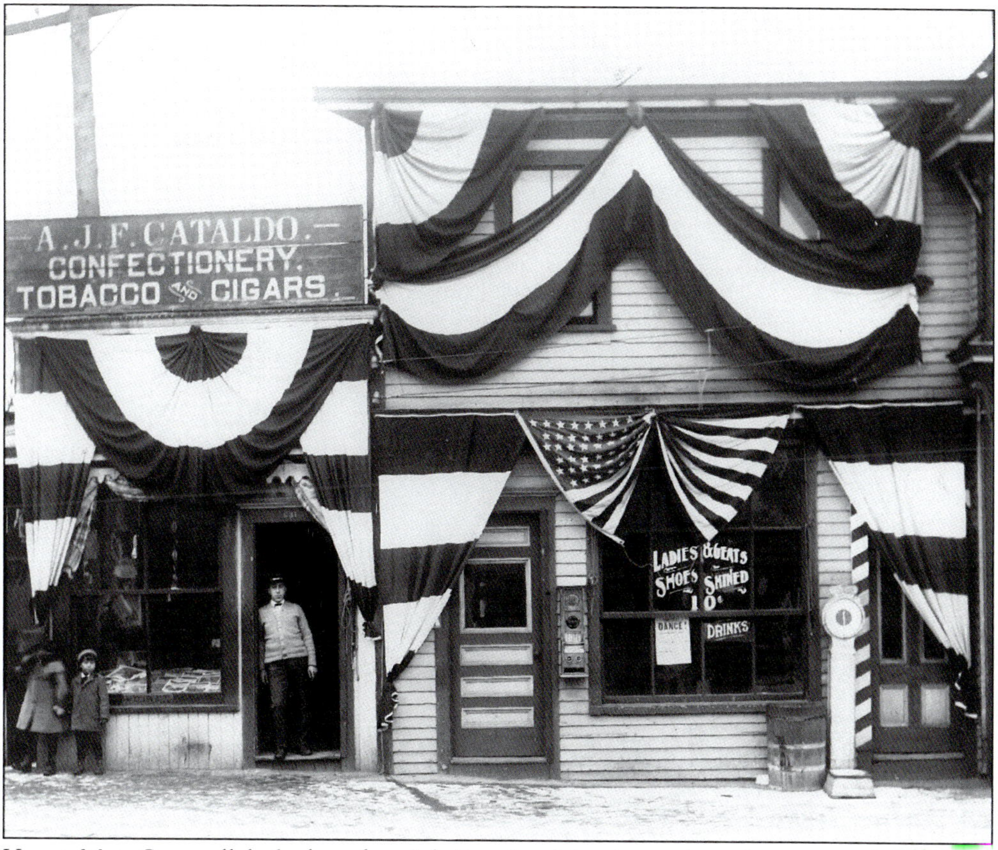


Here is Main Street all decked out for a July Fourth celebration early in the century. A.J. Cataldo can be seen in the doorway of his store.

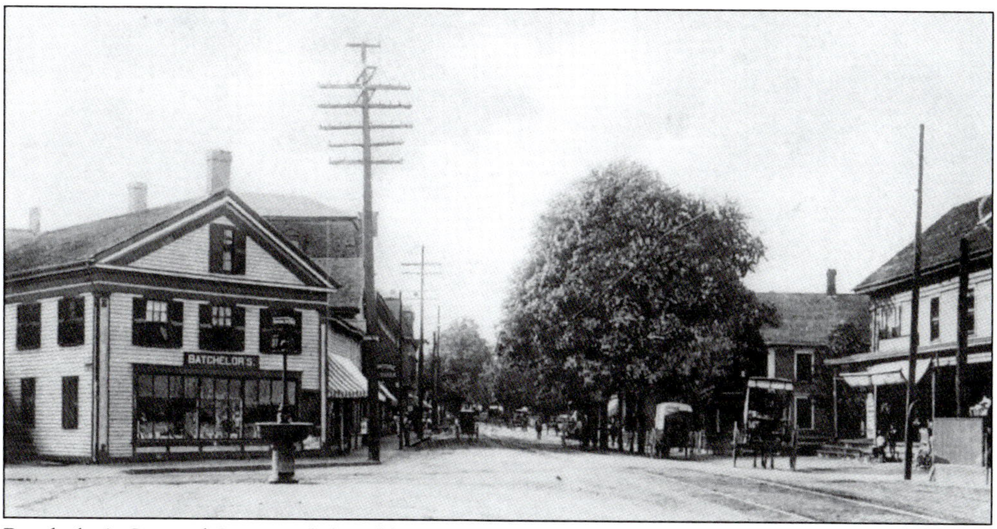


Batchelor's General Store and the old iron watering trough (which still stands on the spot) can be seen in this photograph of "The Square," which looks here much as it did in the 1850s.

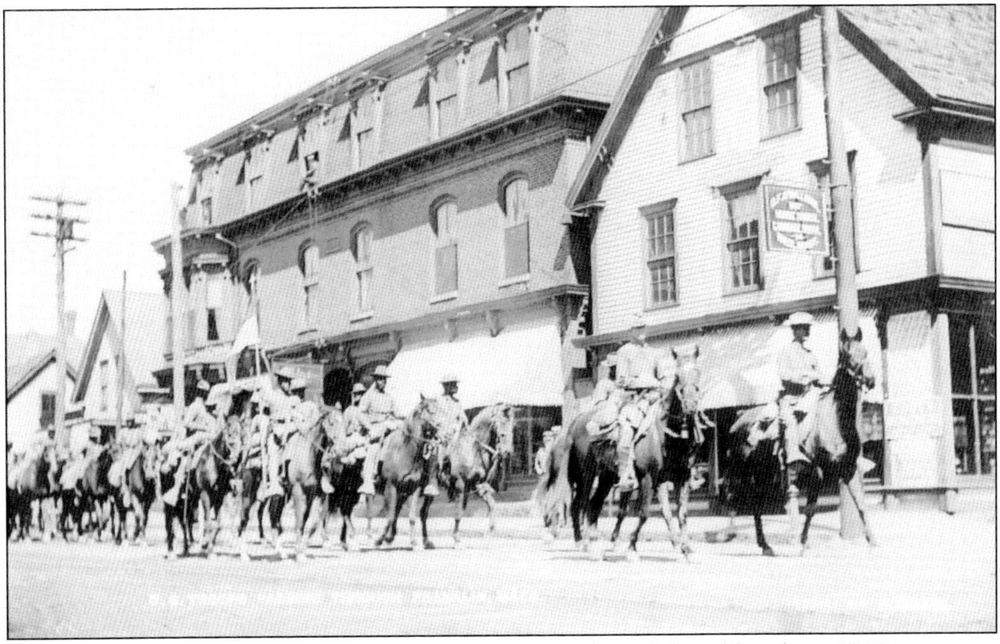

This postcard shows the United States Calvary passing through Franklin about 1908.

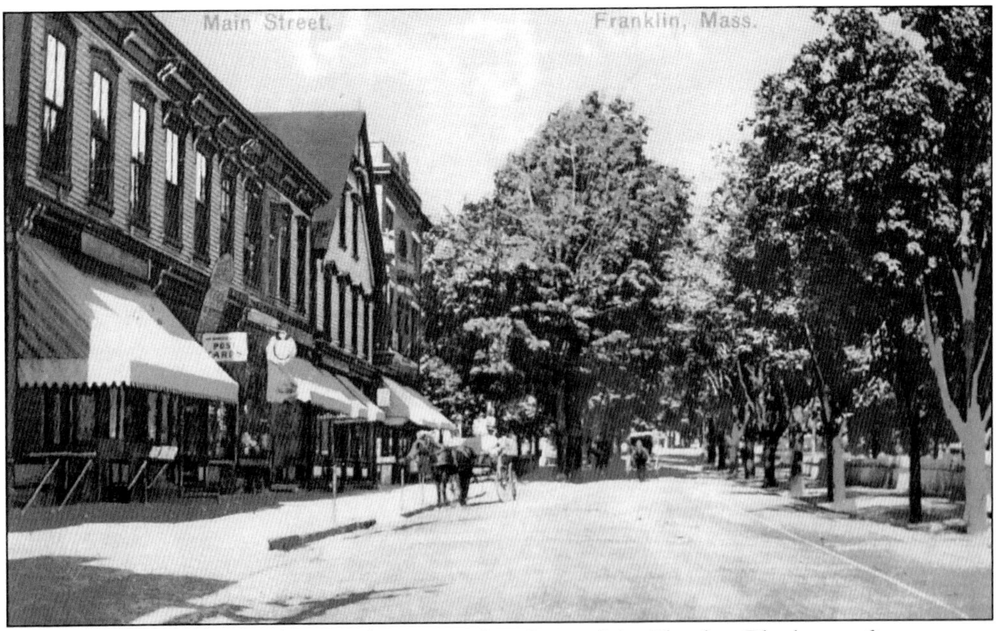


In this picture, a horse and wagon has stopped in front of the Fletcher Block on a fine summer day about 1900. Awnings shade the store windows from the hot summer sun.

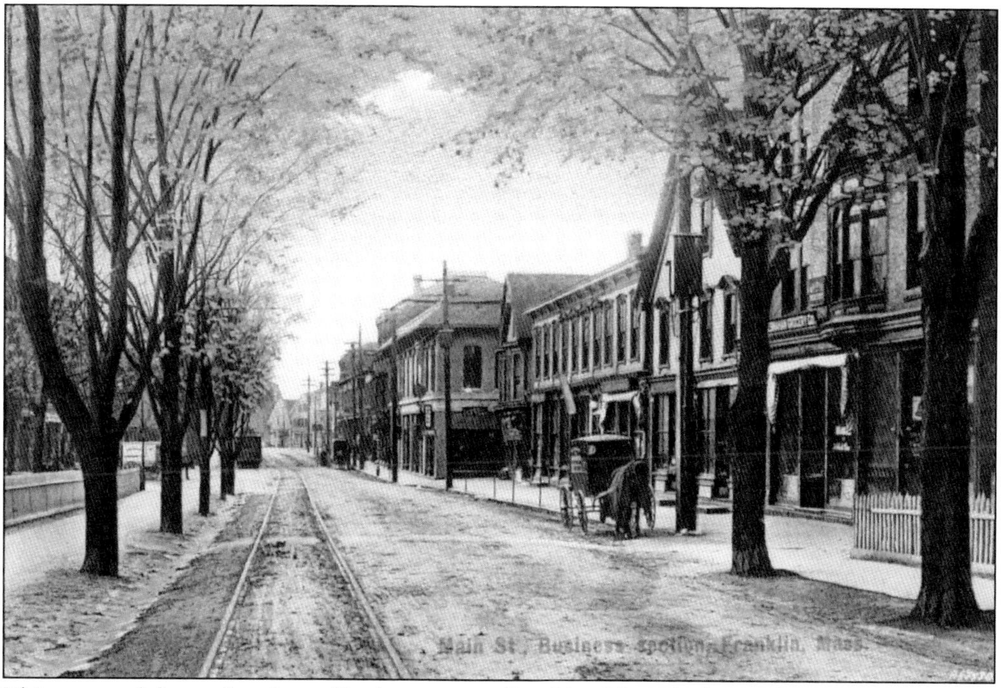

This postcard shows that the trolley has come to Franklin. Note the horse-drawn delivery wagon waiting next to the Fletcher Block.

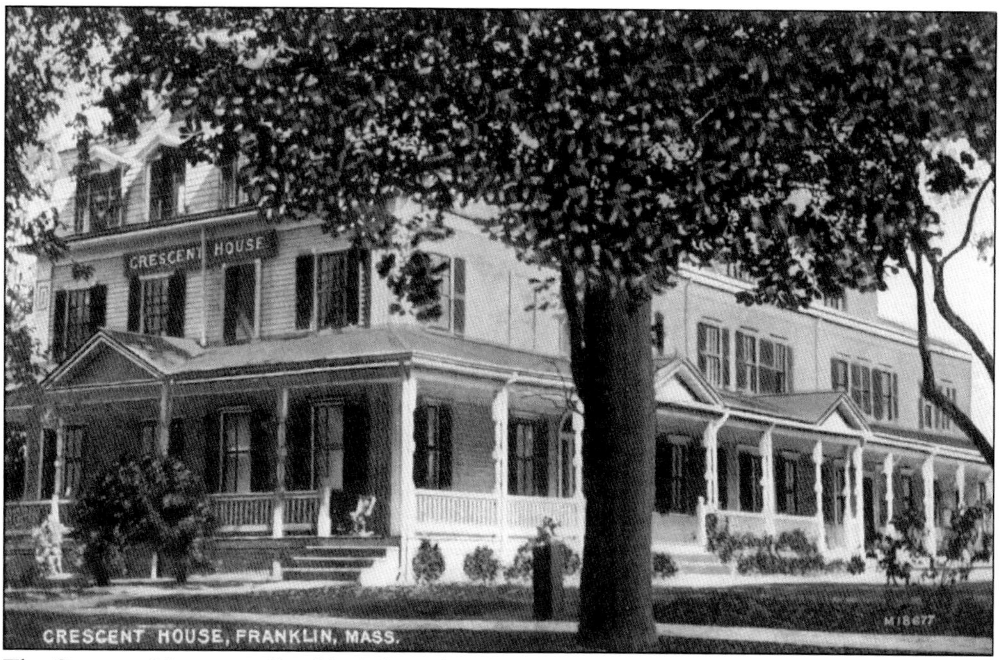


The Crescent House was Franklin's finest hotel. It was the center of social activity for the town for three quarters of a century.

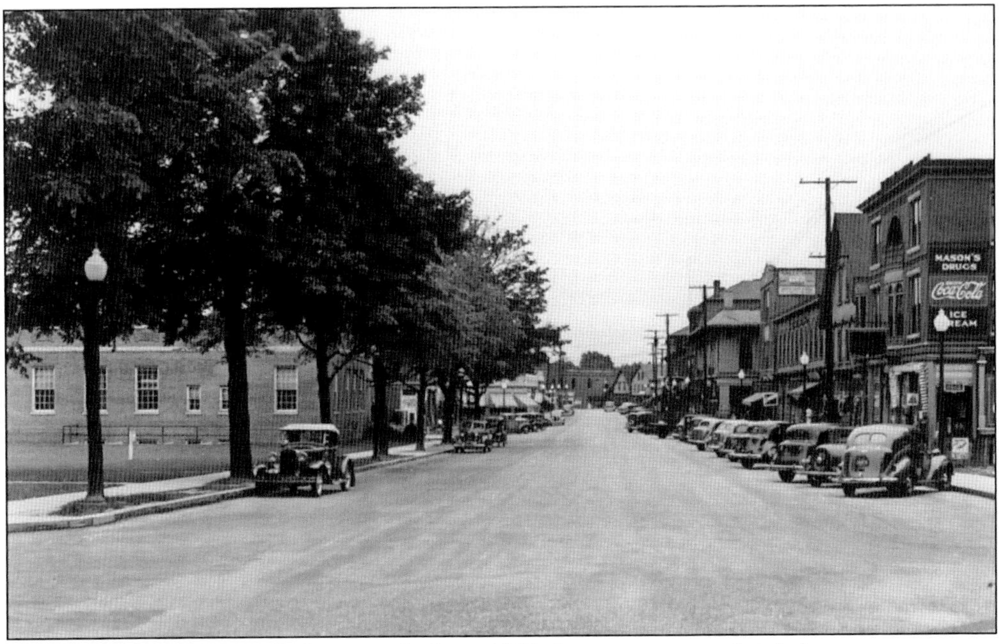

This view of Main Street looking south about 1939 shows some superficial changes.

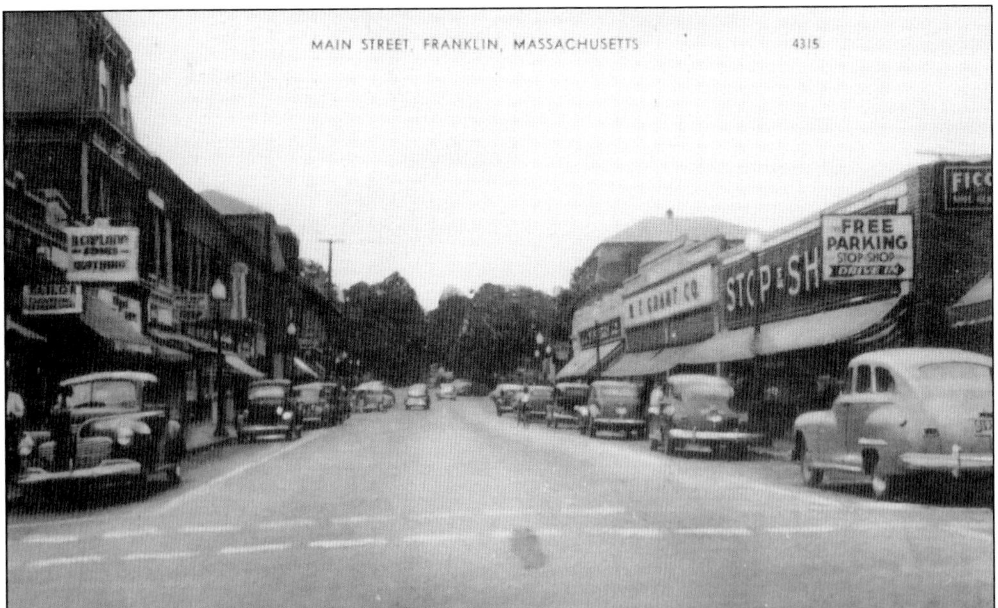

Main Street is still quiet and rural in this c. 1942 view looking north, but the increase in automobiles foretells the many subtle changes that would come with suburban life.

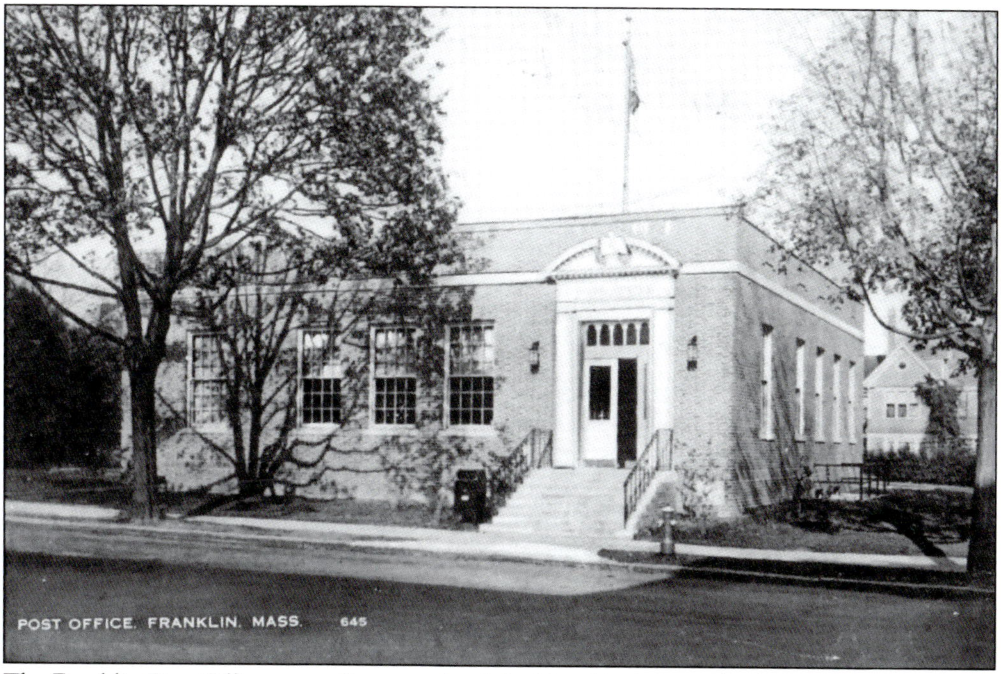


The Franklin Post Office was a direct result of the New Deal. It was built in 1938, and in 1980 it was the post office where the "First Day of Issue" for the Education Stamp took place.

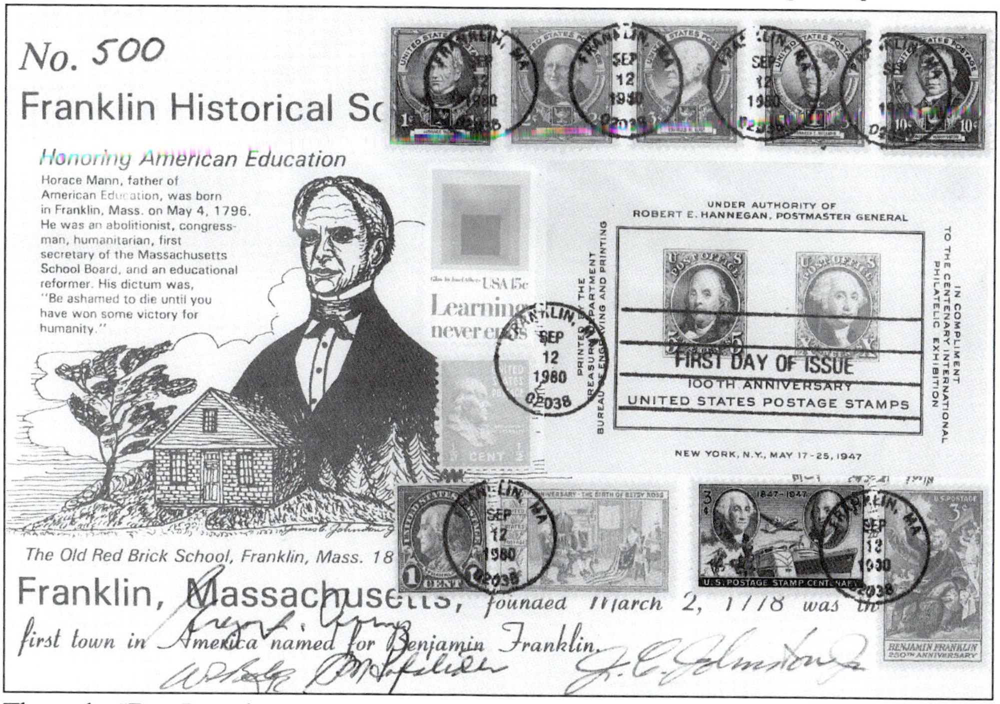


This is the "First Day of Issue" cover of the Education Stamp from the Franklin Post Office. It is autographed by Postmaster General William Bolger, Secretary of Education Shirley M. Hufstedler, Massachusetts Commissioner of Education Gregory Anrig, and James C. Johnston Jr., the cover's cachet artist.

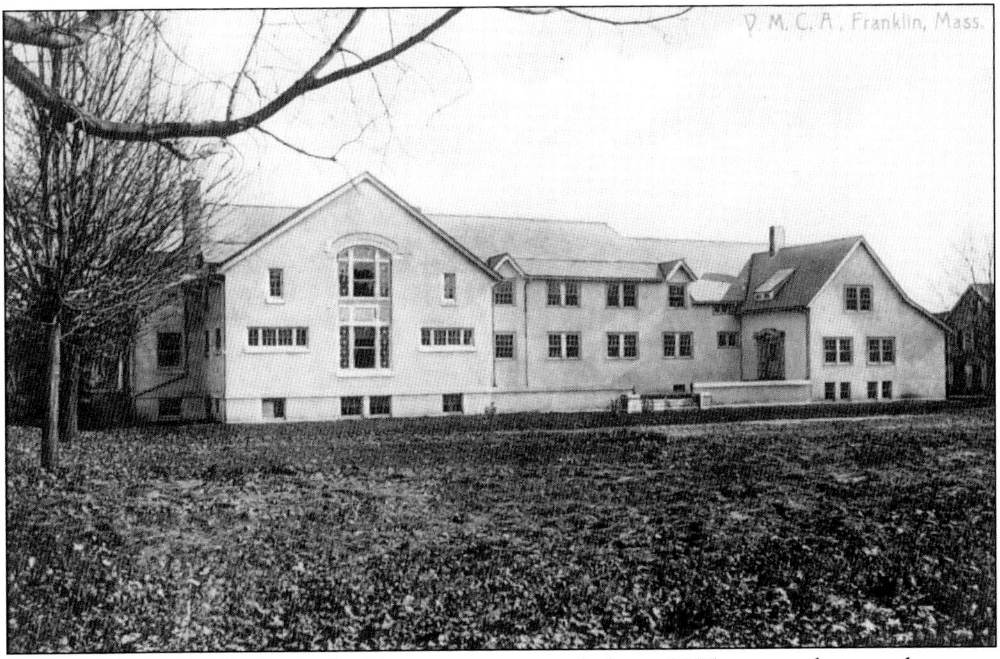


The Franklin YMCA's stucco building, as it appeared about 1935, was to become home to Franklin's Masonic lodge.

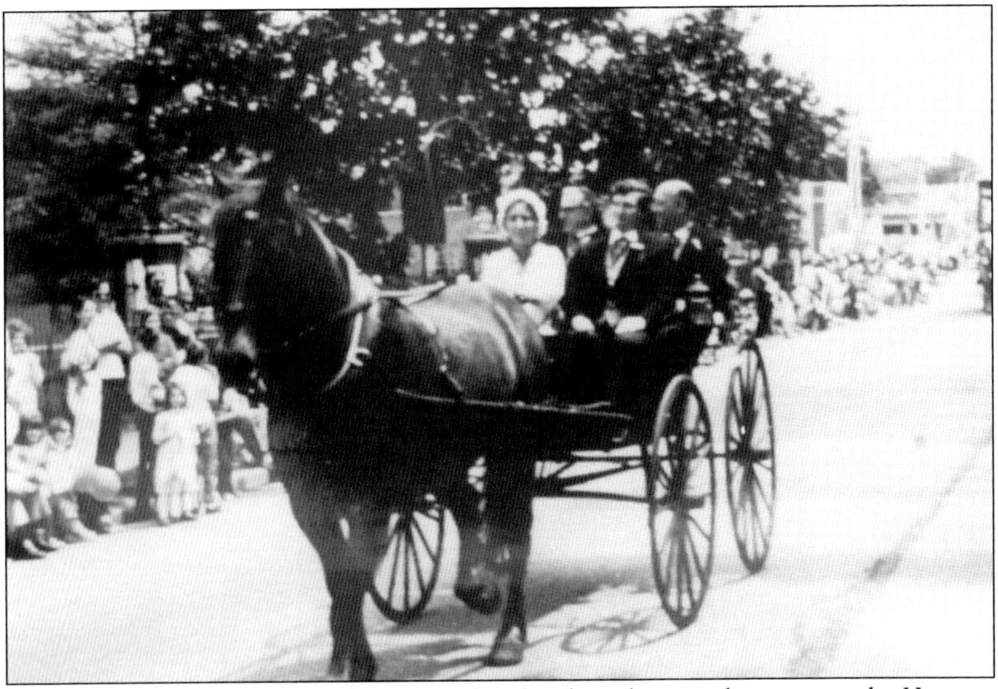

Franklin celebrated the nation's bicentennial with a huge horse and wagon parade. Here are Franklin's Board of Selectmen Herbert A. Vendetti, James C. Johnston Jr., and Albert Pete Brunelli. This photograph, taken by Eileen Vigliante, is courtesy of the *Milford Daily News*.

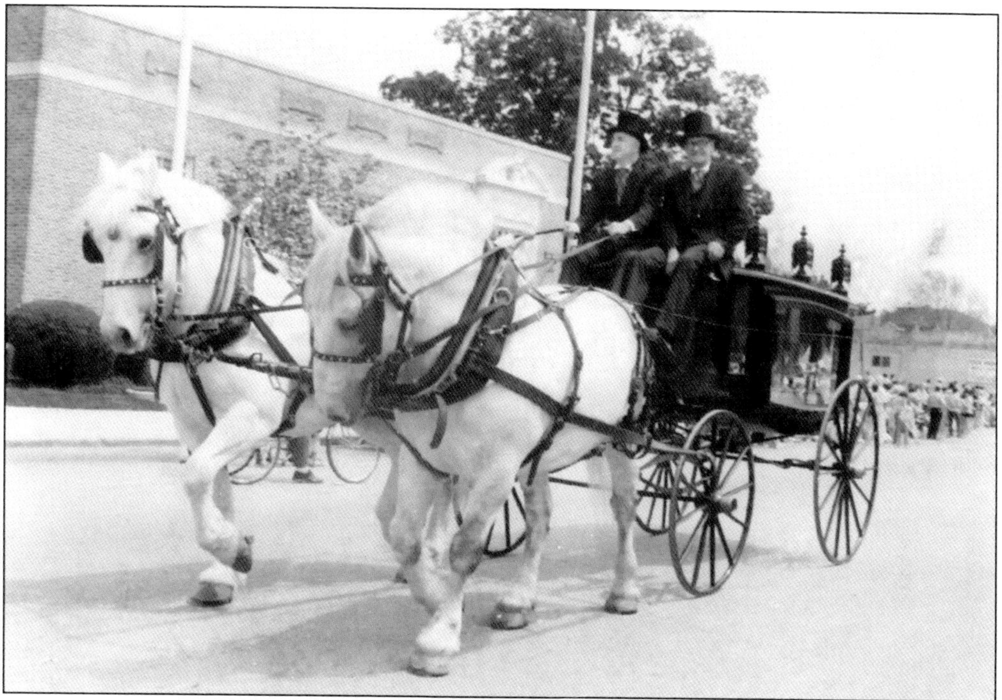

This bicentennial day photograph, also taken by Eileen Vigliante and provided by the *Milford Daily News*, shows the splendid 1850s hearse donated to the parade by Walter Jackson.

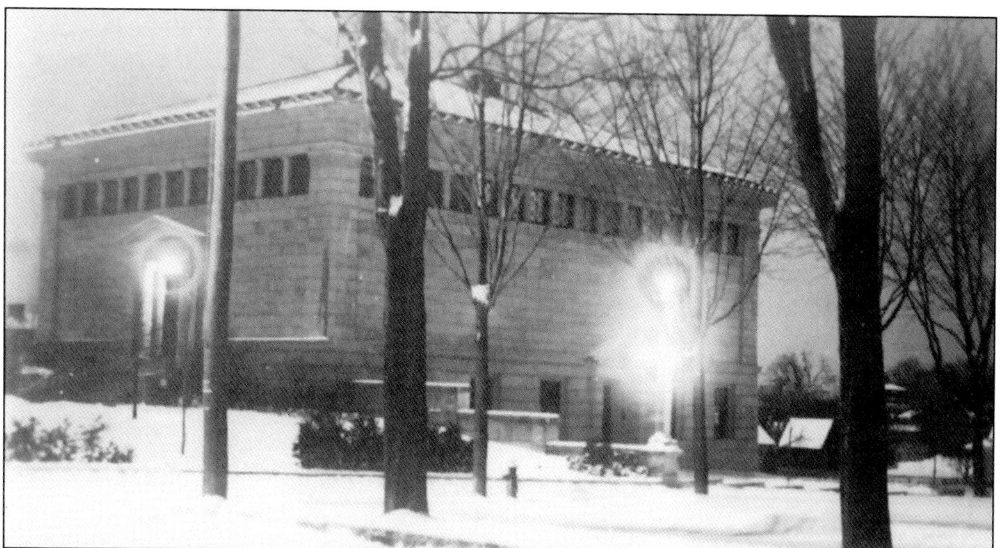

This beautiful Christmas photograph shows a rare seasonal view of the Ray Memorial Library as we look down Main Street to the Common.

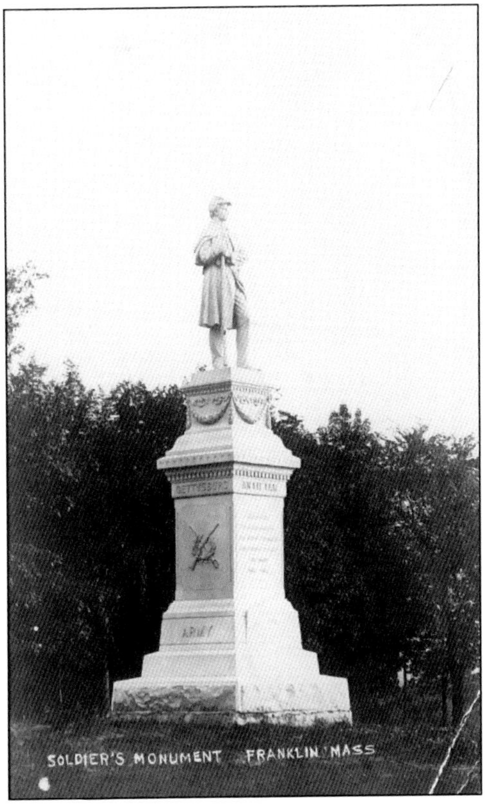


This postcard shows the Civil War Soldier's Monument on the southern end of Franklin Common as it appeared about 1906. It was given to the town by Frederick Newell.

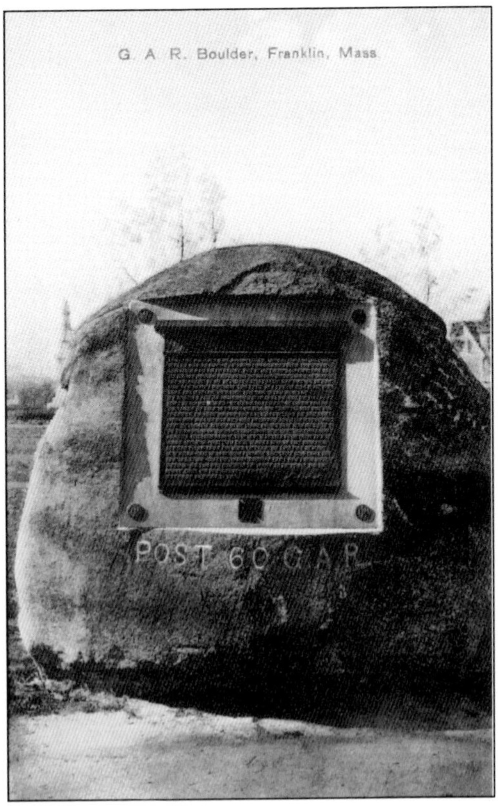


This postcard shows the GAR (Grand Army of the Republic) Memorial Boulder as it appeared on Franklin Common about 1905.

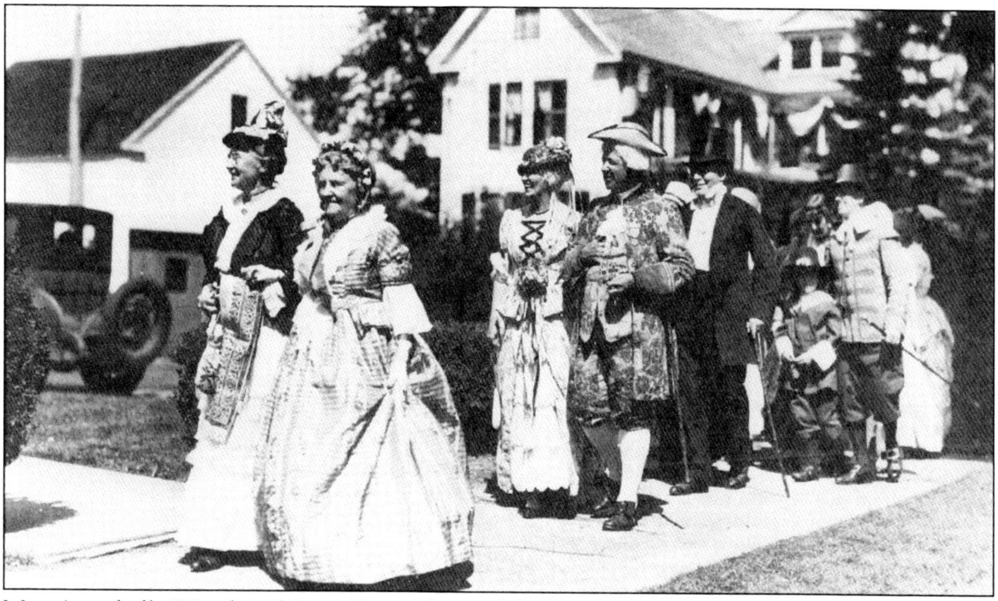

Mrs. Annebelle Woodward, Miss Rene Thayer, Mr. Charles (Doc) Frazer, Mr. Arthur W. Pierce, and Mr. Ray Wycroft lead a little parade of their own as they promenade off to the Common on Sesquicentennial Day in 1928.

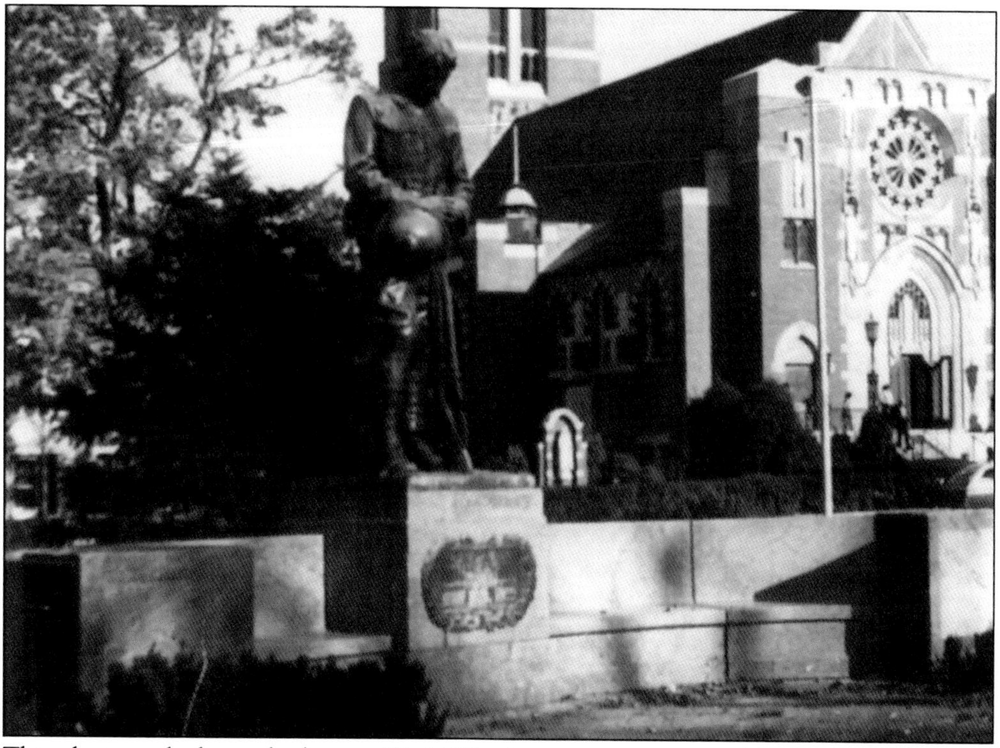

This photograph shows the bronze World War I monument as it used to stand in relation to Saint Mary's Church about 1938. The statue is known as "The Doughboy."

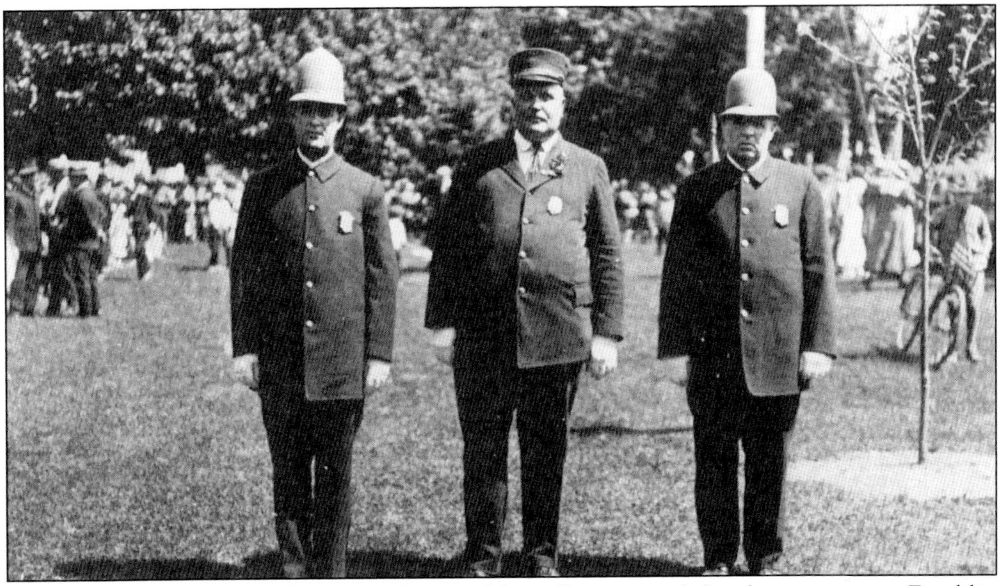

Police Chief John W. Nickerson and two of his officers posed for the camera on Franklin Common on a Fourth of July early in the century. Note the Boy Scout with the flag-decorated bicycle to the right.

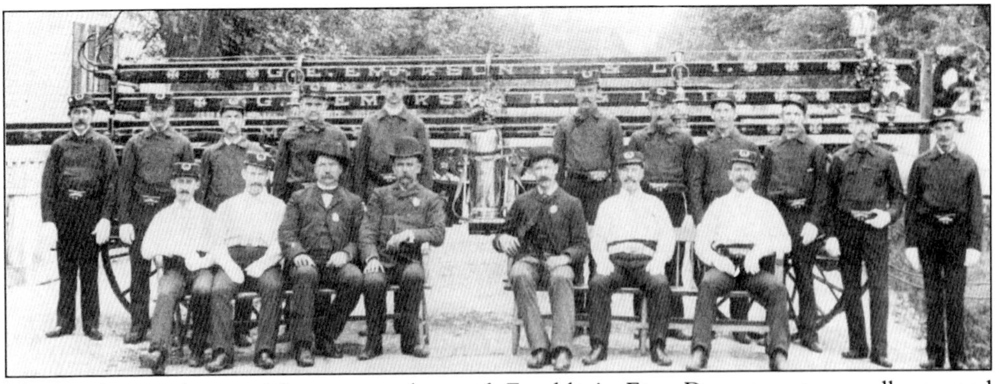

Not to be outdone, eighteen members of Franklin's Fire Department proudly turned out in force.

*Four*

# Franklin's Divine Side: The Churches

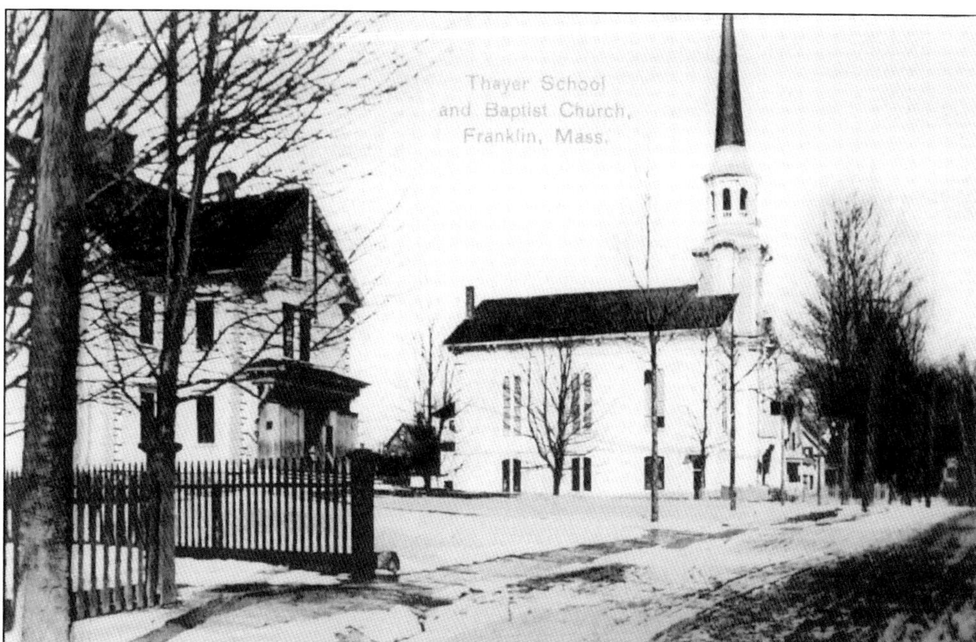


The old Baptist church, in all of its New England splendor, was ruined by the great Hurricane of 1938 (see p. 117).

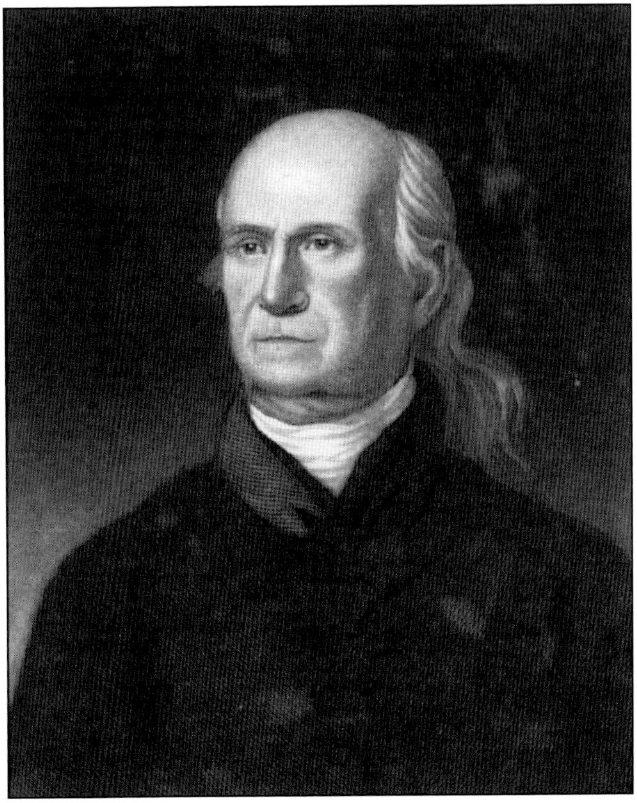

Nathanael Emmonds held the Congregational pulpit in Franklin from 1773 until 1828. His uncompromising Puritanicalism led to his preaching that Horace Mann's brother had gone to Hell because he went swimming rather than attending divine services.

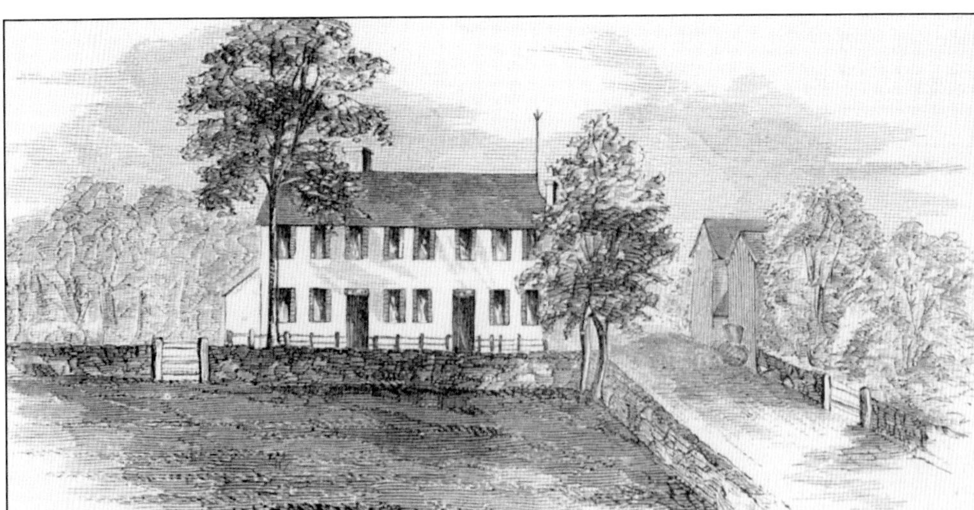

This engraving of Emmon's house appeared in Blake's 1878 history.

This Congregational church burned to the ground in the mid-1890s and was replaced by the beautiful structure at the bottom of the page.

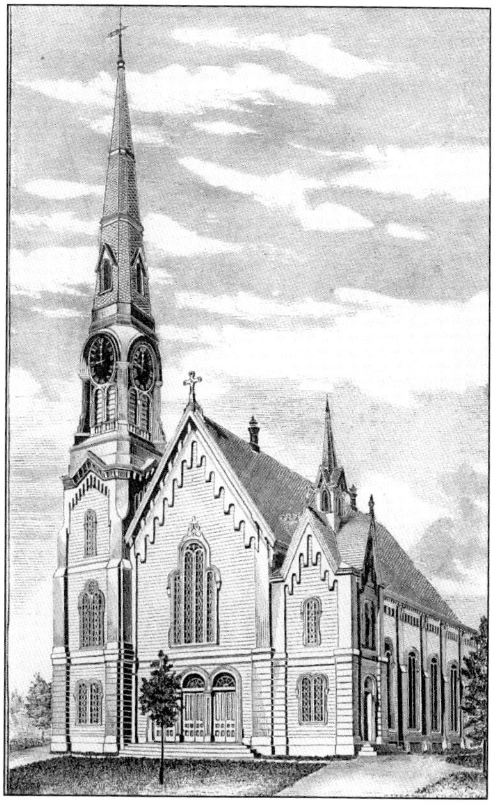

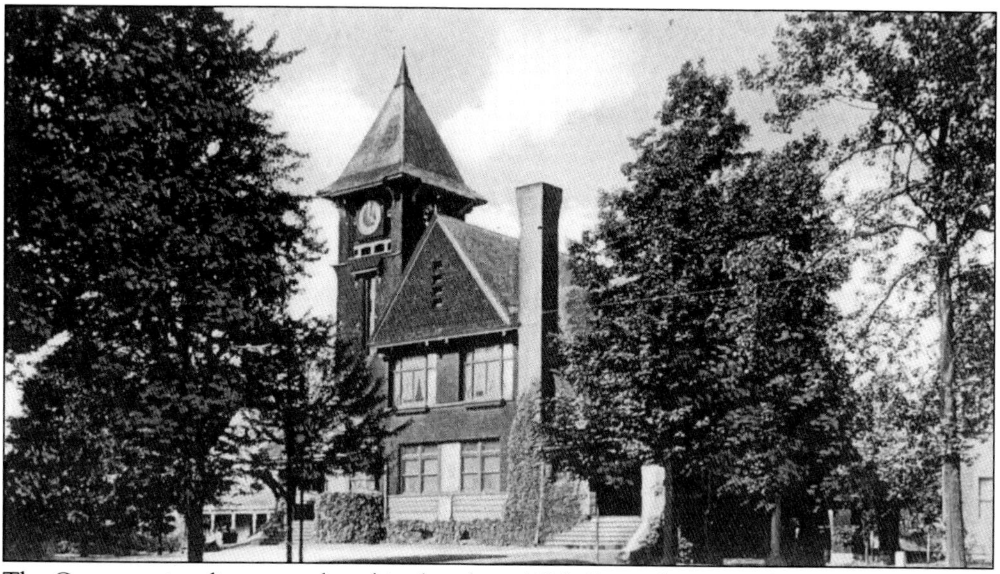

The Congregationalists moved to this church in 1895. Since this 1906 photograph was taken, the tower has been lowered.

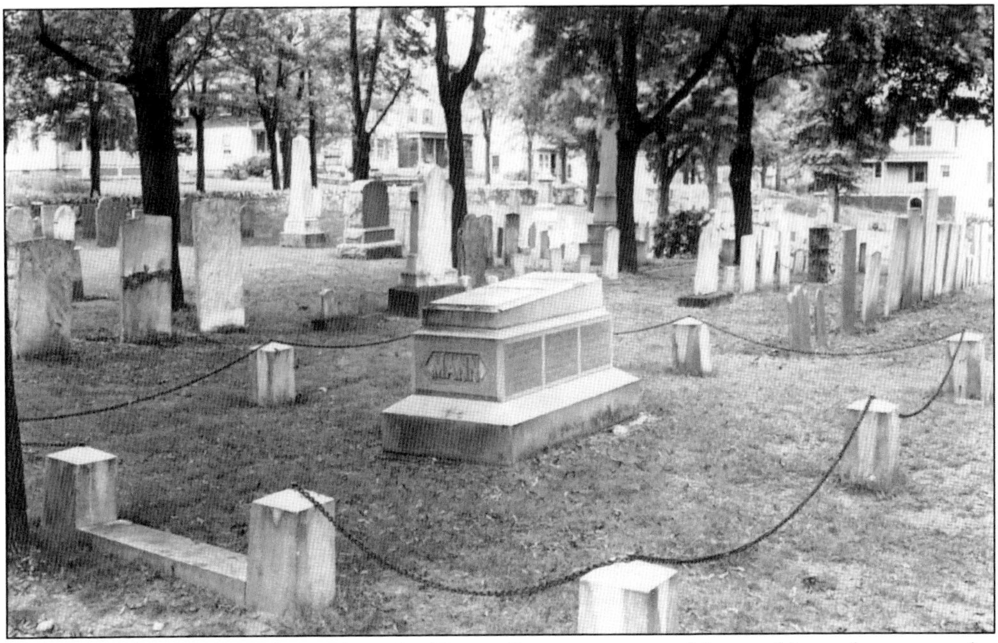

The Mann family plot is located in the Union Street cemetery. Horace Mann, known as the "Father of American Education," is not entombed here, however. Many of the old grave stones date from the 1700s.

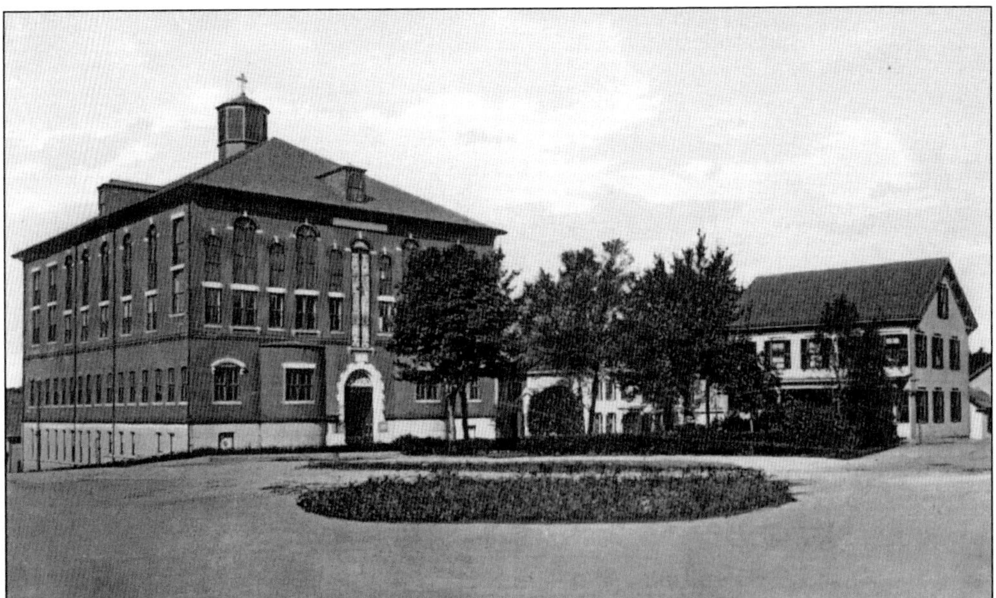

The second St. Mary's Church building suffered the same fate as the first and burned in the early 1920s. It was replaced in 1924.

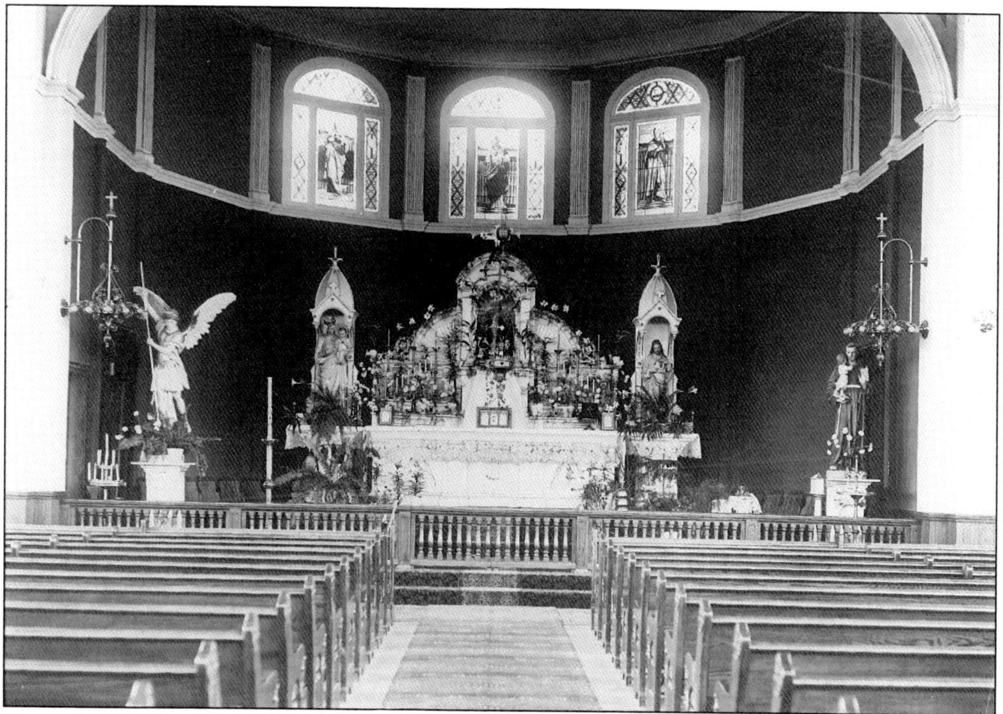

The richly-decorated interior of the second St. Mary's Church was a classic example of Roman beauty. This is how it appeared about 1920.

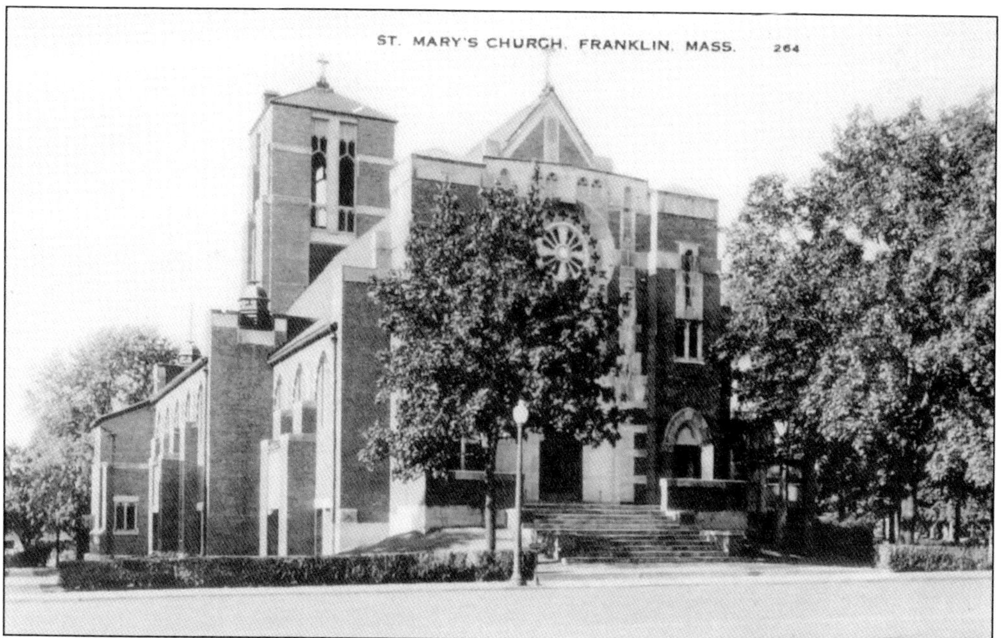


The third St. Mary's Church rose from the ashes in 1924. It has remained substantially unchanged for more than seventy years.

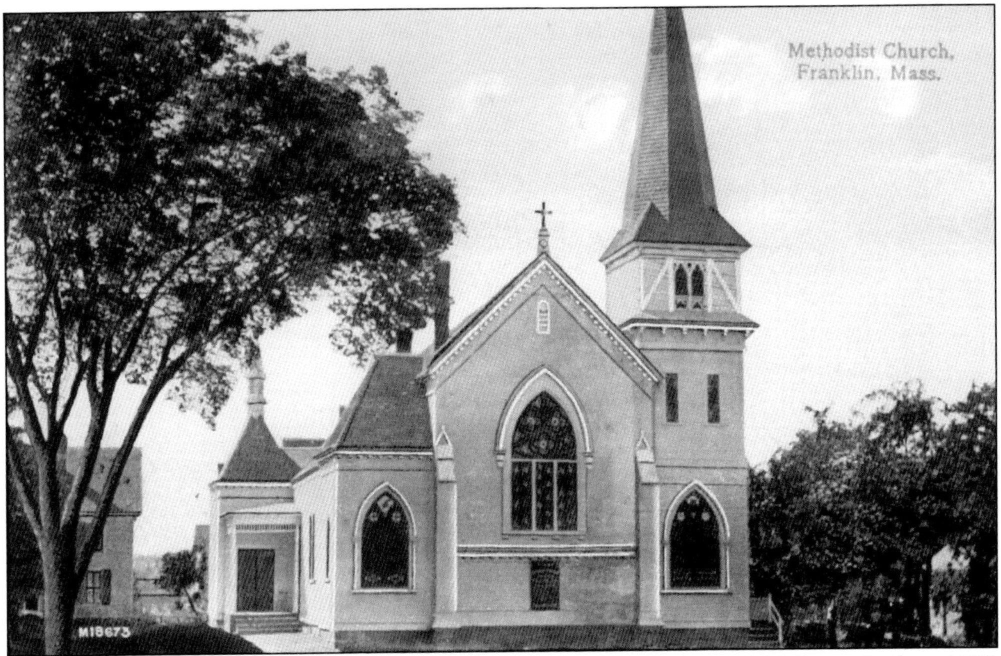


This postcard shows Franklin's Methodist church as it appeared about 1900. It was built in 1872 and has undergone some fine restorations.

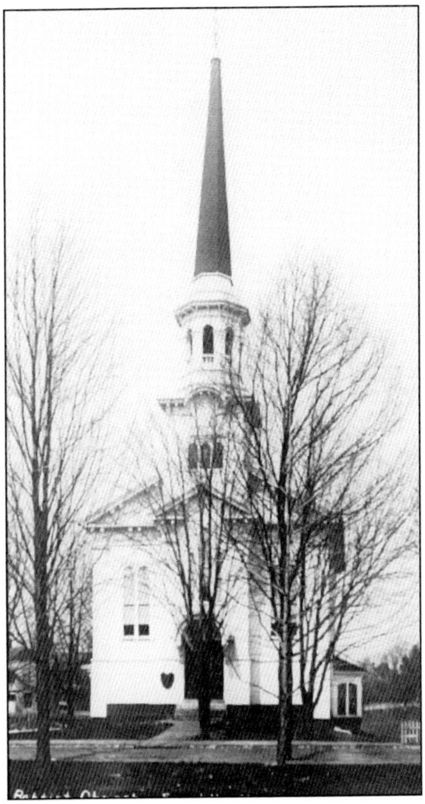

This postcard shows another view of the beautiful old Baptist church which was a victim of the Hurricane of 1938. The Baptists joined with the Congregationalists to form the Franklin Federated Church.

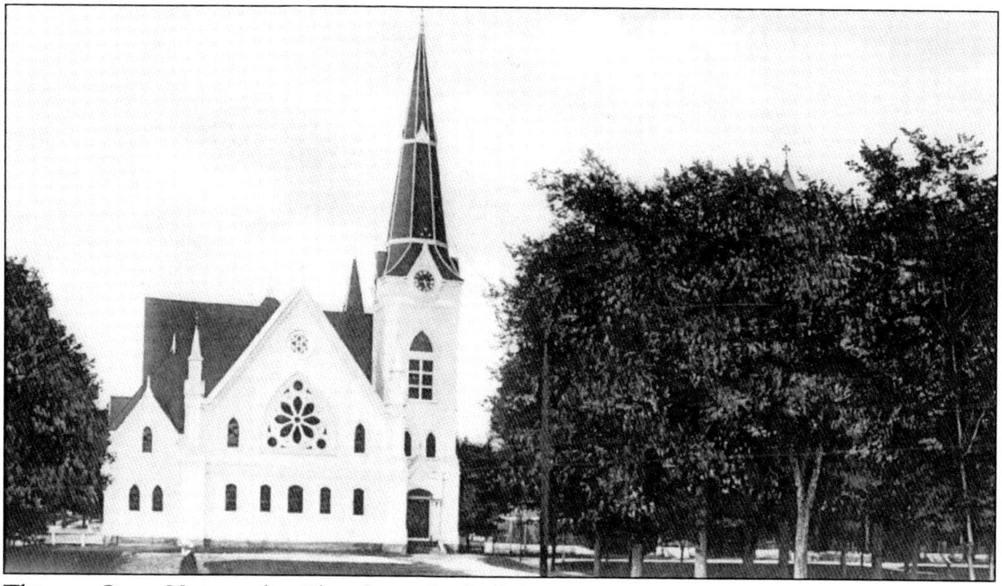

This was Grace Universalist Church as it looked about 1910. It was located on the Dean College campus until the 1960s, when it was taken down to make room for the college library.

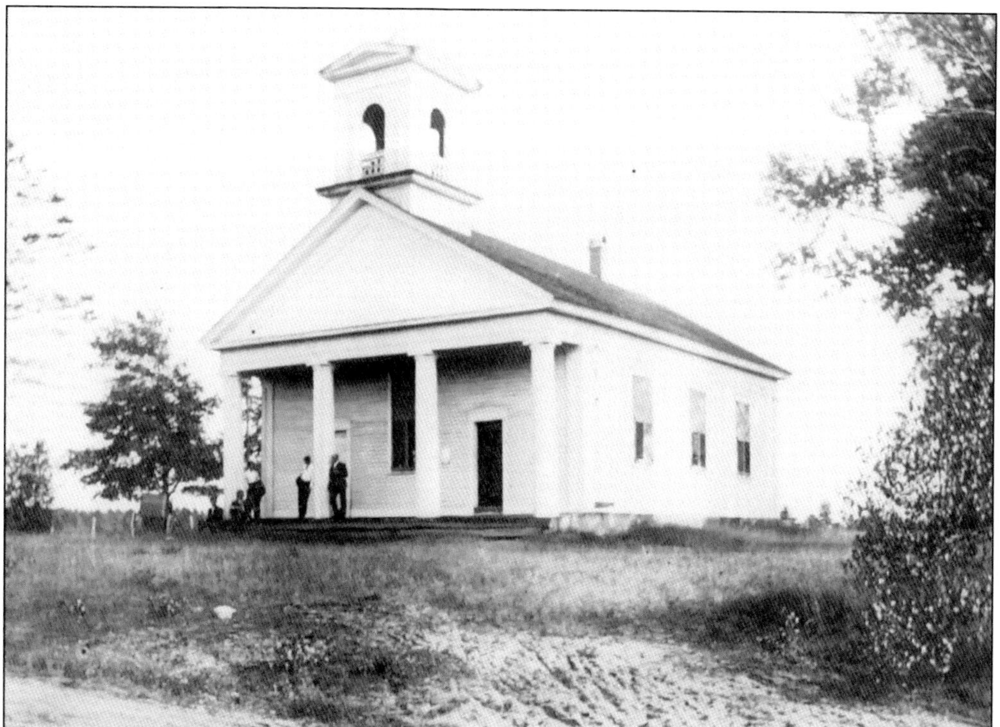

The Old South Meeting House was dedicated about 1856, and it is now the Horace Mann Museum. This photograph was taken in 1900.

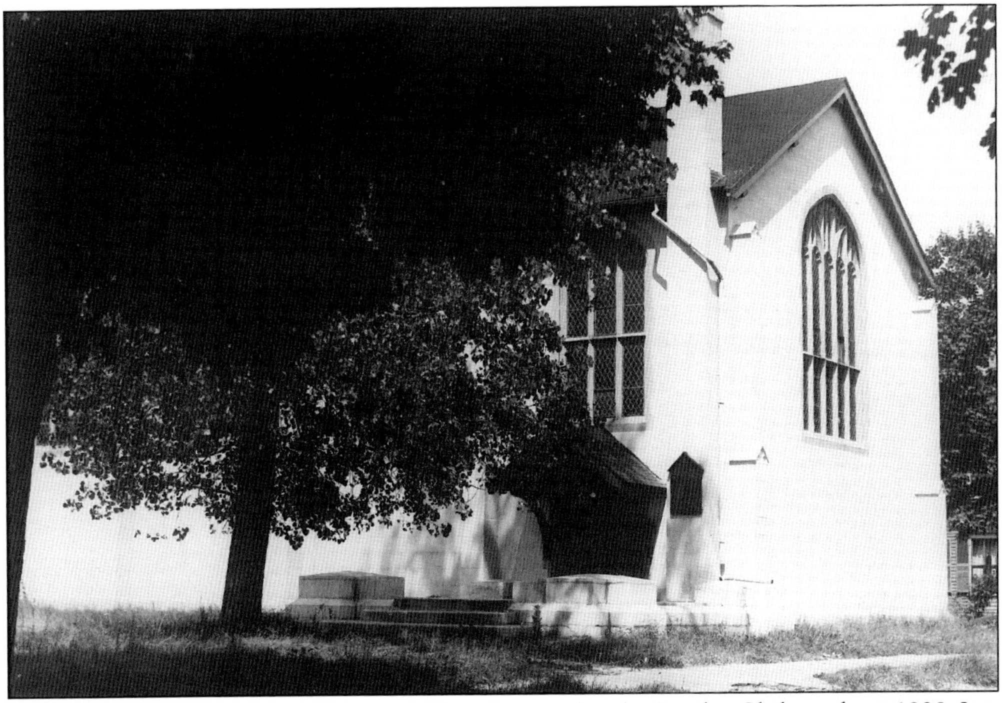

This photograph of St. John's Episcopal Church was taken by Stanley Chilson about 1928. It is now the Dean College Center for Theater Arts.

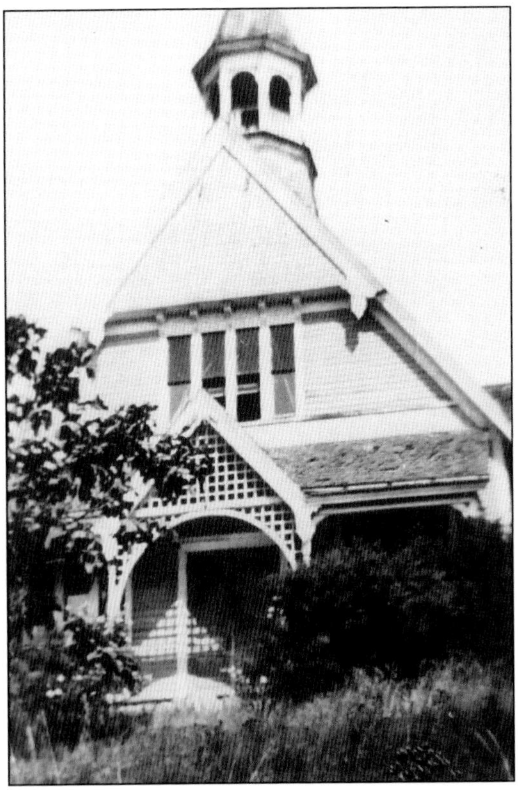

This photograph by Stanley Chilson shows Union Chapel, which was a non-denominational Protestant church from 1894 to 1924. At the end of its thirty-year history, it fell to ruin because of neglect and was torn down.

# *Five*

# Where They Lived: The Homes of Old Franklin

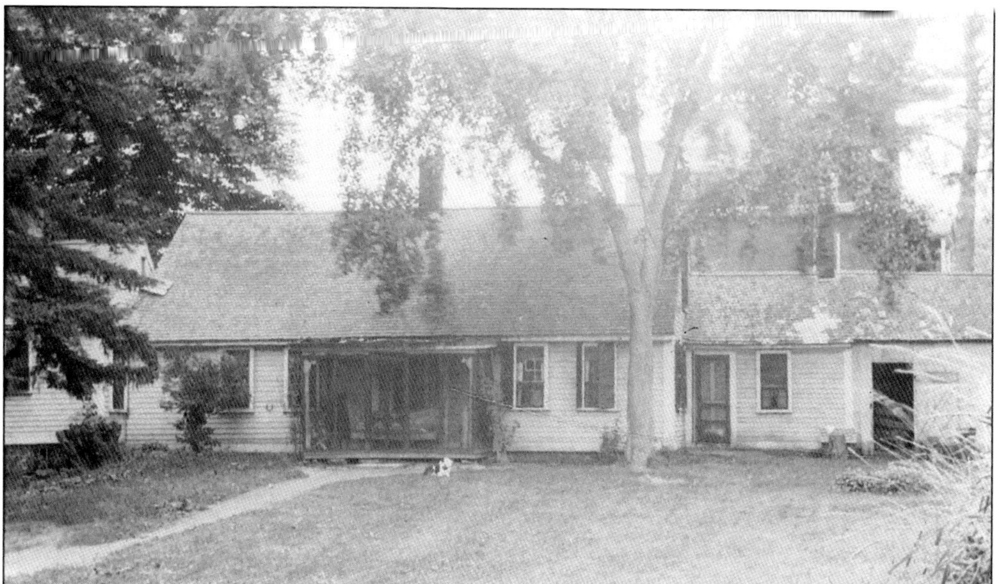

This photograph shows the Oliver Pond House as it appeared about 1900. It was constructed in five stages from 1760 onward to meet the demands of a growing family. Oliver Pond (1725–1799) was a captain of Franklin's Minutemen and participated in the Siege of Boston between 1775 and 1776.

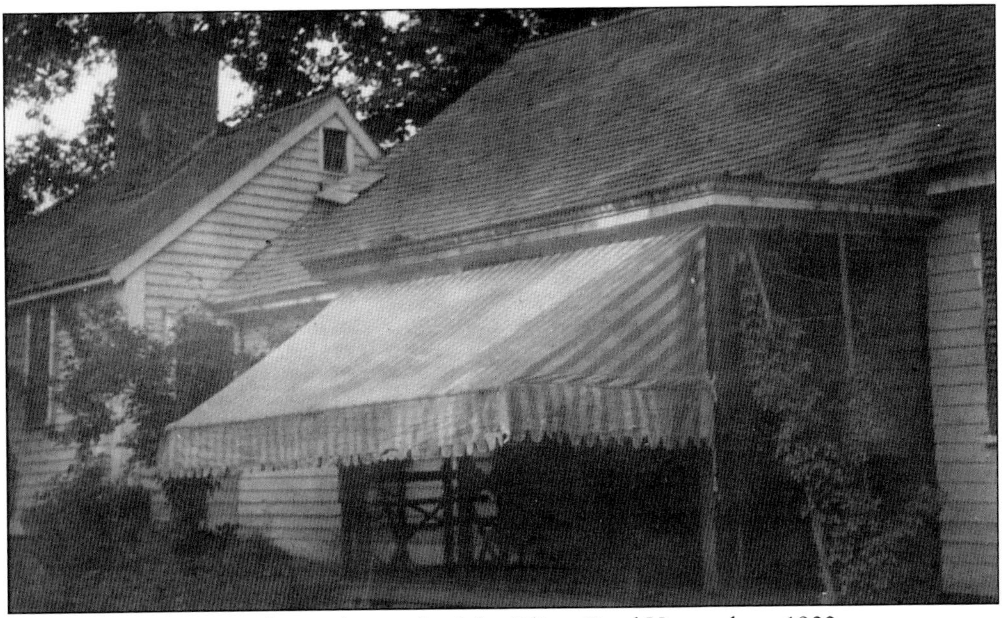

A Victorian awning overhangs the porch of the Oliver Pond House about 1900.

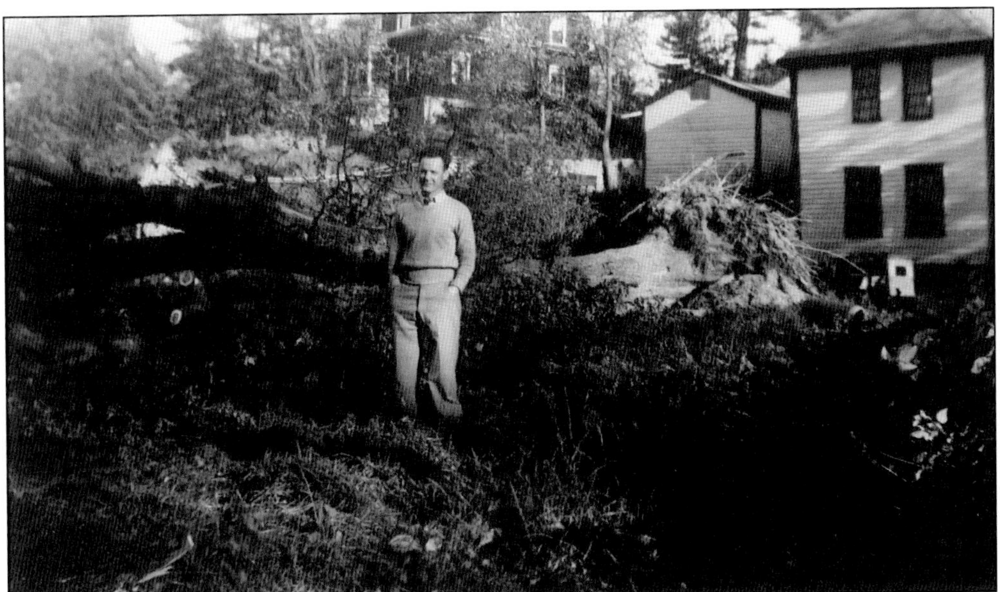

The Oliver Pond House can be seen from the north side in this 1938 photograph. The north wing was almost crushed by a huge tree which fortunately fell away from the house during the "Great Hurricane."

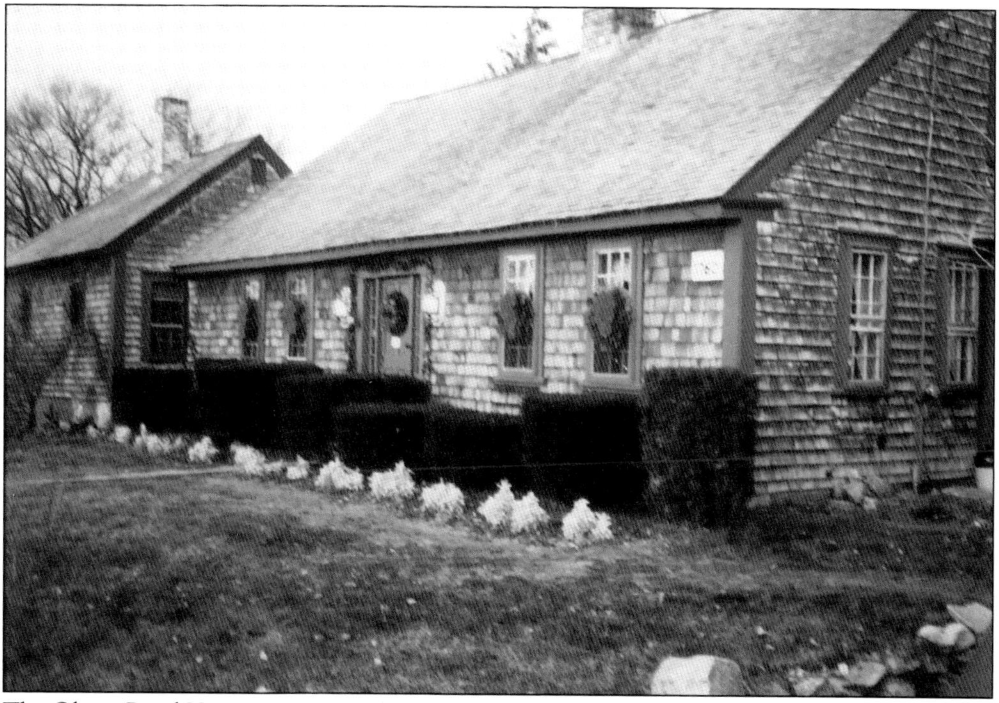

The Oliver Pond House was restored in time for the town's bicentennial as a true Franklin relic of the American Revolutionary period.

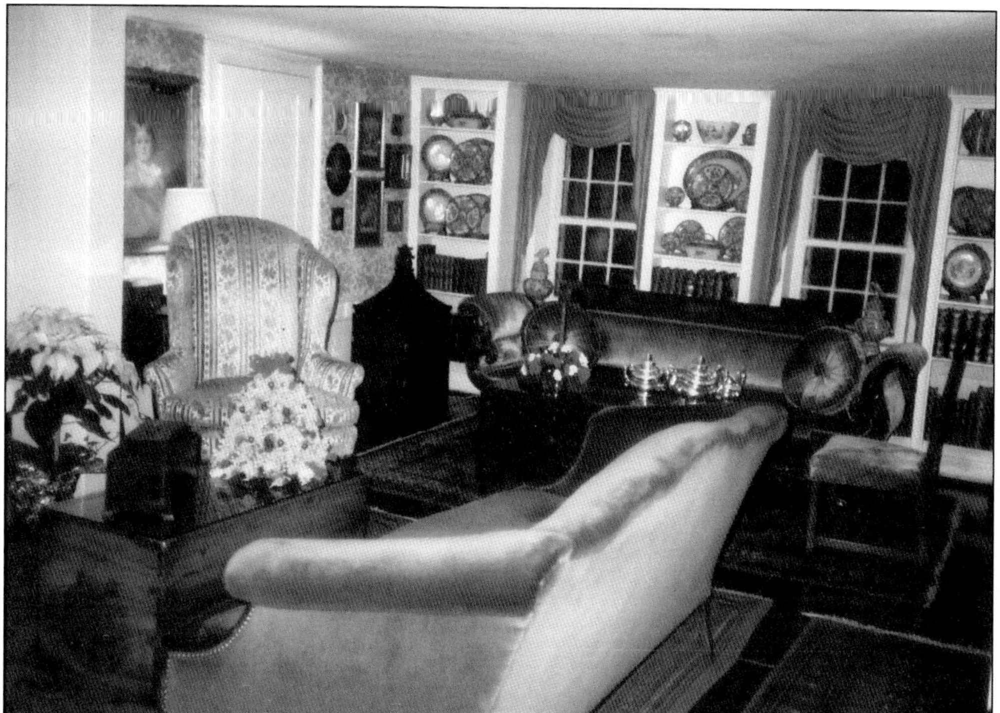

Here is the drawing room in the Oliver Pond House. Andy Warhol's silver service, which dates from 1814, was made by Peter Chiterey of New York and is shown in front of an 1820s sofa.

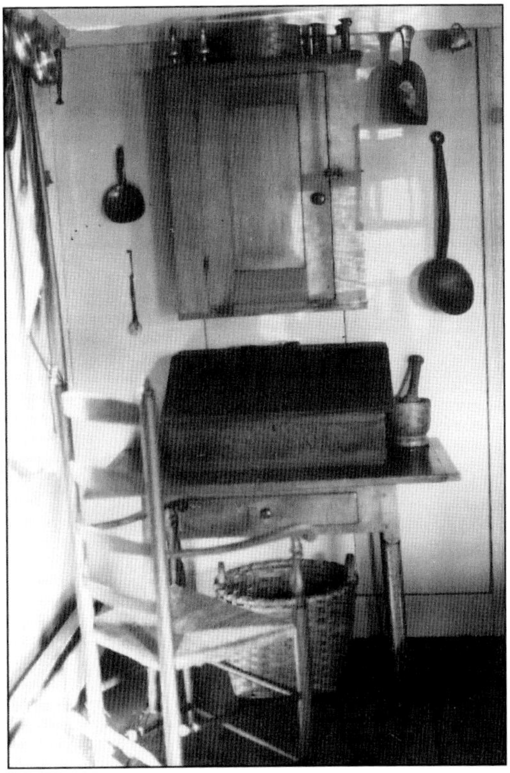

A 1678 Bible box is seen in this photograph sitting on a 1710 Queen and Tavern table at the historic Oliver Pond House.

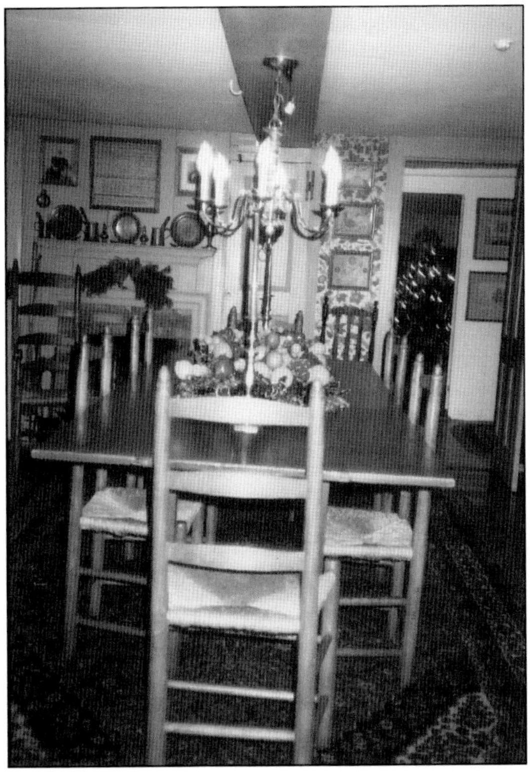

This photograph shows the keeping room (or dining room) of the Oliver Pond House during the Southwood Hospital fund-raising tour of 1990.

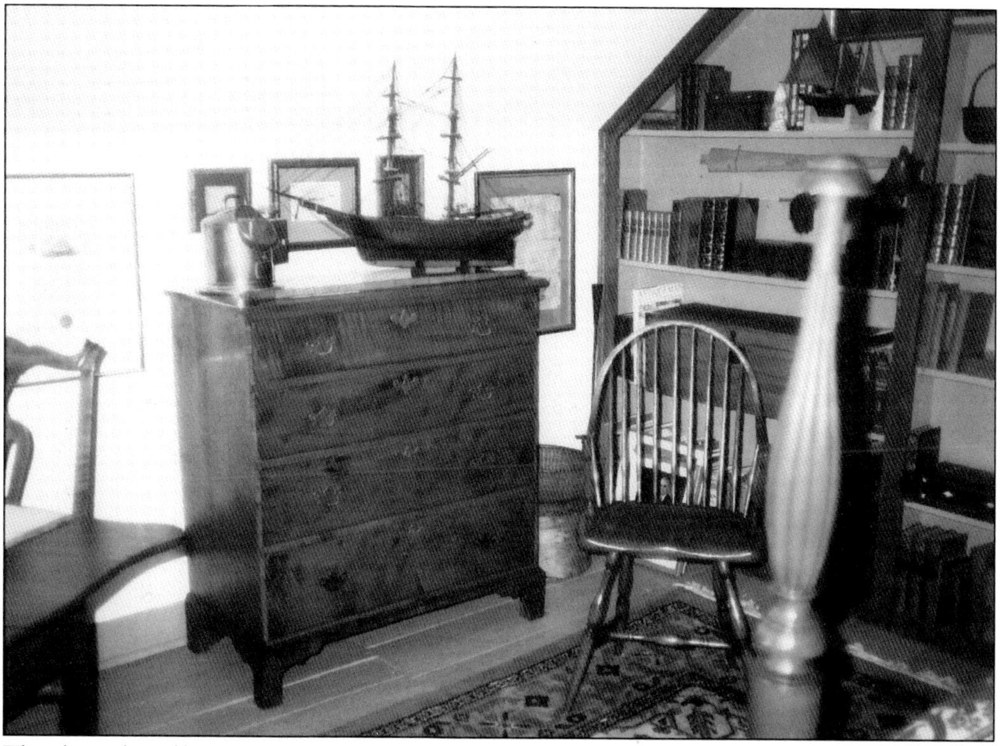

The slanted roof here in the great bed chamber of the Oliver Pond House is typical of New England cottages of the 1630 to 1850 period.

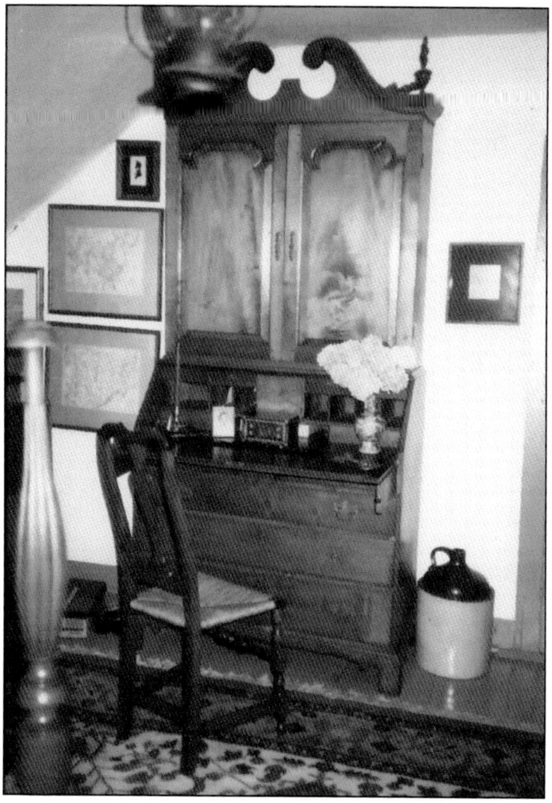

This 1775 Secretary desk dominates the great bed chamber of the Oliver Pond House. The maps to the left of the desk were printed for the use of the British Army in America during the Revolution.

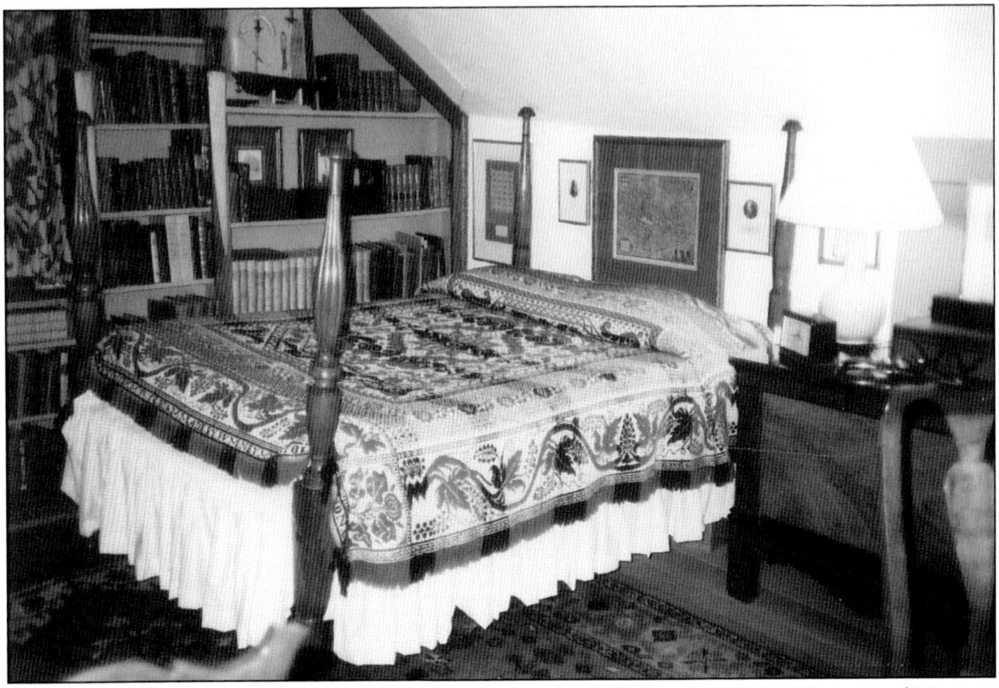

Oliver Pond's bed, built *c.* 1790–95, is preserved in the great bed chamber of the Oliver Pond House.

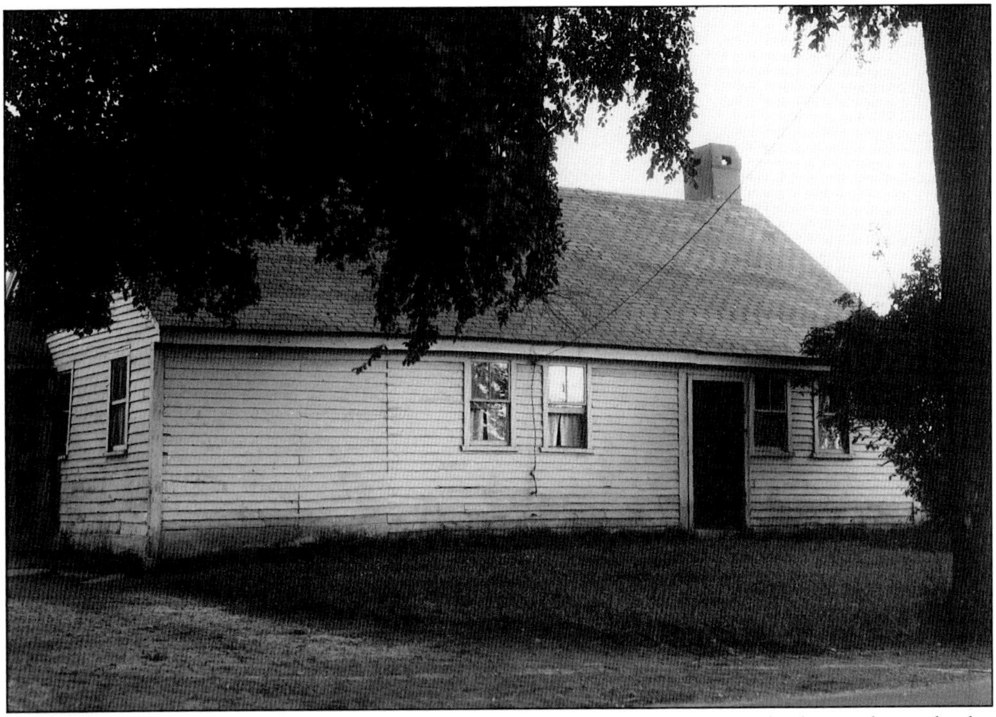

In 1928, Stanley Chilson photographed this pre-Revolutionary cottage, which was formerly the home of Jabez Fisher. Fisher was also a captain of the local Minutemen, Franklin's representative in the Great and General Court, and the town's first moderator in 1778. He was a master politician.

This wonderful old two-story house on Brook Street dates from 1720.

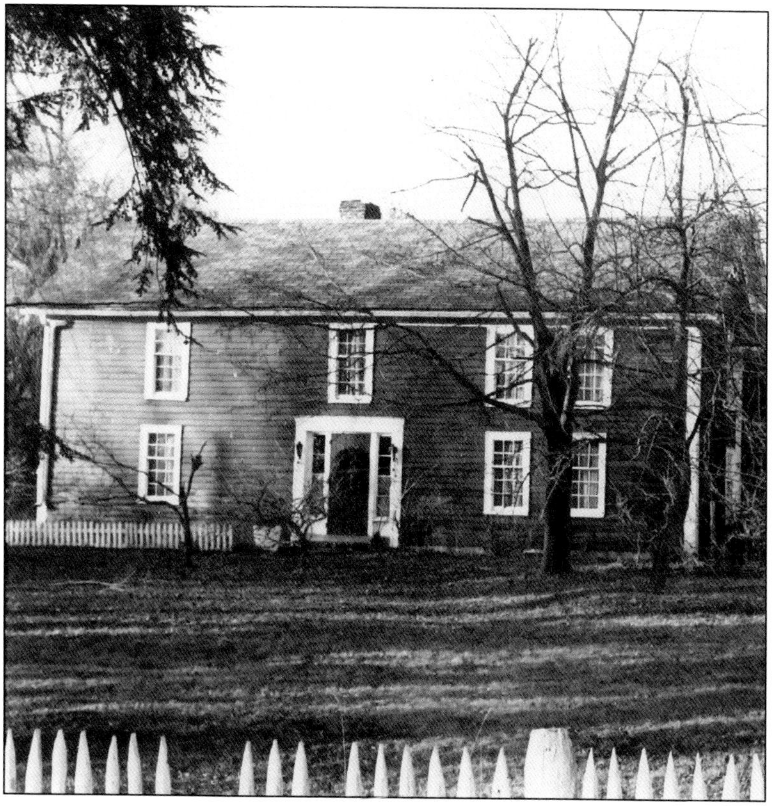

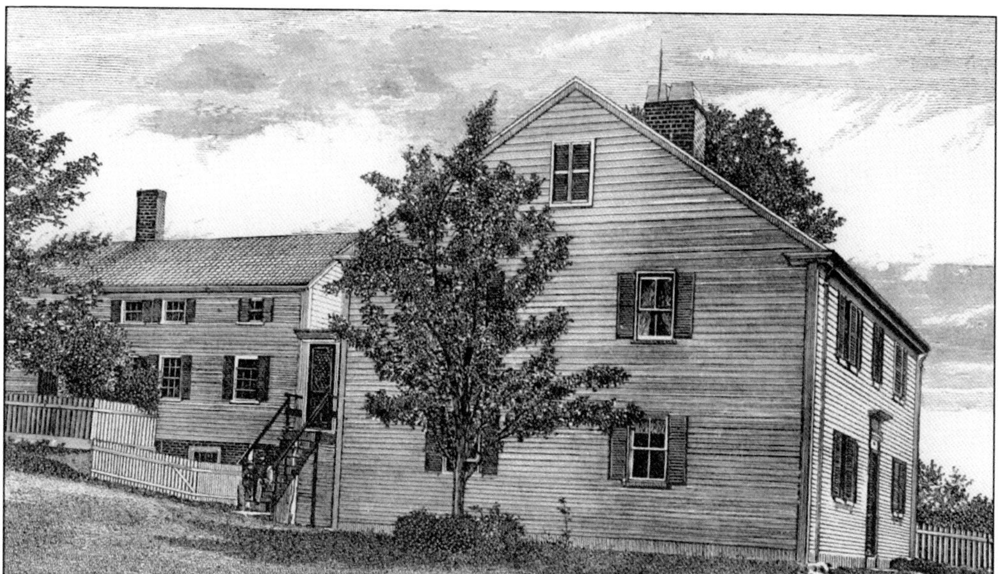

This image shows the historic Richardson Homestead on Lincoln Street as it appeared in 1878. It dates from the mid-1700s and was the home of author and Civil War journalist Albert Richardson. It is now the home of Mr. and Mrs. Frank Locke.

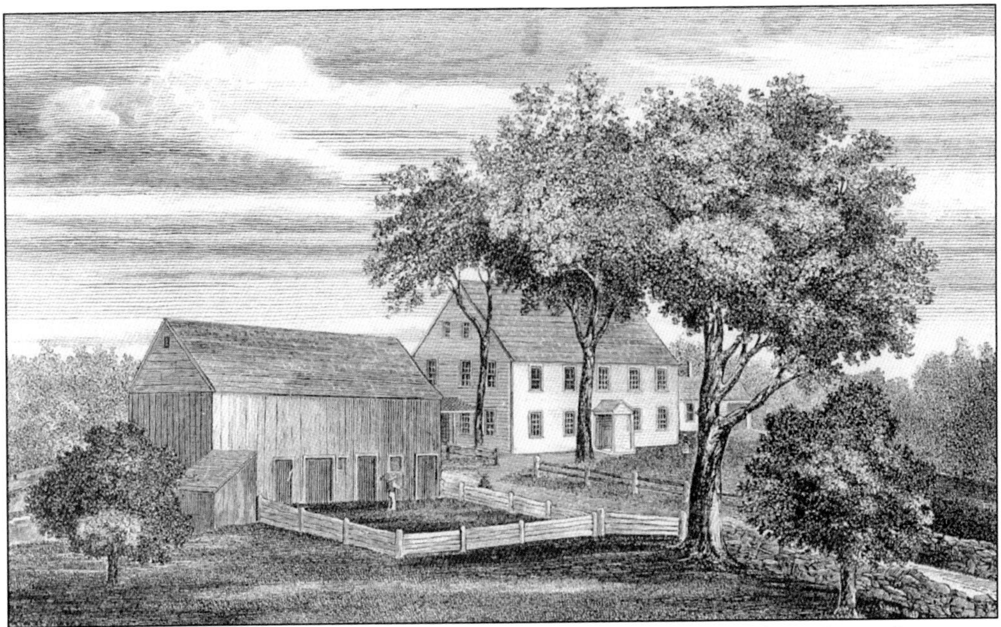

This image of the Fisher Daniels Homestead shows a typical eighteenth-century country Franklin home.

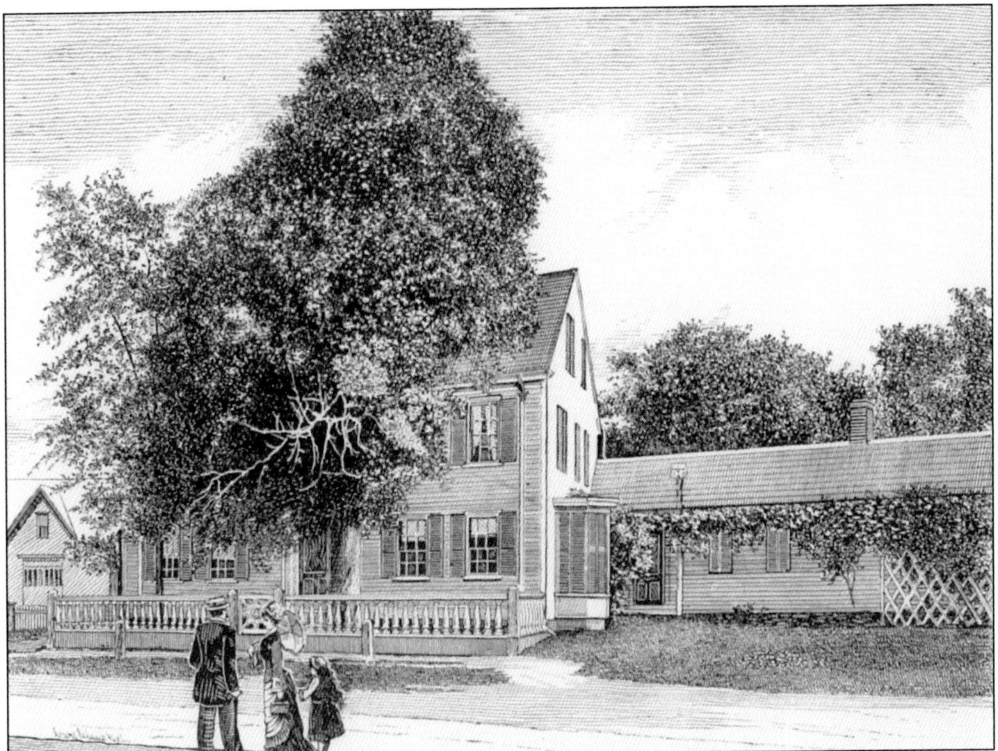

The grandeur of William Makepeace's spacious eighteenth-century home befitted its owner, who was the head of the Massachusetts Christian Temperance Union.

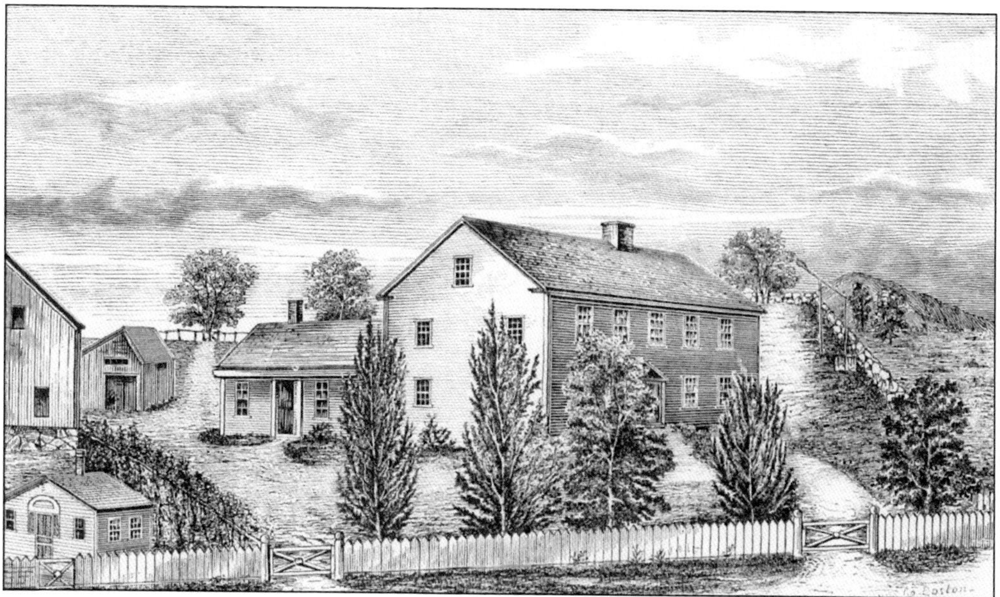

Horace Mann was born in 1796 at the Mann Homestead. This structure was razed in the 1920s. A monument now marks the spot where the the house stood on East Central Street.

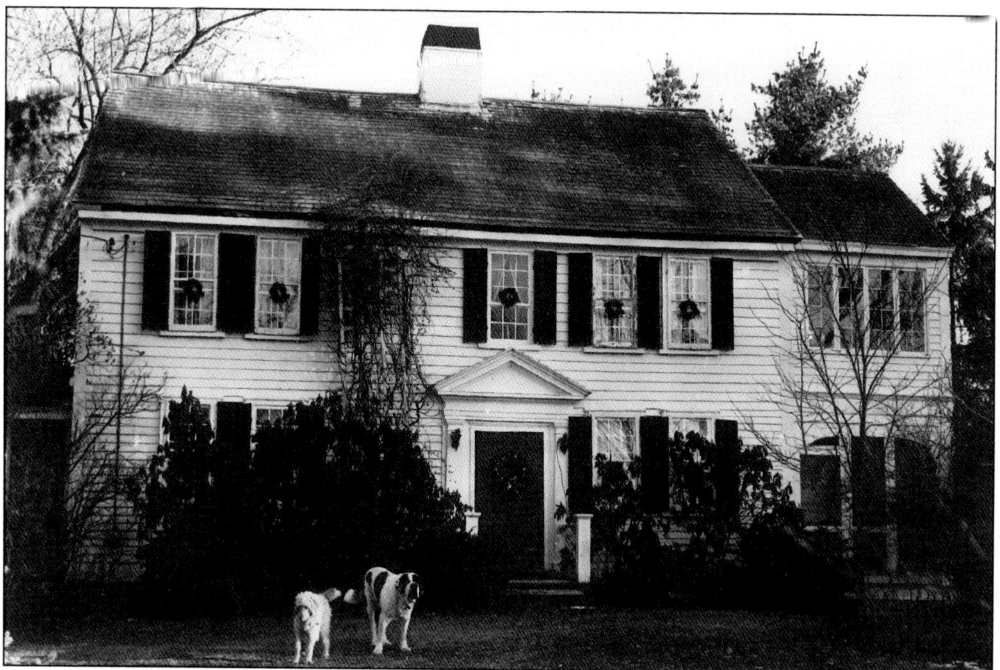

This lovely 1730s house on Forest Street is the home of longtime town official James Nash and his wife Joyce.

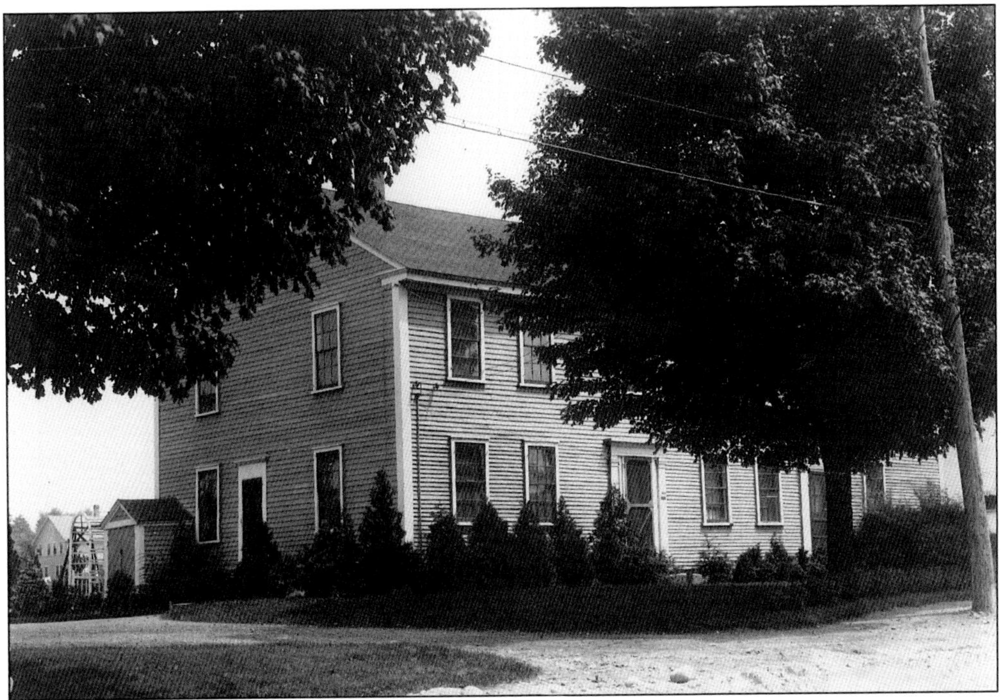

The Van Leewen Homestead was a jewel of eighteenth-century domestic architecture in Franklin.

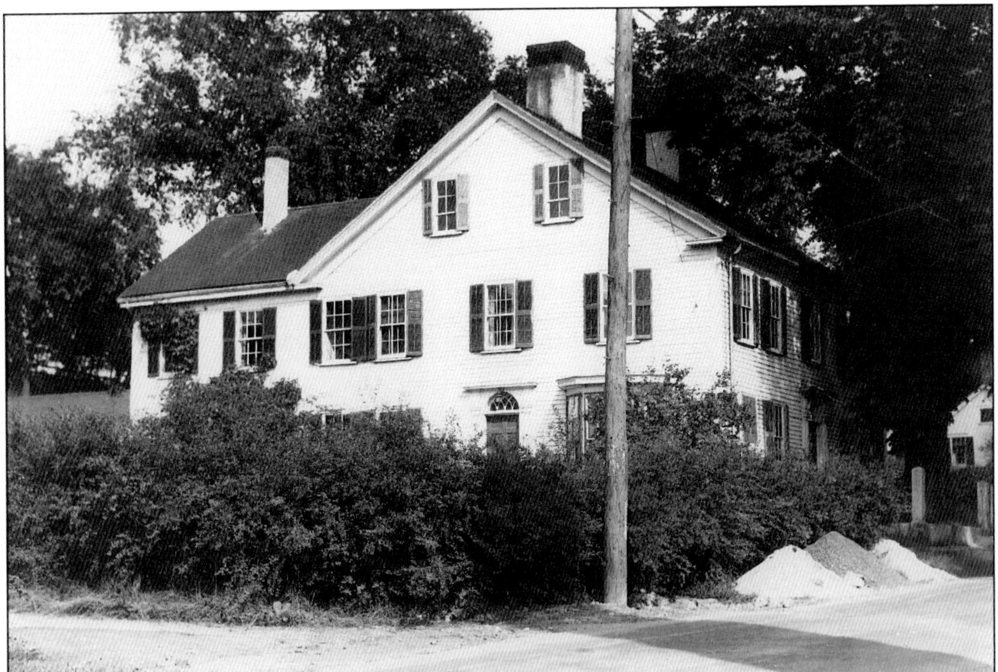

Washington biographer William Makepeace Thayer's beautiful 1760s home was on West Central Street in Franklin. It was photographed by Stanley Chilson about 1928 and was ripped down in the 1940s.

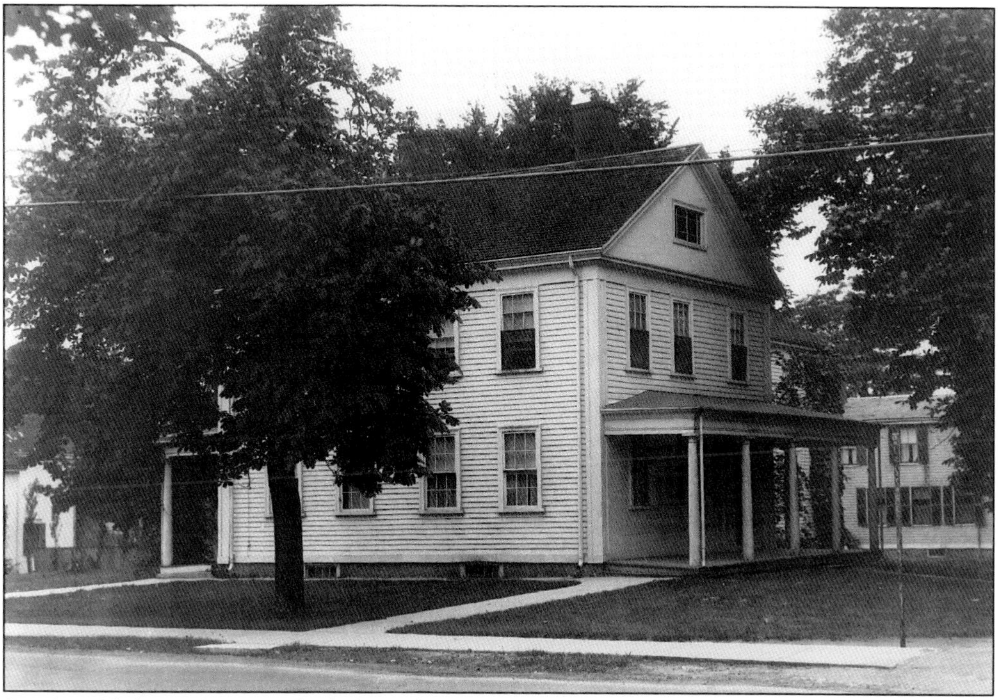

Stanley Chilson photographed the Oliver Dean House about 1928. Oliver Dean was the richest man in town in 1865, which was the year he founded Dean Academy, now known as Dean College.

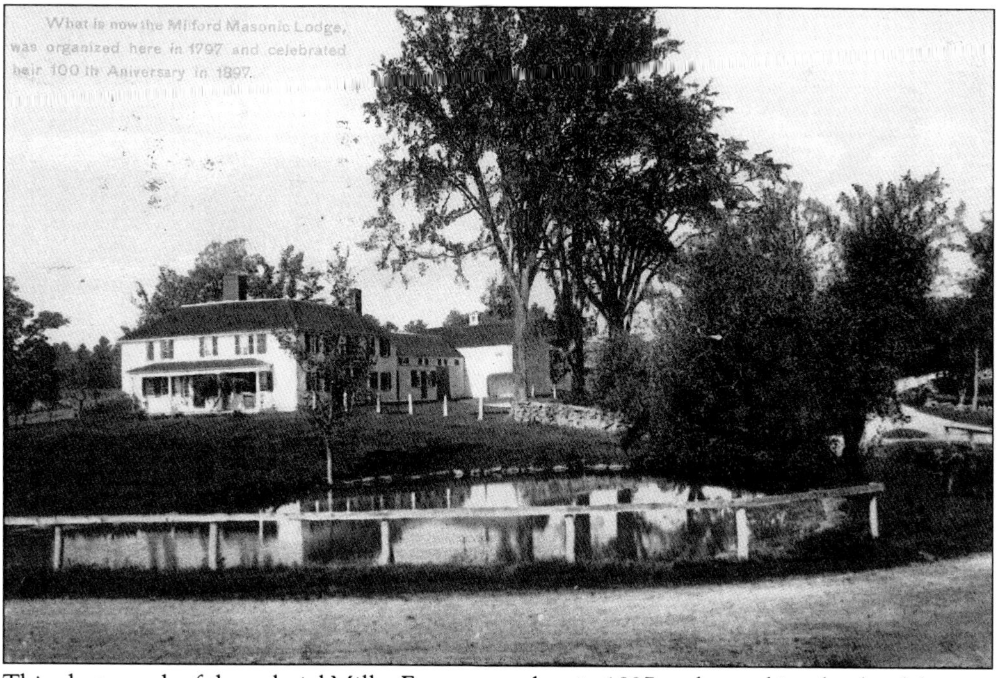



This photograph of the palatial Miller Estate was taken in 1897, to be used in a book celebrating the centennial of the Montgomery Lodge of Masons. The Miller Mansion was a classic eighteenth-century hipped-roof structure.

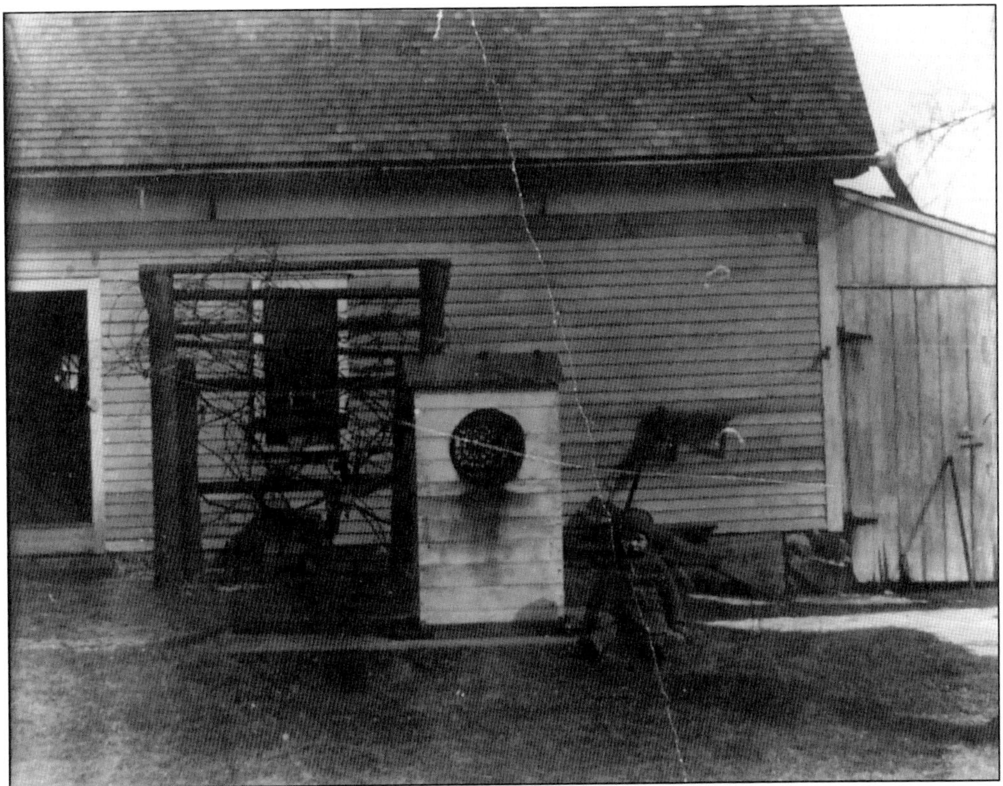

This Franklin well house was a typical fixture of domestic life throughout the nineteenth and early twentieth centuries. This one was located to the rear of the Clark cottage.

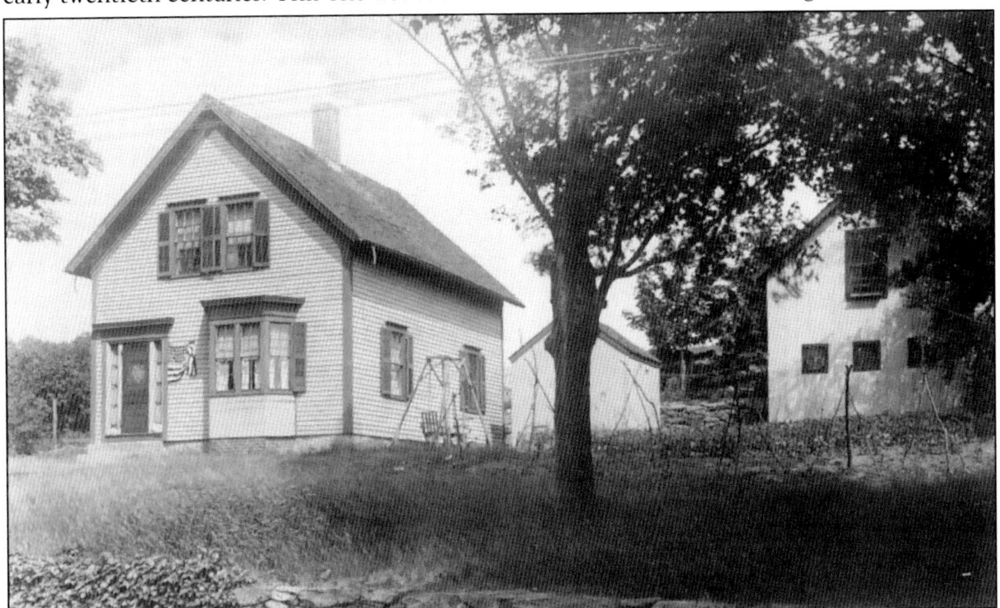

This 1830s cottage located on West Central Street was typical of its time. The ceilings were higher and a "bay window," added later, gives it style. The Federal doorway also gives it a little grandeur. It was the Barton Homestead.

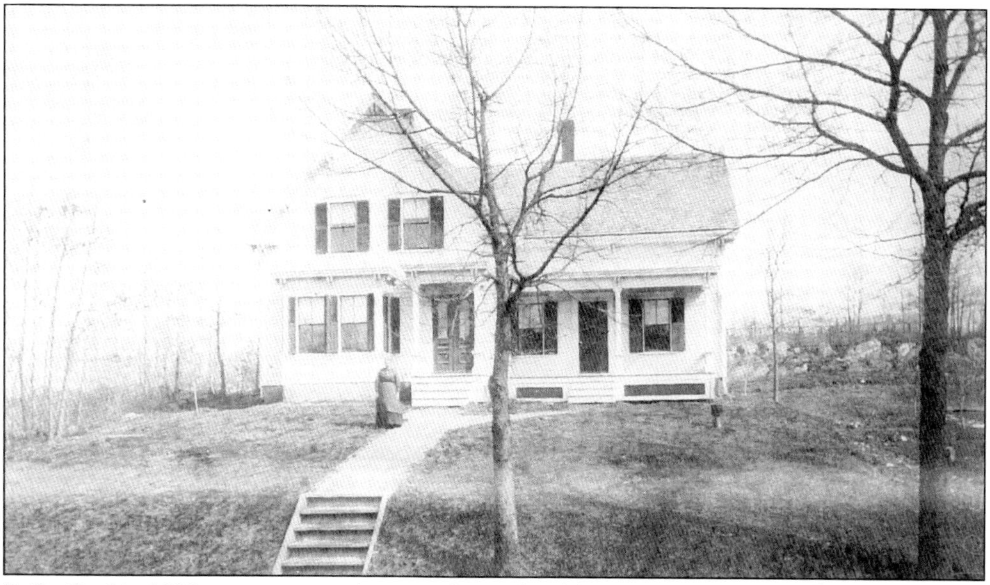

D.C. Cook's 1850s cottage was large and comfortable and an obvious source of pride to Mrs. Cook, who posed in front of it in this 1888 cabinet photograph. The Cook home was located at 111 East Central Street.

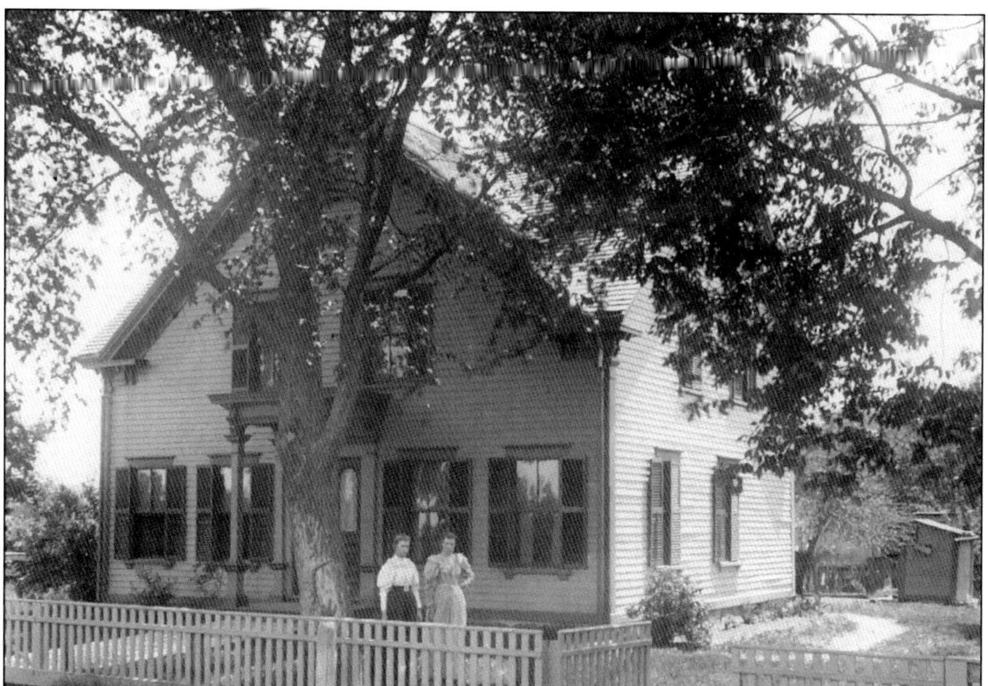

Louise Clark and her sister look over their property about 1880. Louise was a gifted amateur oil painter. Note the well house at the rear of this dwelling on West Central Street.

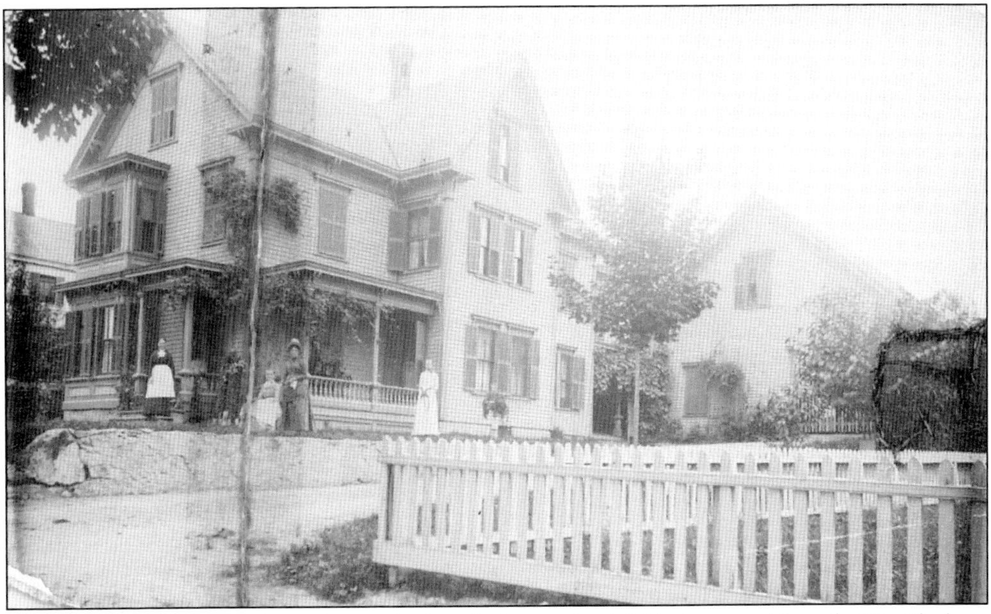

This photograph was taken about 1875 and shows the 1850s home of Joseph W. Clark at 214 Union Street. Clark was a leader of the Industrial Revolution in Franklin, making textile machinery in his factory on Union Street. Members of the Clark family lived in this house until the 1980s.

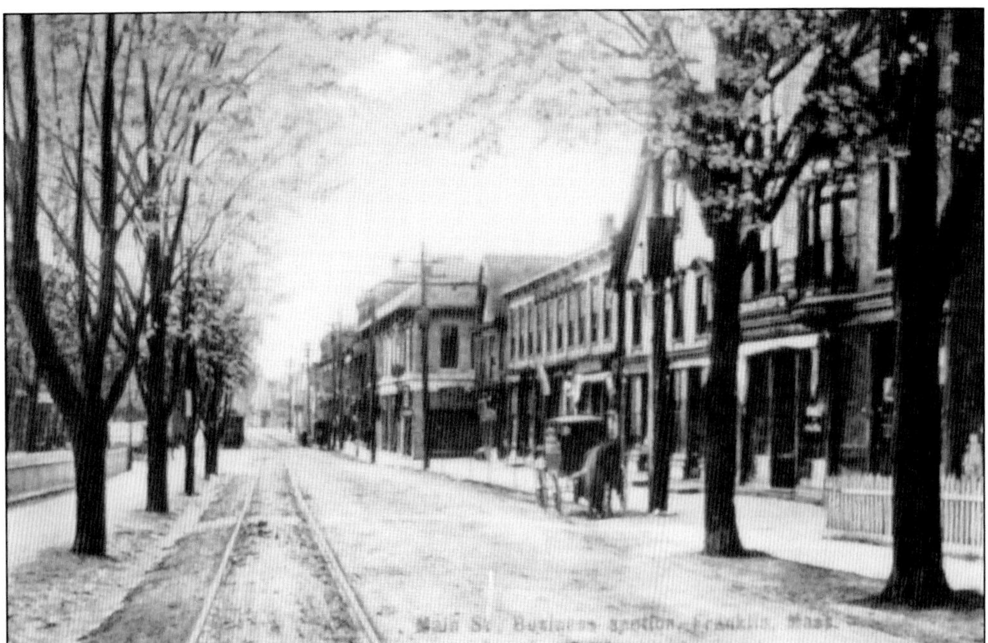

The stores on Main Street often rented the upper floors of their buildings out as apartments.

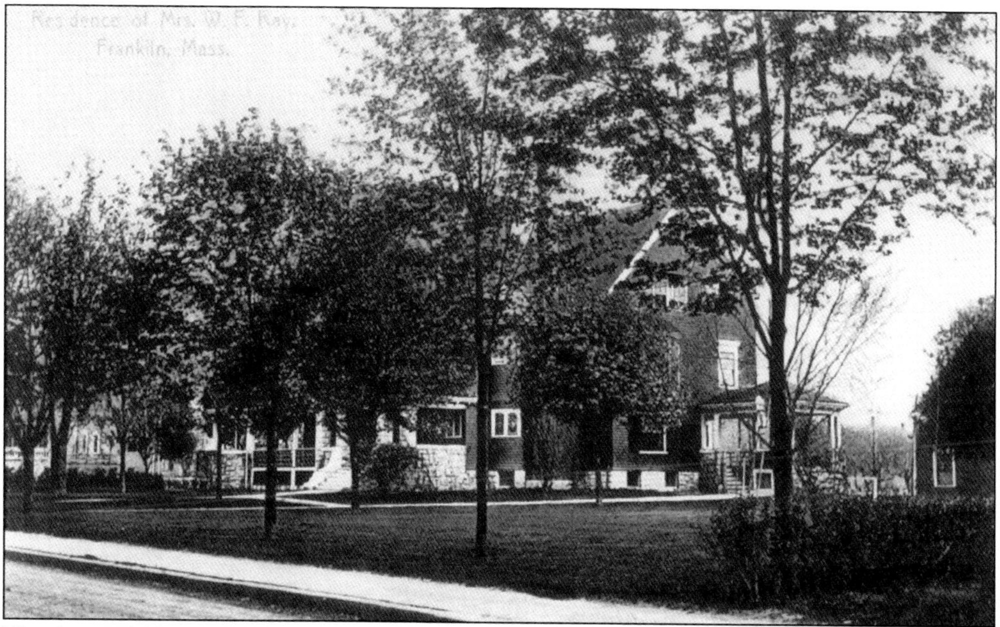


This beautiful Victorian mansion on West Central Street was the home of Mrs. William F. Ray. The building now belongs to Dean College and is called the Mitchell House. This photographic postcard dates from 1902.

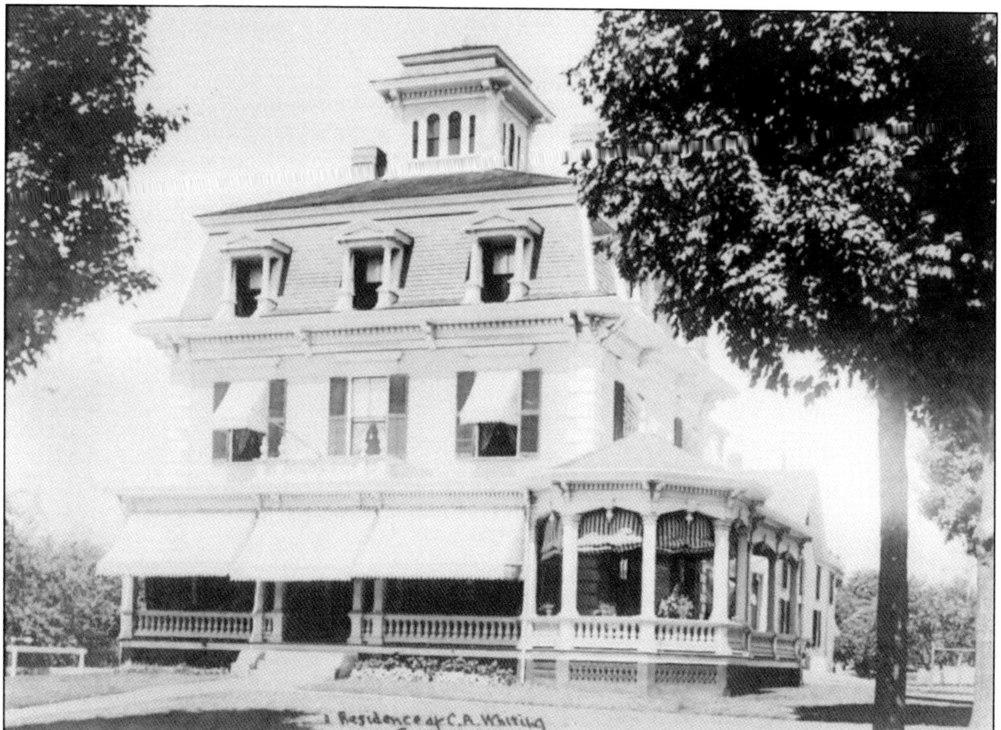


This Second Empire mansion was the home of the Whitings on West Central Street. It eventually passed into the ownership of Dean College, which ripped it down in the 1960s to create a student parking lot.

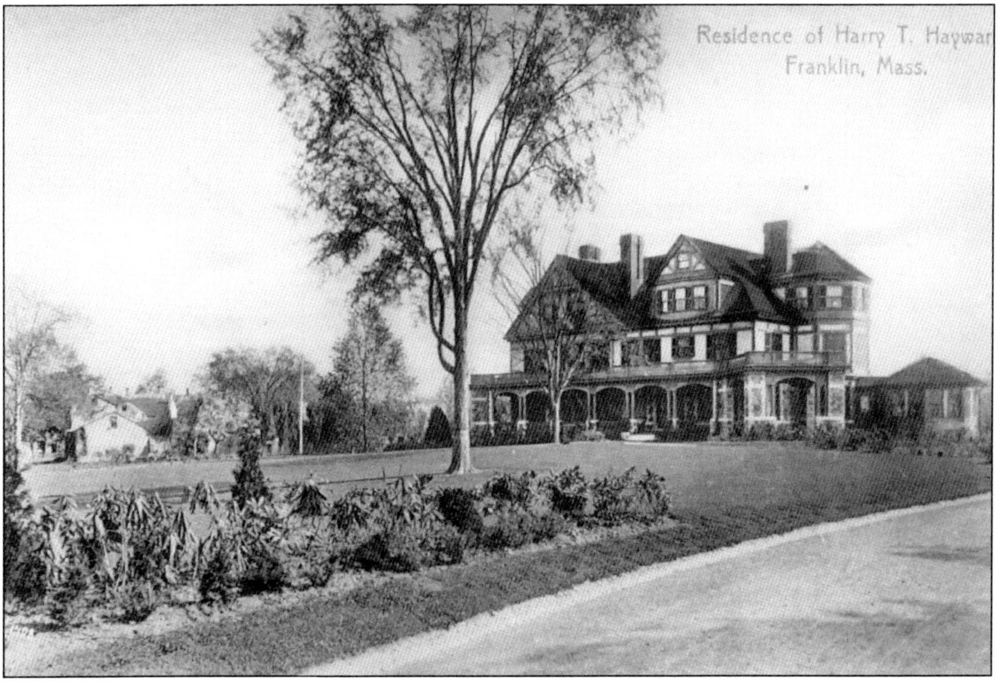


Mr. and Mrs. Harry J. Haywood's half-timbered Victorian mansion is shown in this postcard and the one below about 1905.

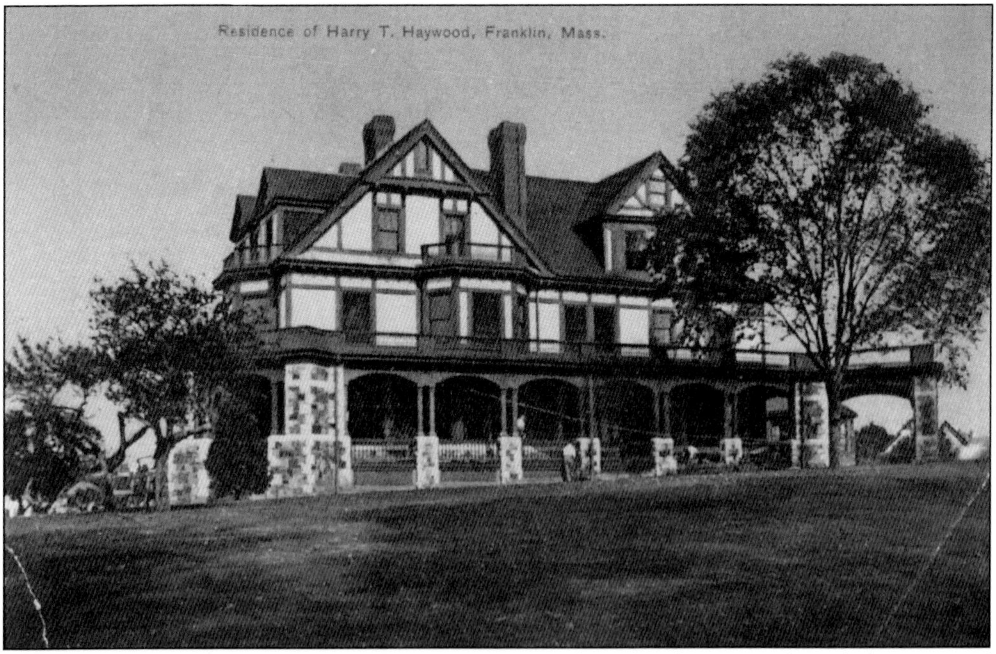


The Haywood Mansion did not please Mrs. Haywood to the degree it pleased the postcard makers. She ripped it down in the 1920s and built a splendid Georgian brick mansion in its place, which became a convent after her death.

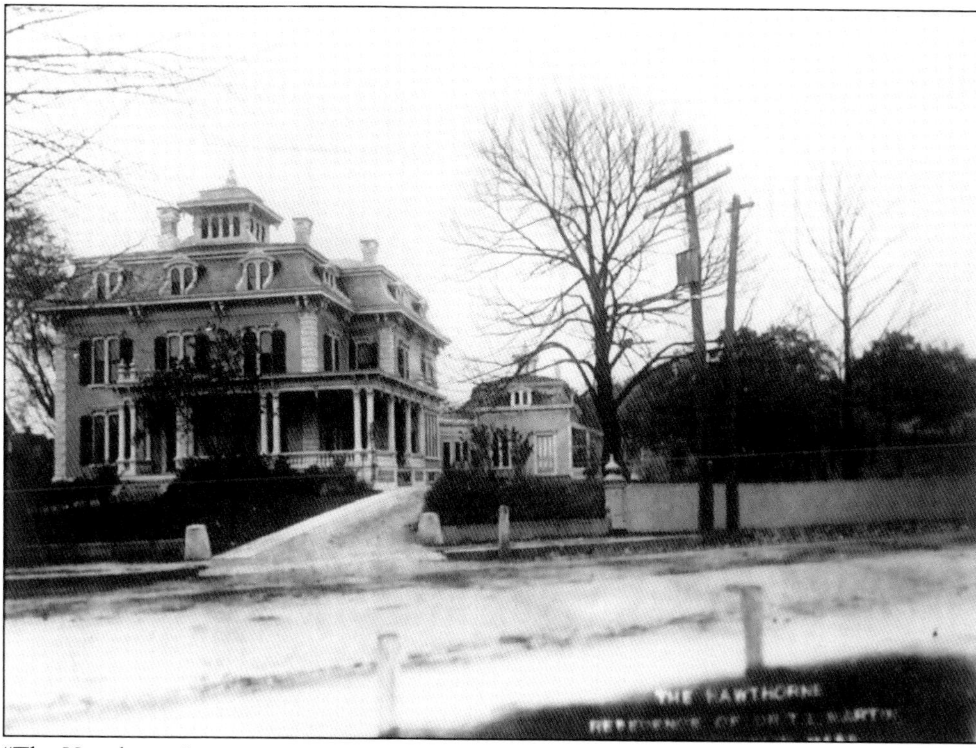


"The Hawthorne" was yet another Second Empire mansion gracing the town's center. It is shown here in a 1905 postcard.

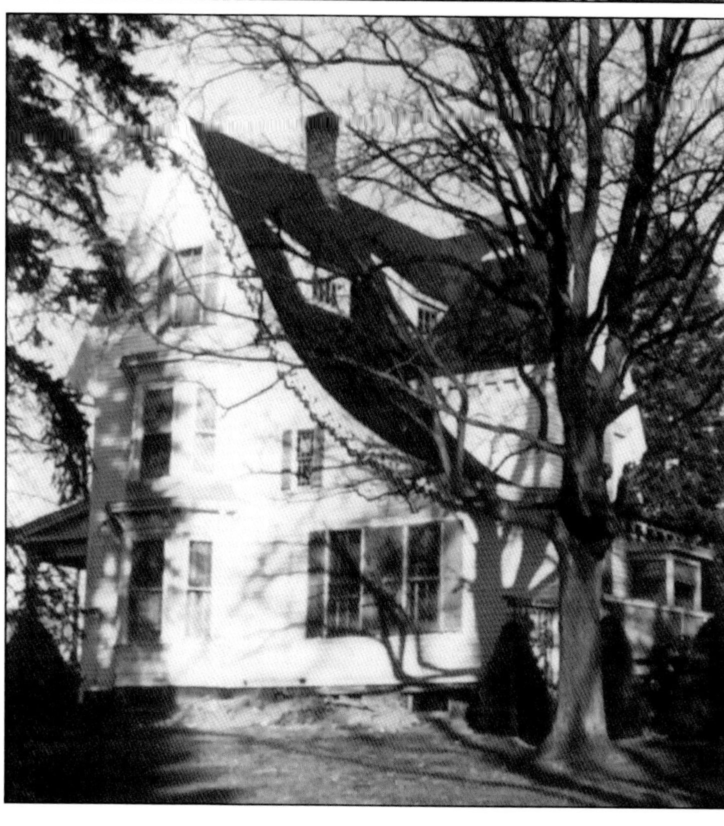

This lovely Victorian gingerbread cottage occupies the corner of Union and High Streets. It was the home of E.H. Sherman, and later, of Franklin businessman Harry Geb.

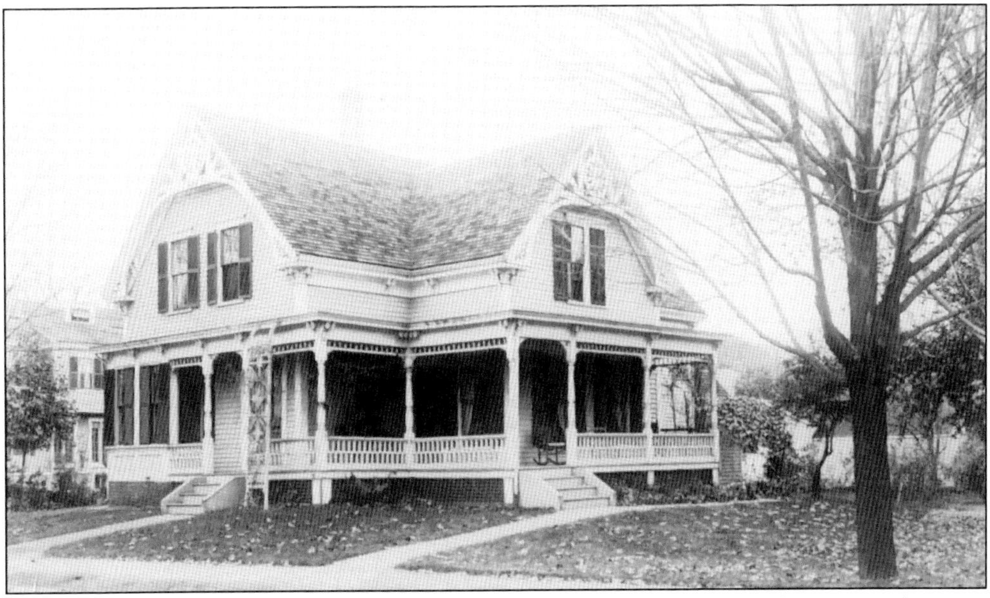

This Victorian cottage, with its well-cut gingerbread decoration, had a good near-town location and was considered pretty enough to be reproduced on this 1900 postcard.

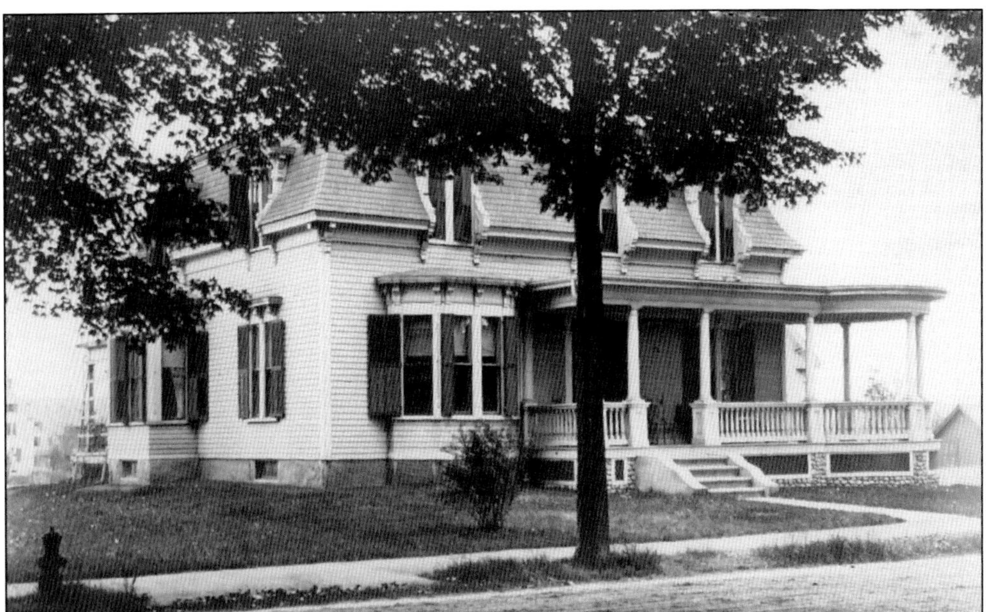

This Second Empire cottage was a mere ten rooms in size, and hardly in the same league with its bigger and more showy brothers, but it was featured on this 1900 postcard as the proud home of C.E. Craig of Cottage Street.

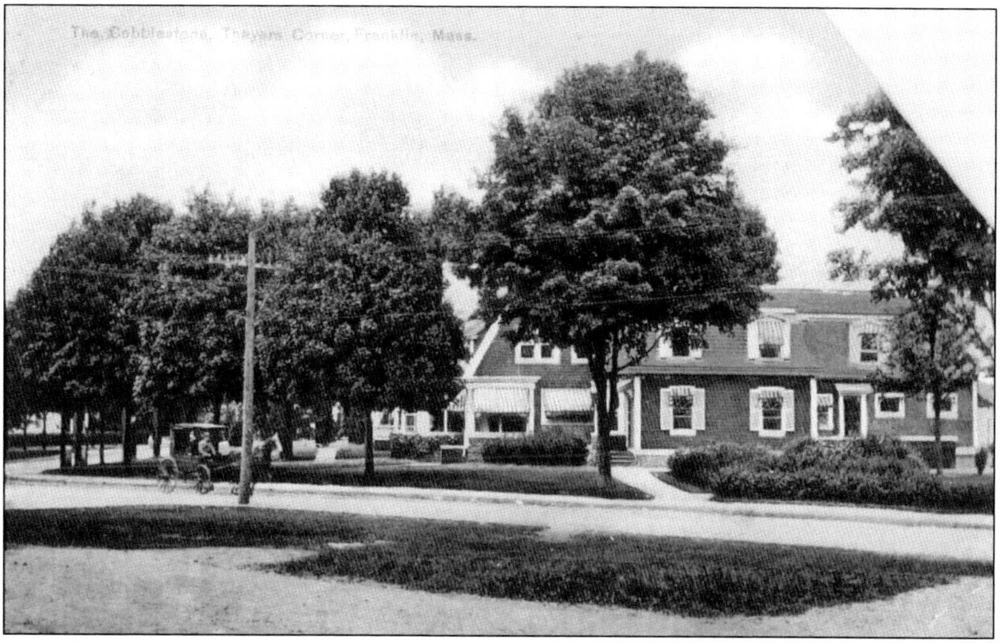

"The Cablestone," another Thayer home, occupied Thayer's Corner. Note the horse and buggy in this 1895 photograph.

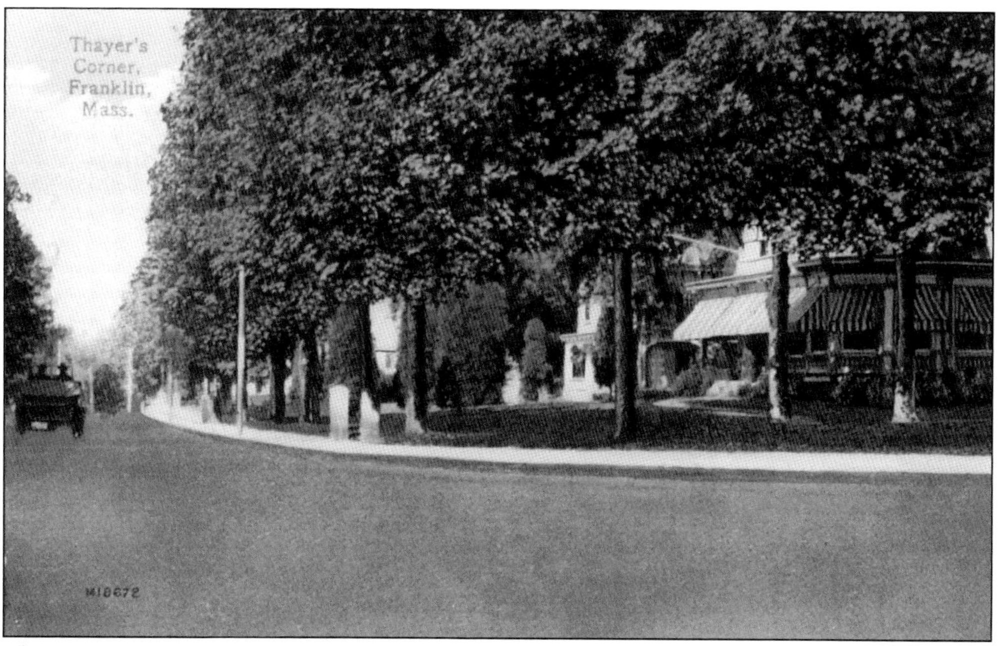


This 1900 summertime photographic postcard shows another view of Thayer's Corner.

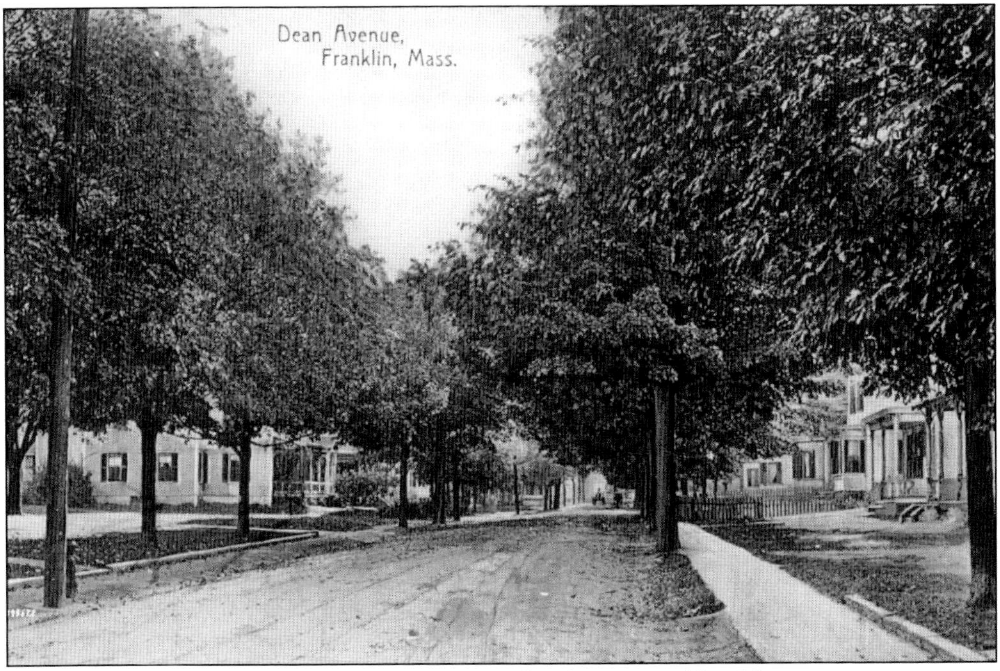


Dean Avenue, shown here about 1905, was considered a respectable address.

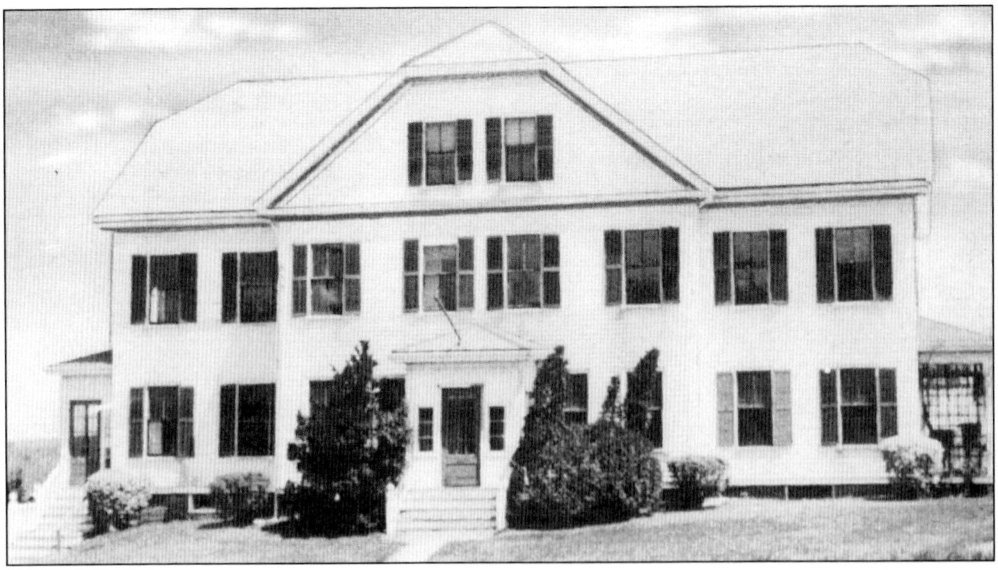

This building was the last Franklin "Poor Farm," where elderly down-and-out Franklin citizens could go to live on the slight charity of the town. It was later operated by the Ober family as the Hillcrest Convalescent Home.

# *Six*

# Franklin at Play: The Sporting Life

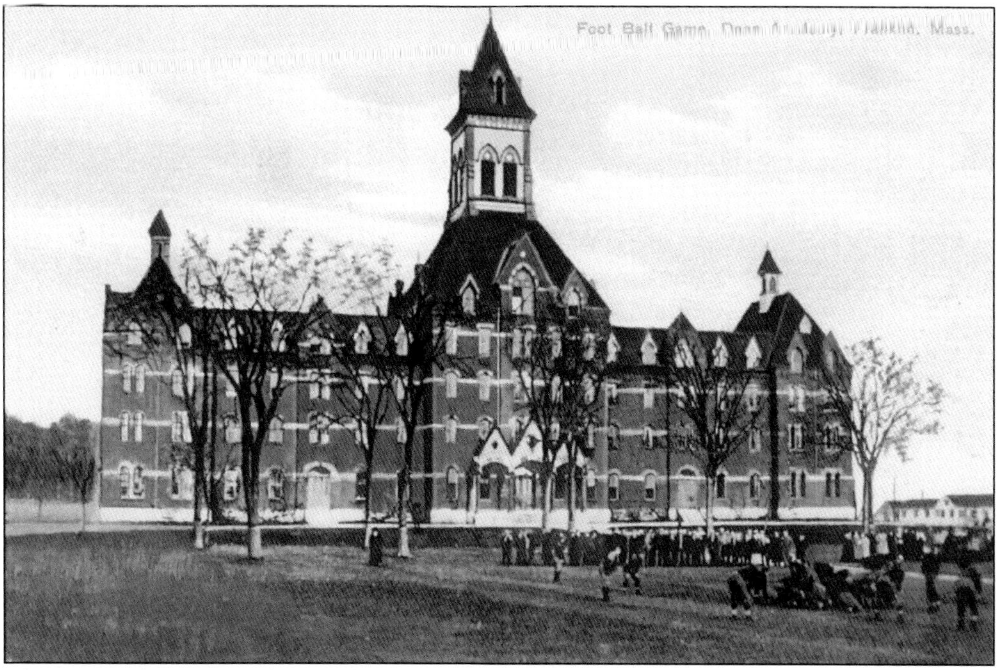


This postcard was made from a photograph of a football game played in front of Dean Hall in 1904. The "Dean Demons" have played football for a century.

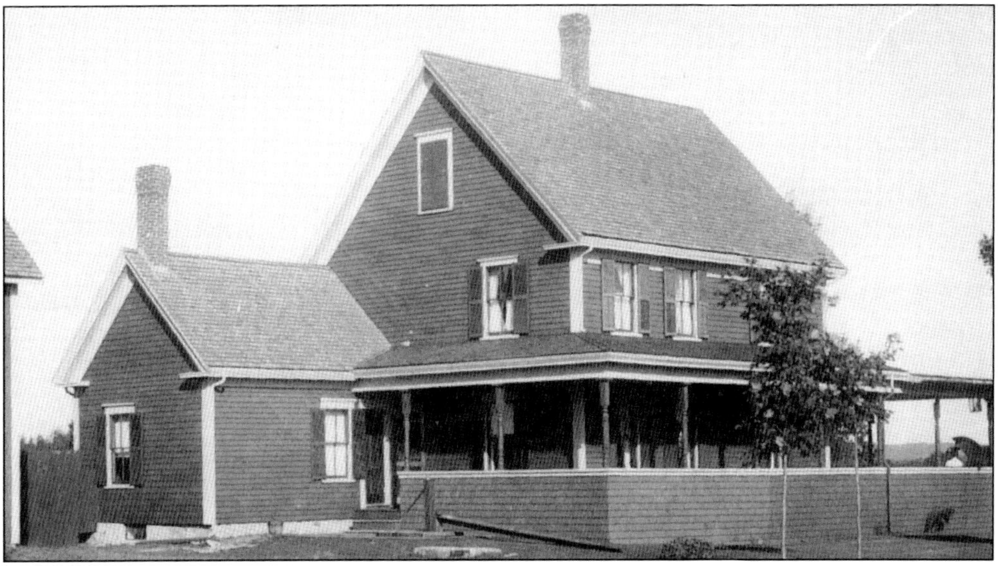

In 1899, the Franklin Country Club was organized for the "First Families" of Franklin. Golf mania was sweeping the country, spawning the "country club" as an upper and upper-middle-class fixture.

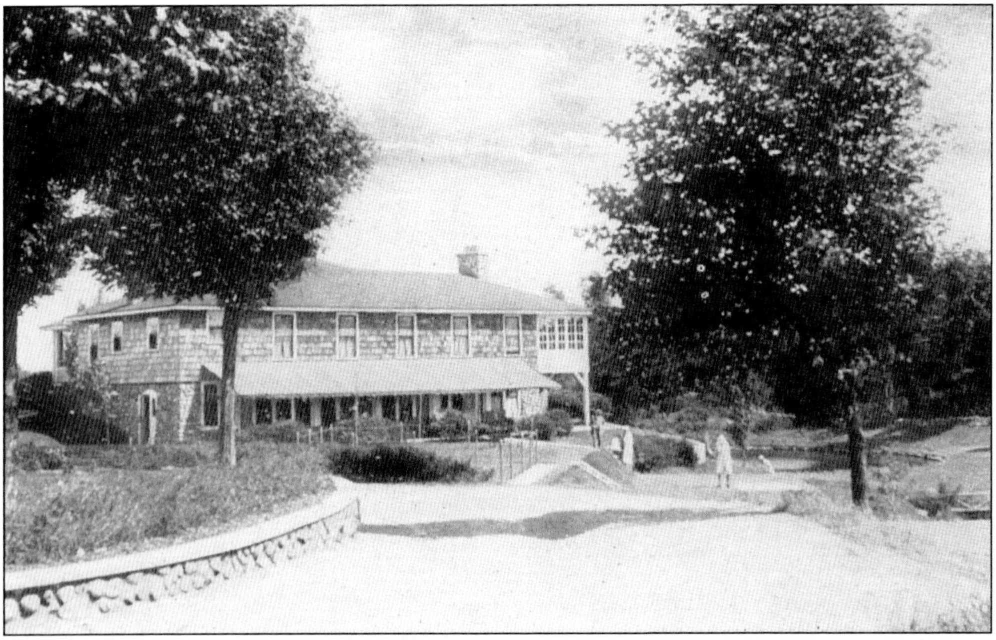

By the 1920s, the clubhouse was expanded, and chaps sporting "plus-fours," the golfer's knee pants, could be seen putting away.

This is a baseball patch featuring Ty Cobb, who once played a game of baseball at Woodland Park in Franklin. Eddie Grant also played baseball there while in the New England League.

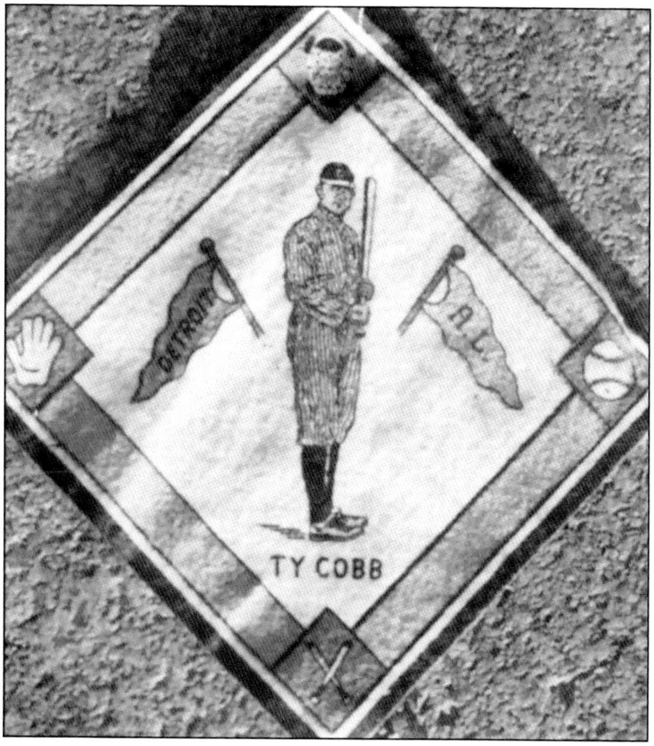


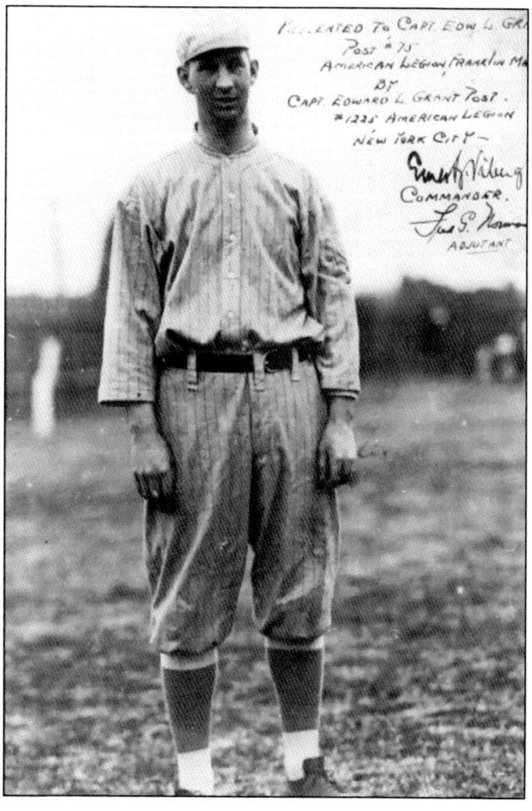


Eddie Grant, known in the major leagues as "Harvard Eddy," was an authentic hero. He was the only major league baseball player to fight in World War I. He rose to the rank of major and was killed leading his men while looking for "the Lost Battalion" during the Battle of the Argonne.

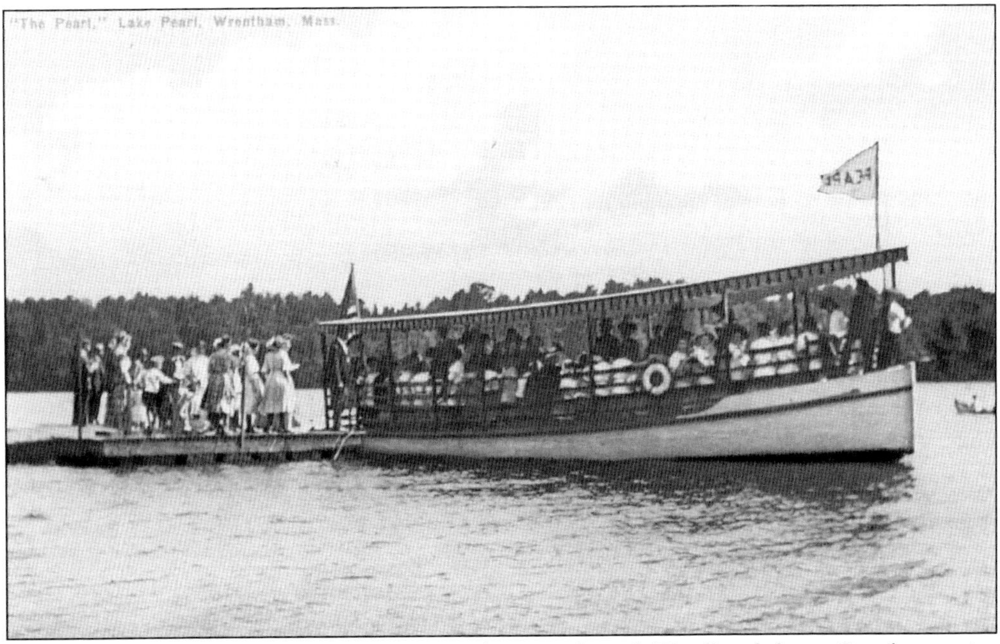


This Franklin group went over to Wrentham to board *The Pearl* for a Sunday cruise around Lake Pearl.

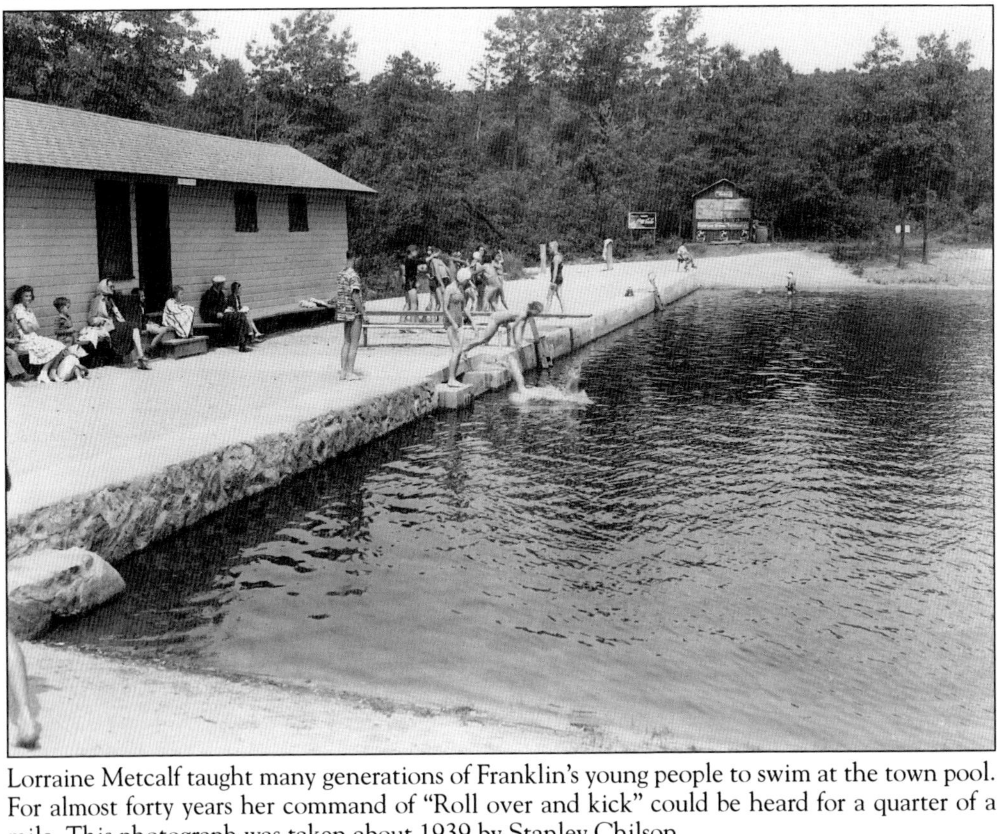

Lorraine Metcalf taught many generations of Franklin's young people to swim at the town pool. For almost forty years her command of "Roll over and kick" could be heard for a quarter of a mile. This photograph was taken about 1939 by Stanley Chilson.

In this 1928 photograph, Ada Melin demonstrates the fine art of snow-shoeing, which was not a bad way of getting around snow-bound Franklin.

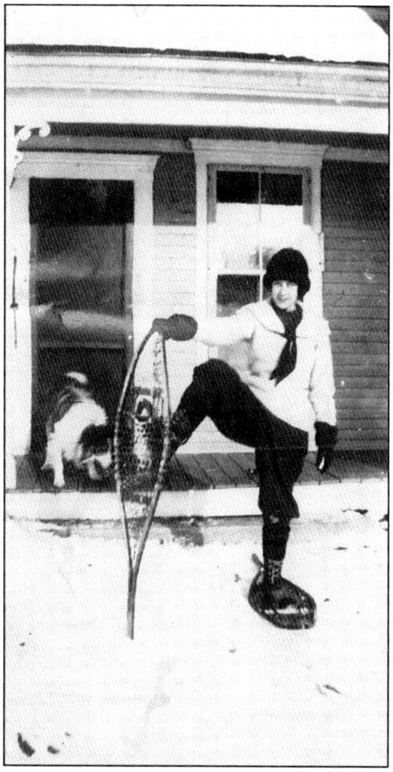

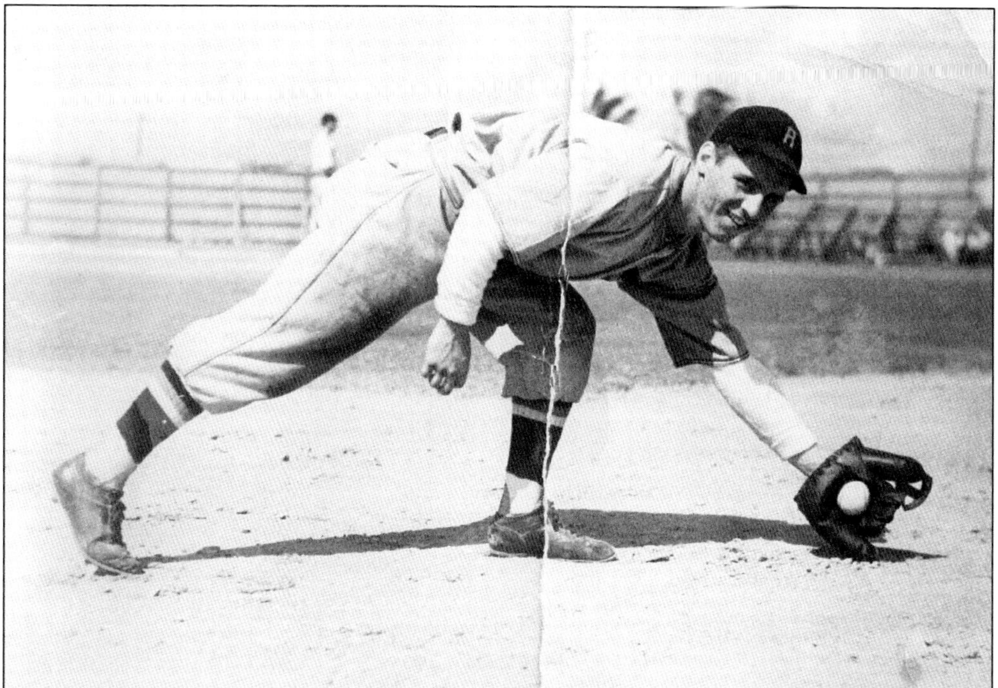

Fran Bartolomei grew up in the baseball tradition of Franklin. He was one of Franklin's great players, and spent some time with the Cardinals organization in the early 1940s.

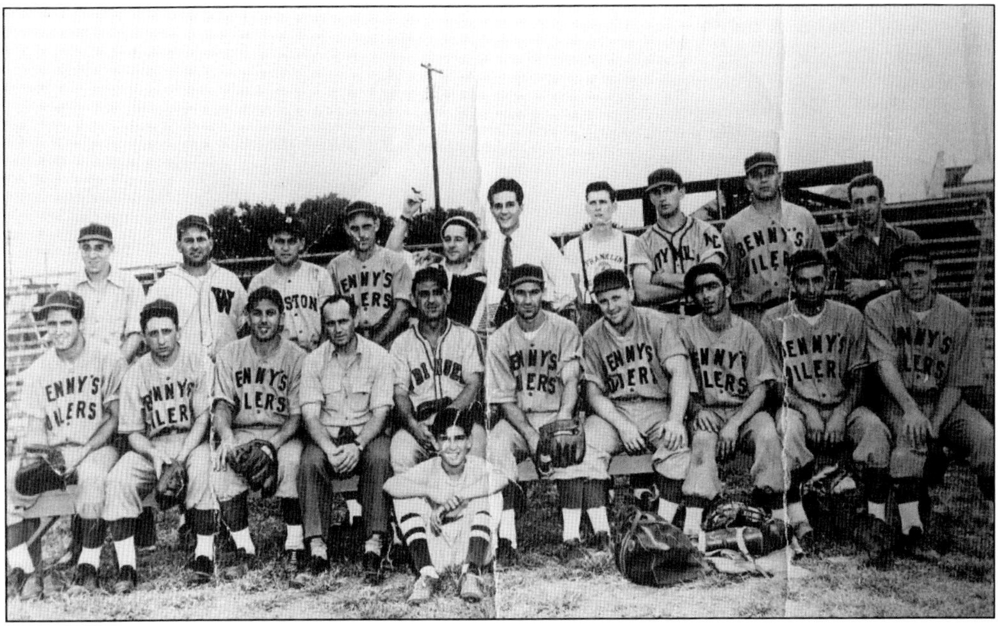

Baseball was to grow to be bigger than ever in Franklin. "The Claremacks" and "Benny's Oilers" (pictured here) competed in the 1940s for semipro national championships.

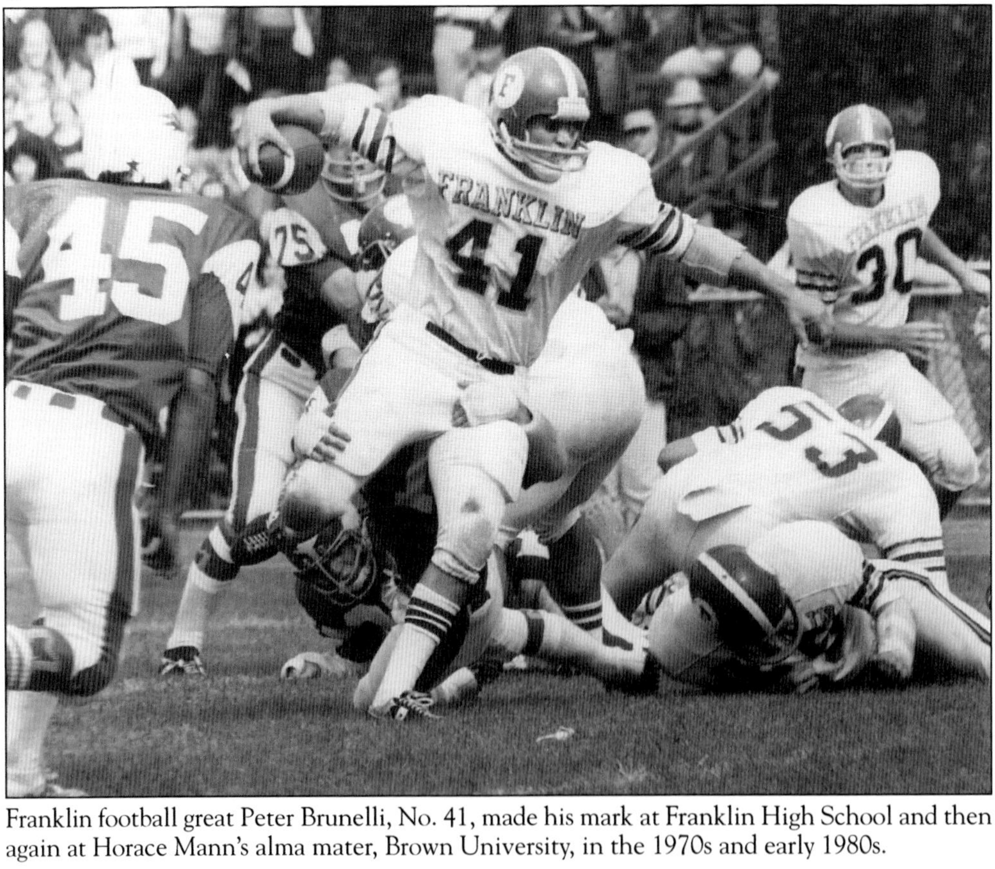


Franklin football great Peter Brunelli, No. 41, made his mark at Franklin High School and then again at Horace Mann's alma mater, Brown University, in the 1970s and early 1980s.

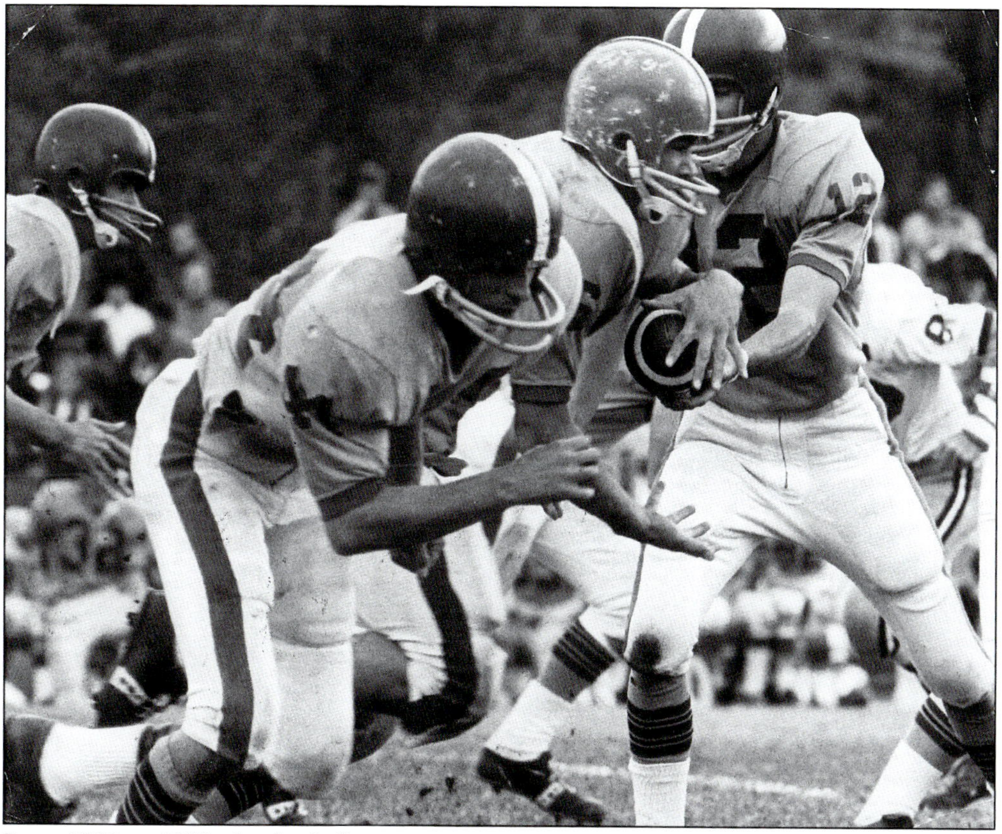

From 1969 to 1972, the football teams of Franklin's great coach Gerry Leone never lost a game.

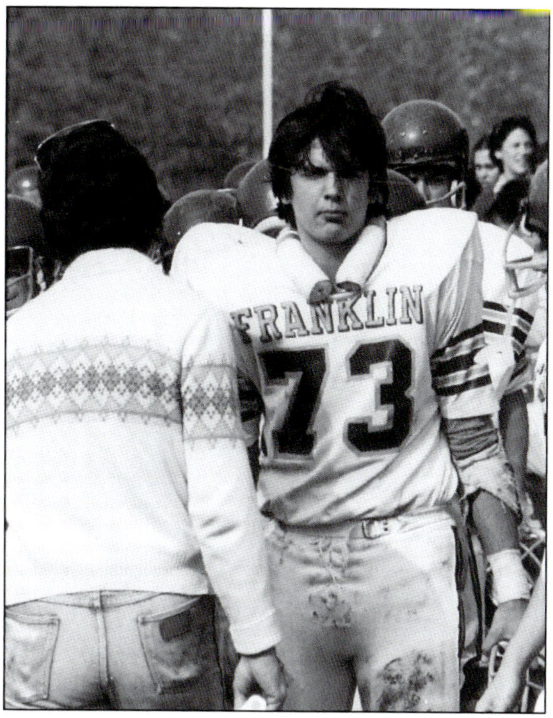


George Danello, No. 73, was an outstanding player of the 1976 bicentennial season. After college, he returned to Franklin and became the vice-president of the Benjamin Franklin Savings Bank.

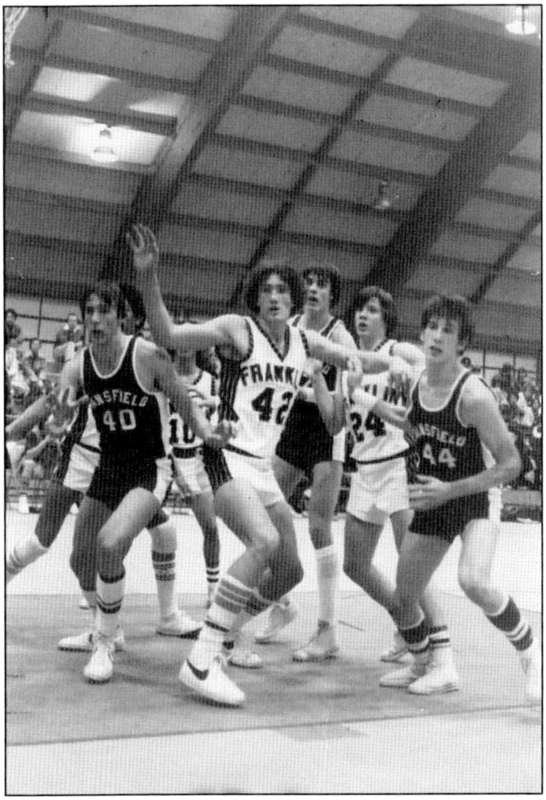

Franklin also had a great championship basketball team during the bicentennial season, led by John Walls, No. 42.

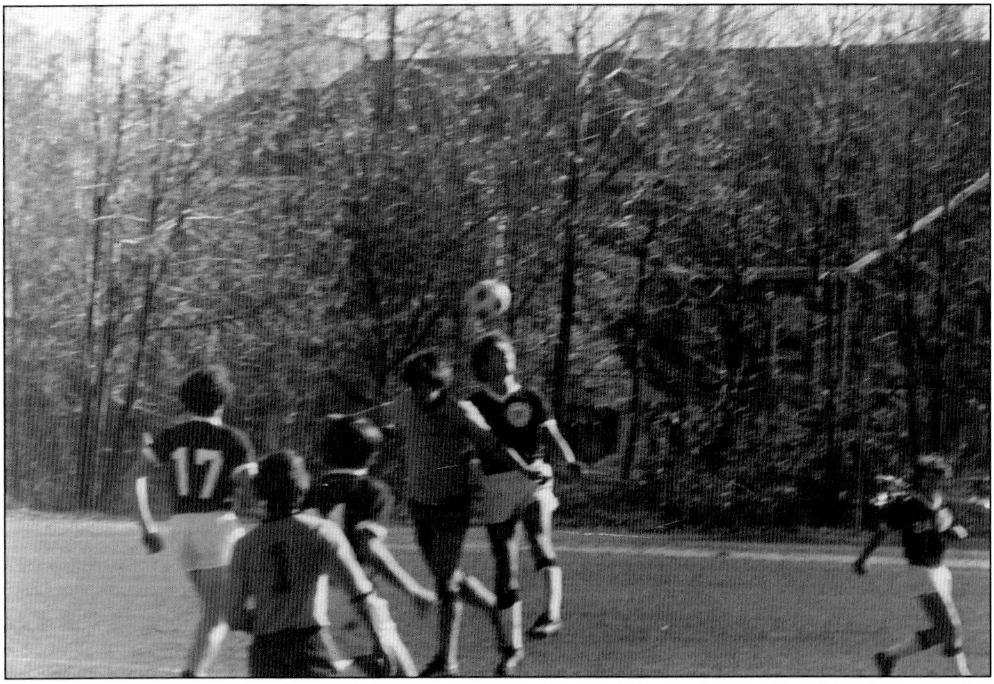

Dave Harrington "heads" the ball during a season that ended in glory as Franklin became the Division I champions during the bicentennial season of 1976.

*Seven*

# Franklin at School

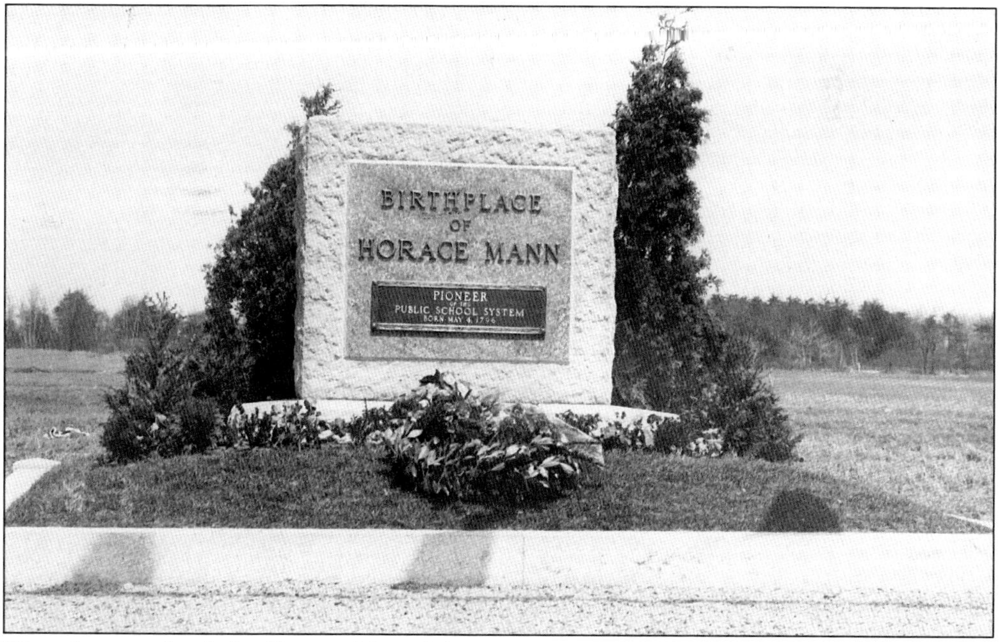


This photograph of the Horace Mann Monument was taken in 1928. It marks the spot on East Central Street where the Mann Homestead stood. This marker honors Horace Mann as a "Pioneer of the Public School System." He was born here on May 4, 1796.

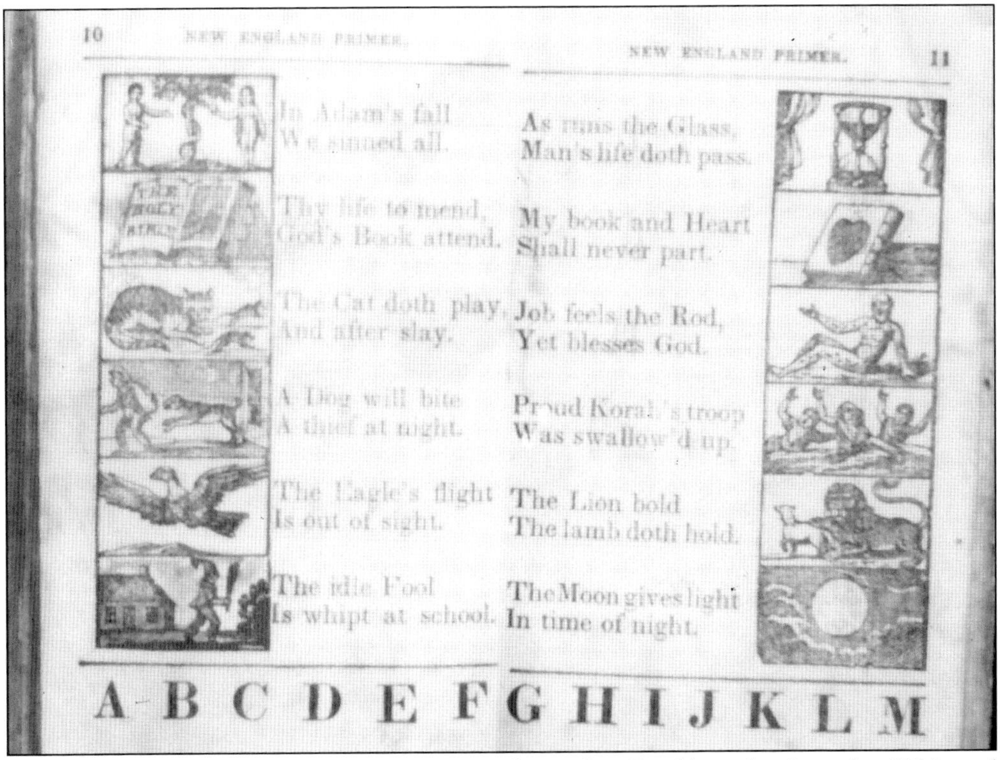

10 NEW ENGLAND PRIMER. NEW ENGLAND PRIMER. 11

In Adam's fall
We sinned all.

Thy life to mend,
God's Book attend.

The Cat doth play,
And after slay.

A Dog will bite
A thief at night.

The Eagle's flight
Is out of sight.

The idle Fool
Is whipt at school.

As runs the Glass,
Man's life doth pass.

My book and Heart
Shall never part.

Job feels the Rod,
Yet blesses God.

Proud Korah's troop
Was swallow'd up.

The Lion bold
The lamb doth hold.

The Moon gives light
In time of night.

A B C D E F G H I J K L M

This book, *The New England Primer*, was actually used in Franklin schools in the 1820s and 1830s. Little children learned that "A" stood for "Adam," and, "In Adam's fall, We sinned all." The Puritan ethic dominated education for three hundred years.

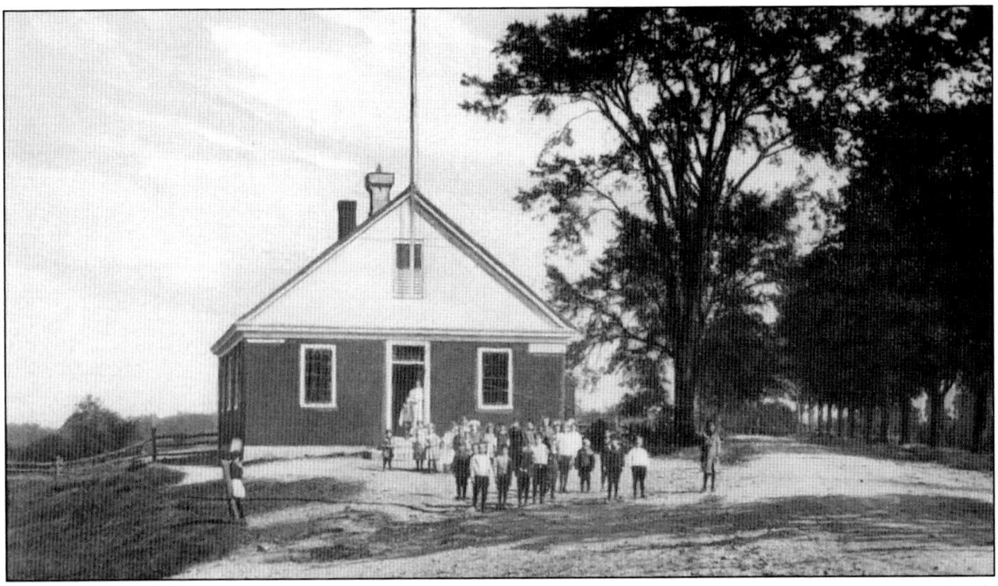

This 1906 postcard shows the "Red Brick School," which is the oldest operating one-room brick school in the United States. This is ironic, because Horace Mann hated the concept of the one-room schoolhouse, in which all of six to eight grade levels were taught in one room. This school has operated since 1832.

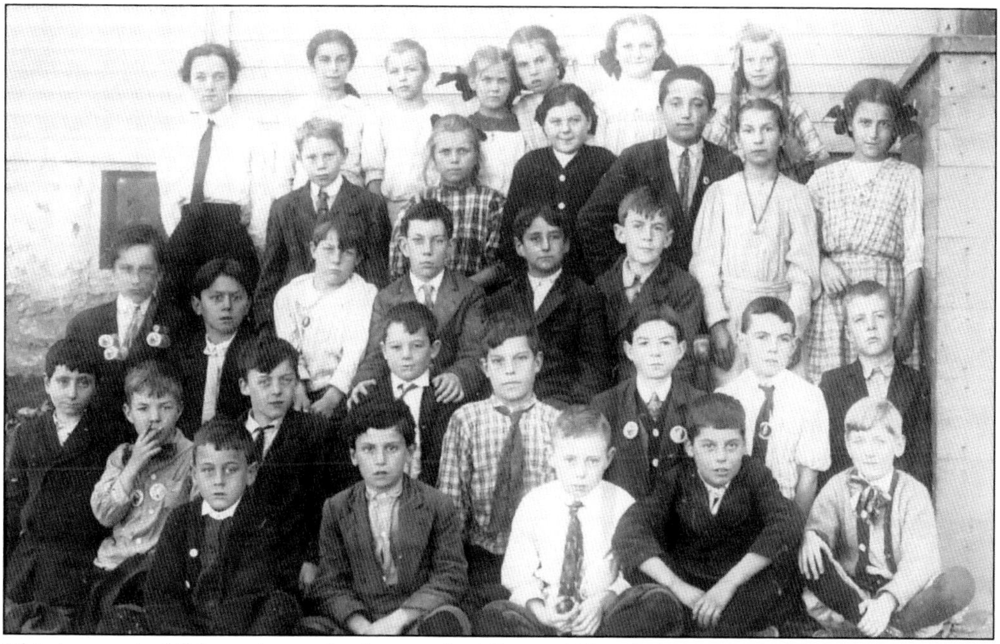

This is a typical "class picture," taken at the Thayer School about 1915. They are all in their places with bright shiny faces, these little scholars.

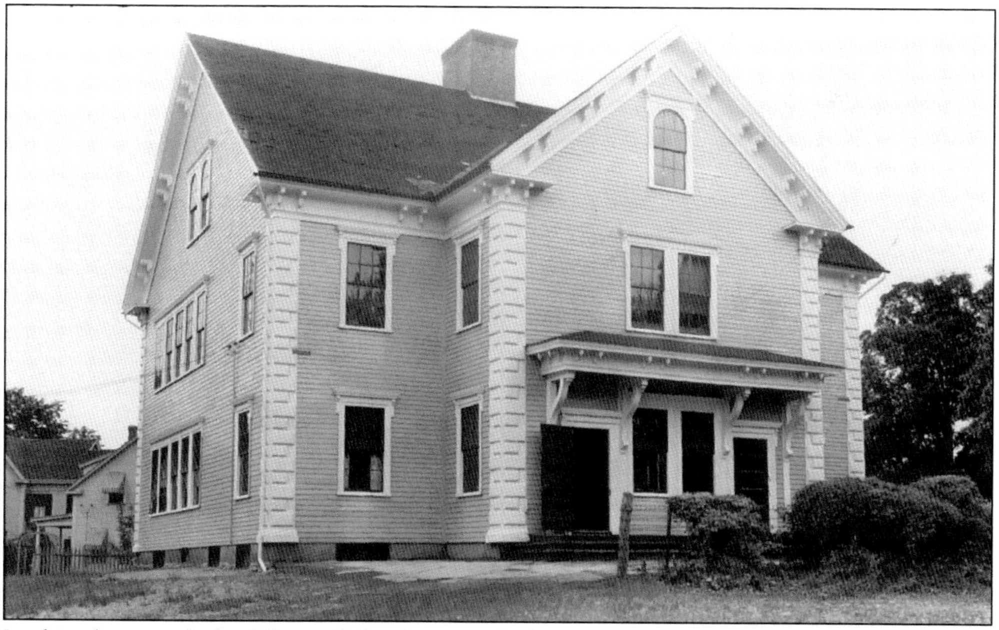

In this photograph the Thayer School tries to hide its antiquity under a coat of new paint. It was photographed by Stanley Chilson on August 21, 1931. The next decade would see the old structure razed.

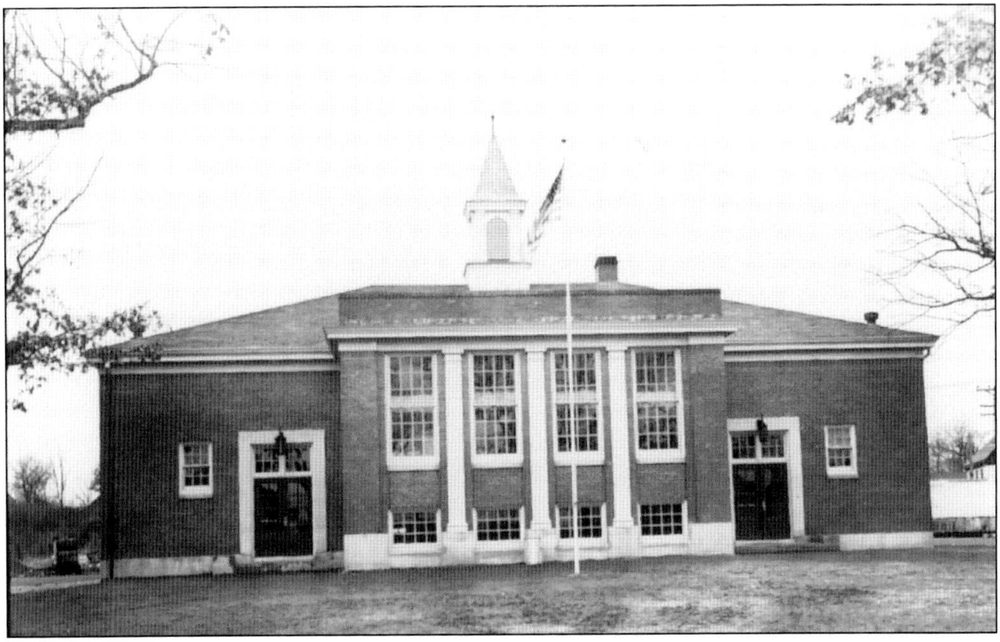

This 1936 photograph shows the latest of three schools to be built on this site. Each one was known as the "Four Corners School." The first was a one-room school; the second had two rooms, and this New Deal project had four.

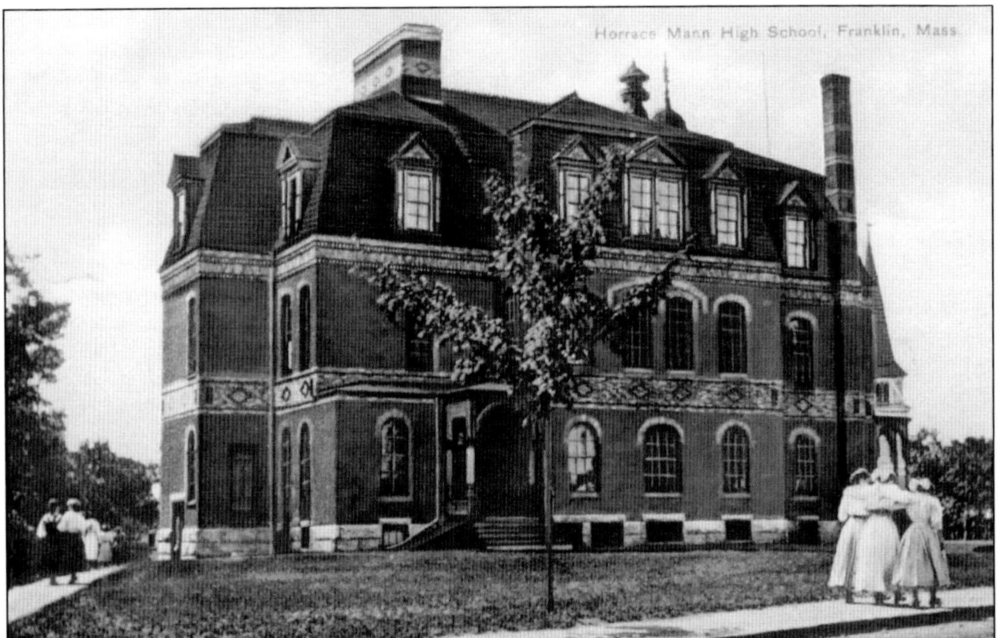


"Three Little Maids From School" walk in an embrace of friendship past the ten-year-old Horace Mann High School about 1905. This building is now the Franklin Municipal Building.

This is a fine view of the Horace Mann High School as it looked in the late 1890s. Later its mansard roof would be removed, as well as the tower, which was unsafe. Stanley Chilson, who was a graduate, told me that the third floor of the chemistry lab would bounce and shake when he walked across it.

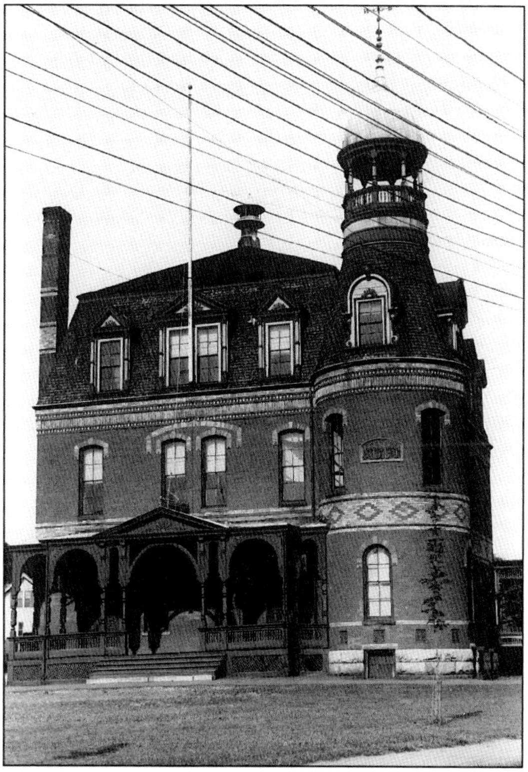

This photograph shows Franklin High School students about 1910 at the front of the building.

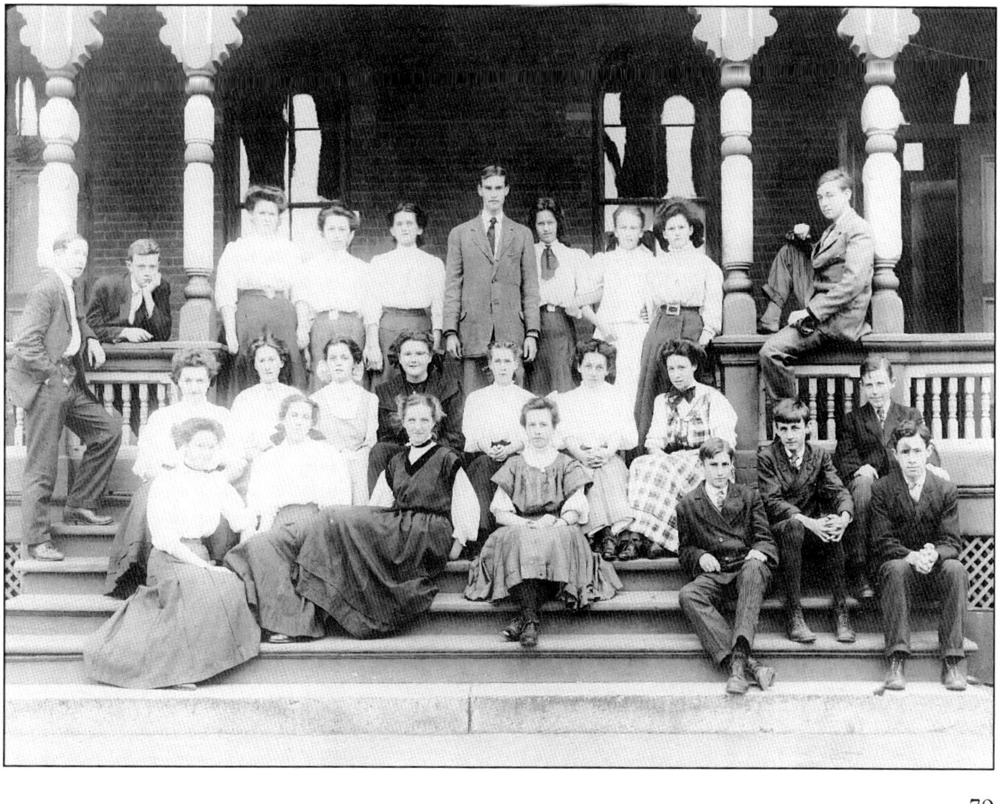

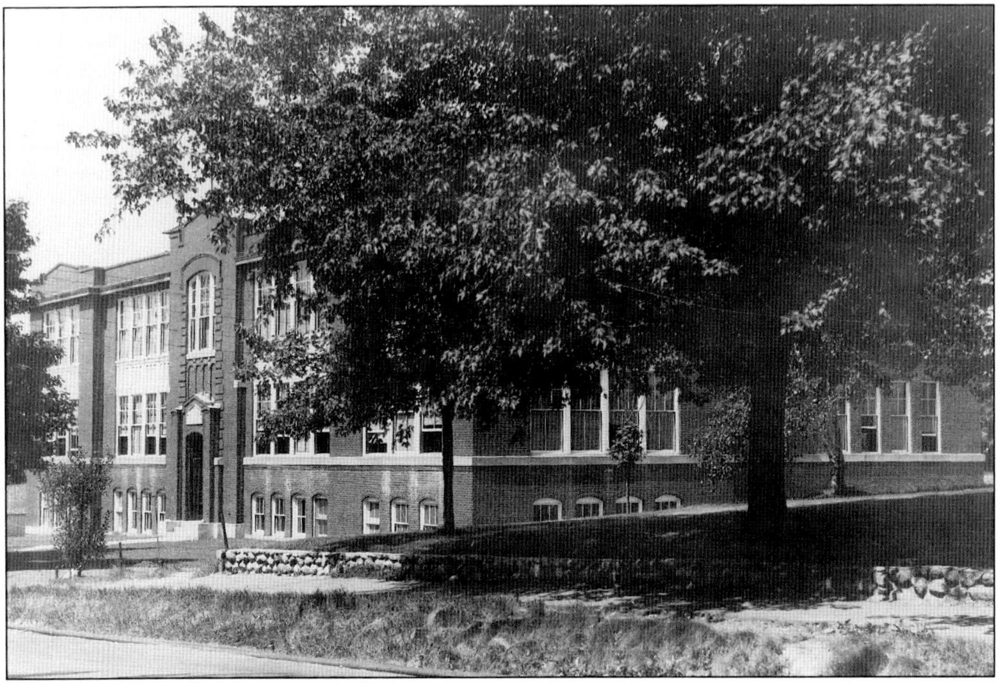

Theron Metcalf Junior High School was built in 1912. It is now houses senior citizens.

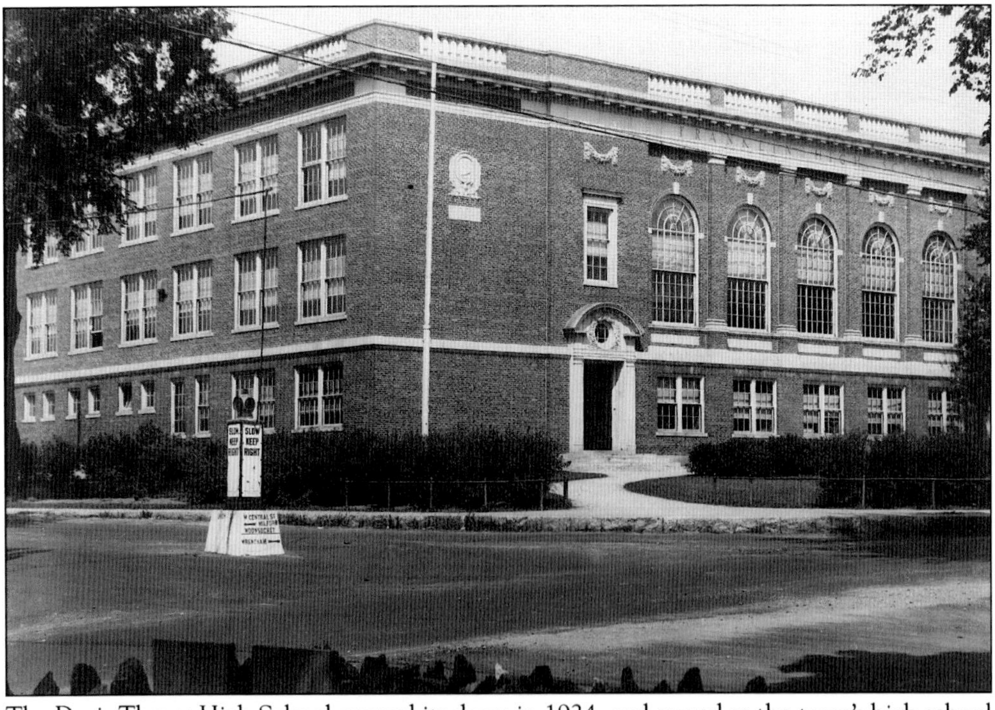


The Davis Thayer High School opened its doors in 1924, and served as the town's high school until 1962. It is now an elementary school.

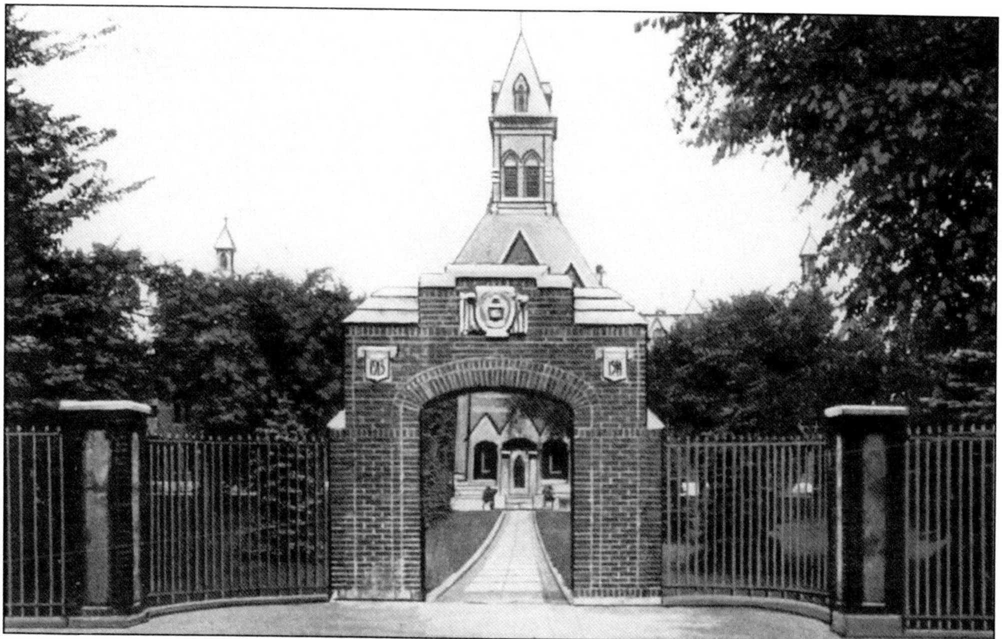

Dean Academy was founded in 1865 as a private institution by Dr. Oliver Dean, who had made a fortune in textiles. It later became Dean Junior College, and has recently changed its name to Dean College.

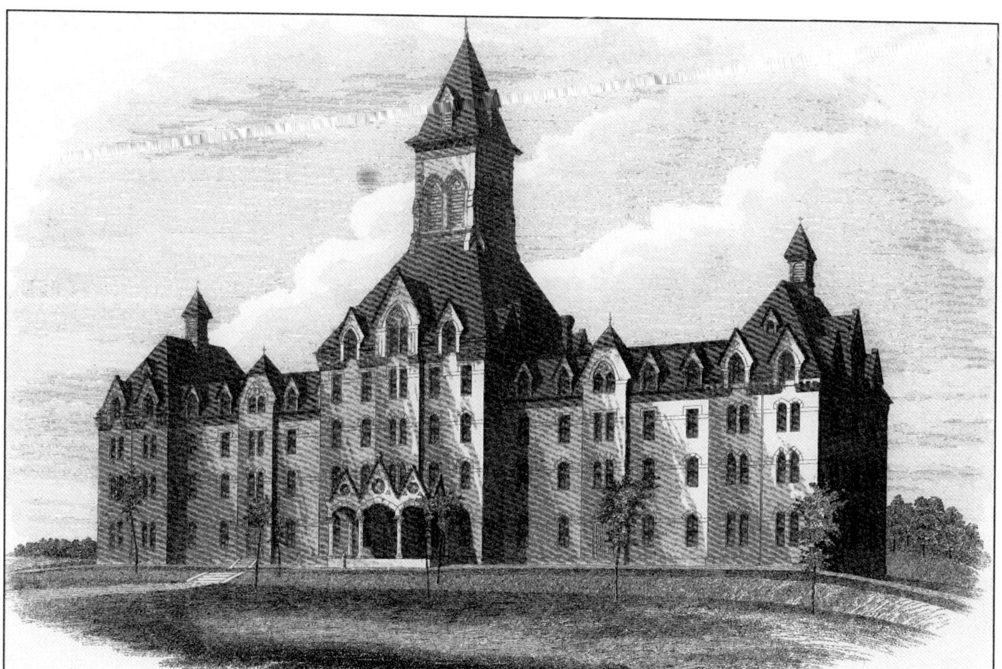

This picture shows Dean Academy as it appeared in 1878. Actor Broderick Crawford, whose greatest film role was the character of Huey Long in *All the King's Men*, was a Dean graduate.

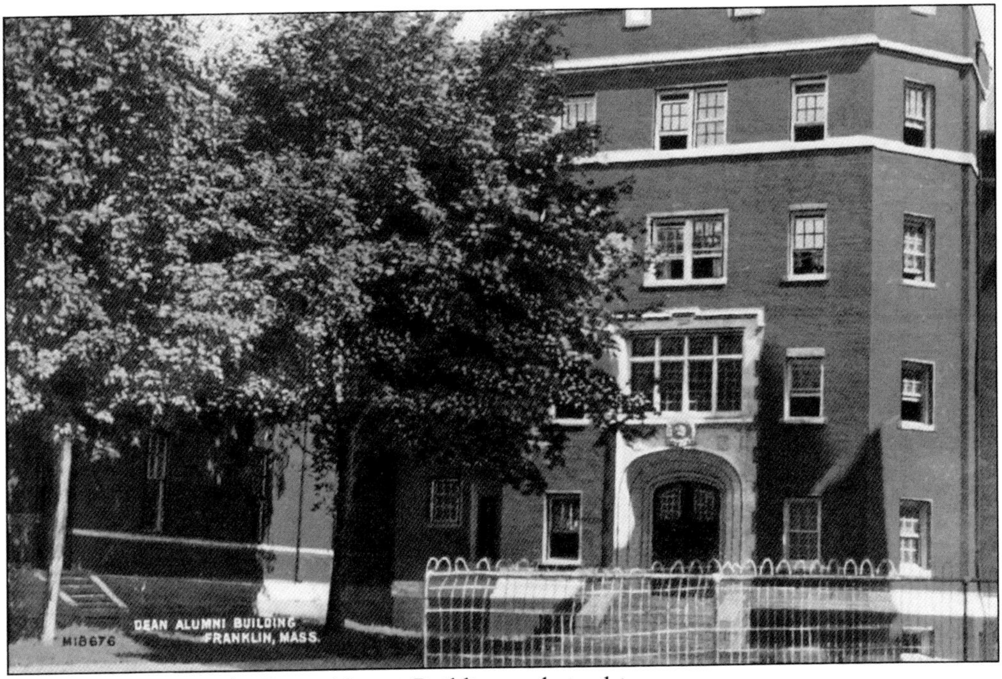

This postcard shows the Dean Alumni Building early in this century.

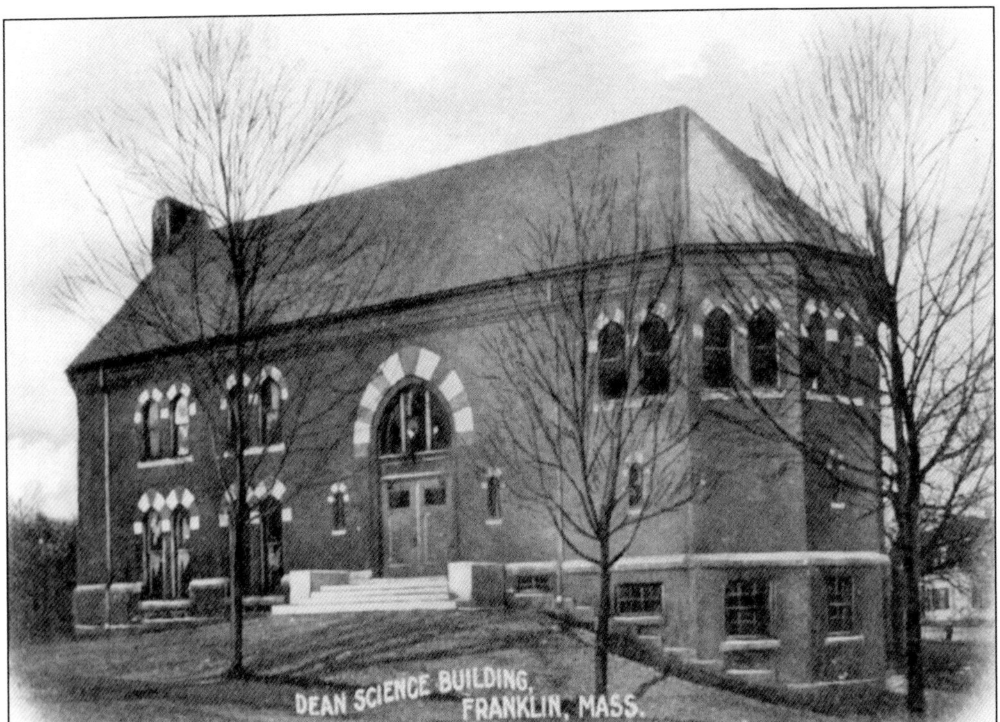

The Dean Science Building is shown here in a *c.* 1906 photograph. It still serves as the science building today.

*Eight*

# Franklin Folks in Peace and War

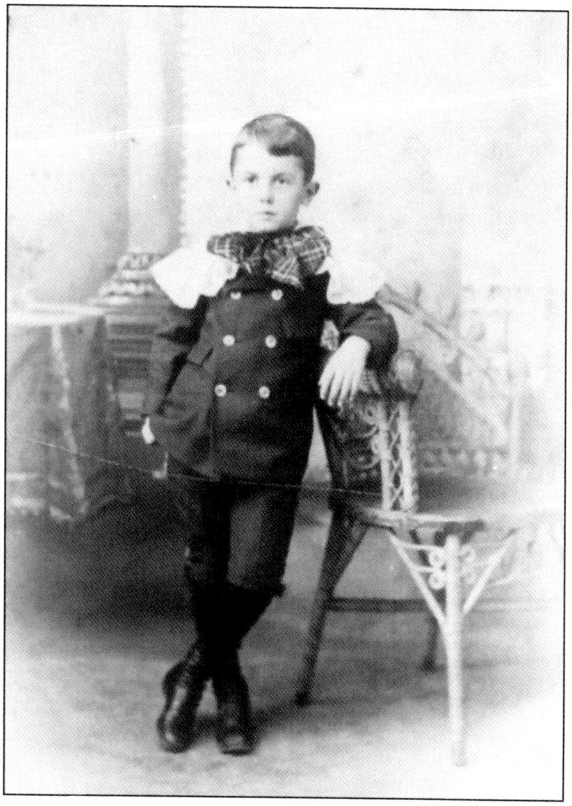

This photograph of Master Stanley Grant Chilson was taken in 1895. Stanley was the great photographer/historian of Franklin. He took thousands of photographs of the town until his eyes began to fail him. He also produced a fine collection of moving pictures of events in Franklin which spanned the 1920s through the early 1960s.

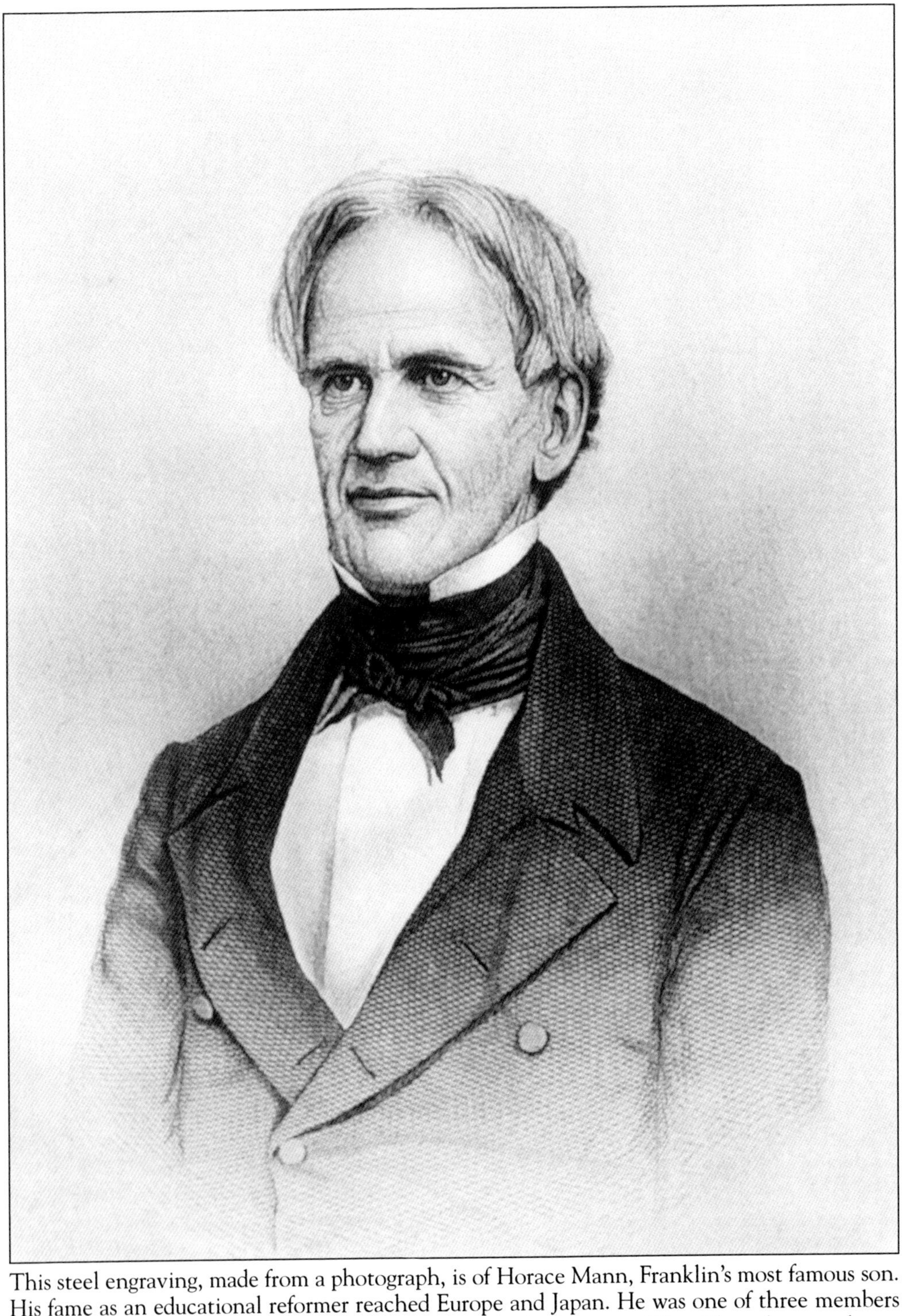

This steel engraving, made from a photograph, is of Horace Mann, Franklin's most famous son. His fame as an educational reformer reached Europe and Japan. He was one of three members of Congress to vote against the U.S. participation in the Mexican War. The other two brave souls were Abraham Lincoln and the congressman that Horace Mann succeeded in the House, John Quincy Adams.

This is a portrait of Dr. Nathaniel Miller Sr., who was Franklin's premier medical doctor. His home was the first meeting place of the Montgomery Lodge of Masons in 1797.

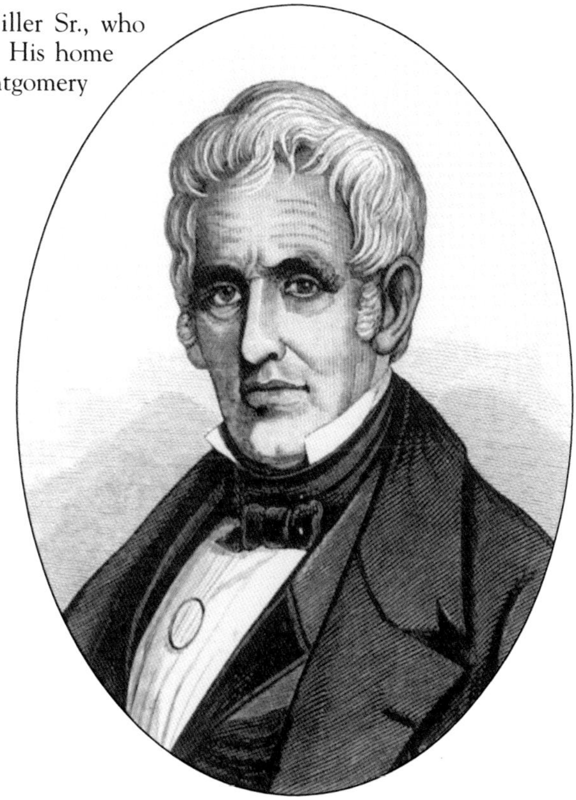

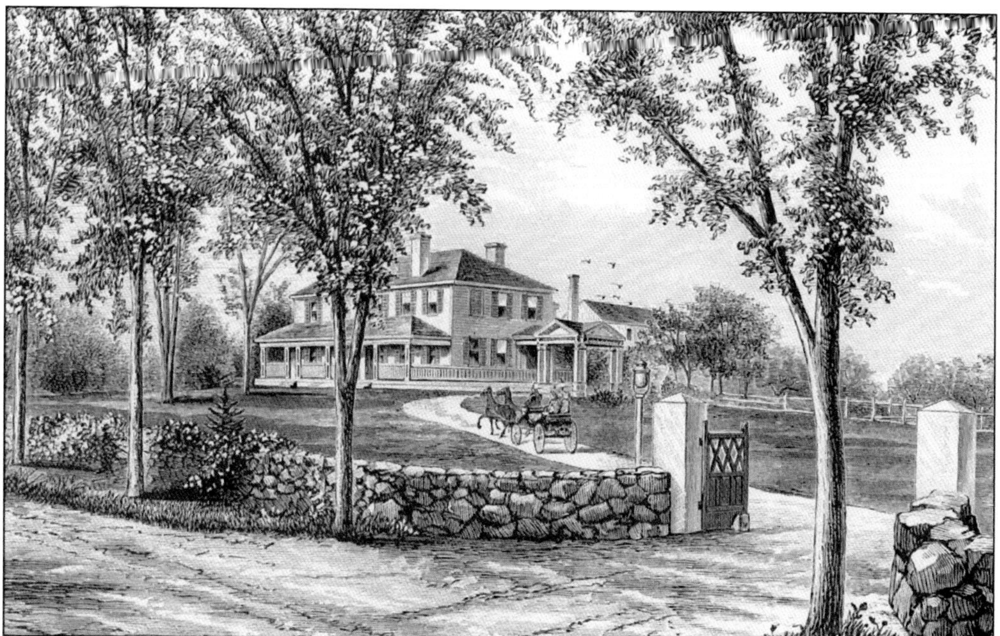

This 1878 engraving of "Miller Hall," which still stands on Miller Street, was Dr. Miller's private hospital. The town also had a "pest house" to which people with serious illnesses were sent. The "pest house" existed well into the 1920s.

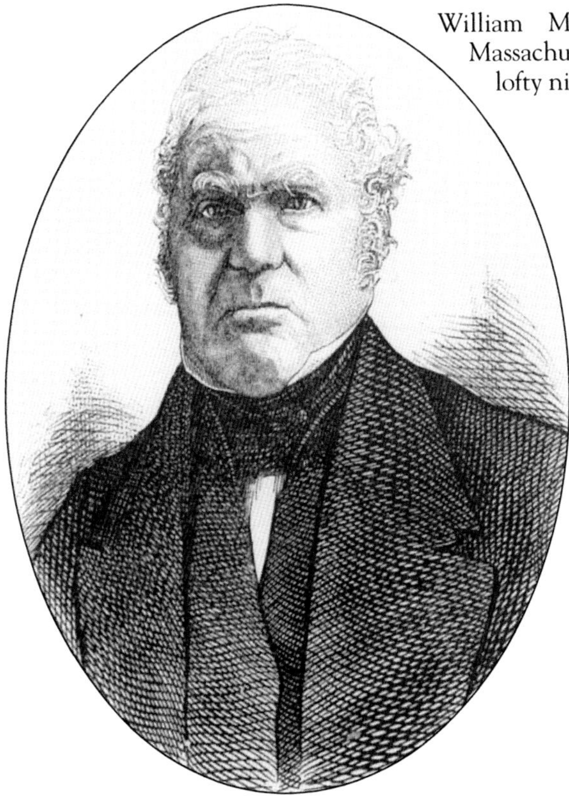

William Makepeace was a president of the Massachusetts's Temperance Union. This was a lofty nineteenth-century position indeed.

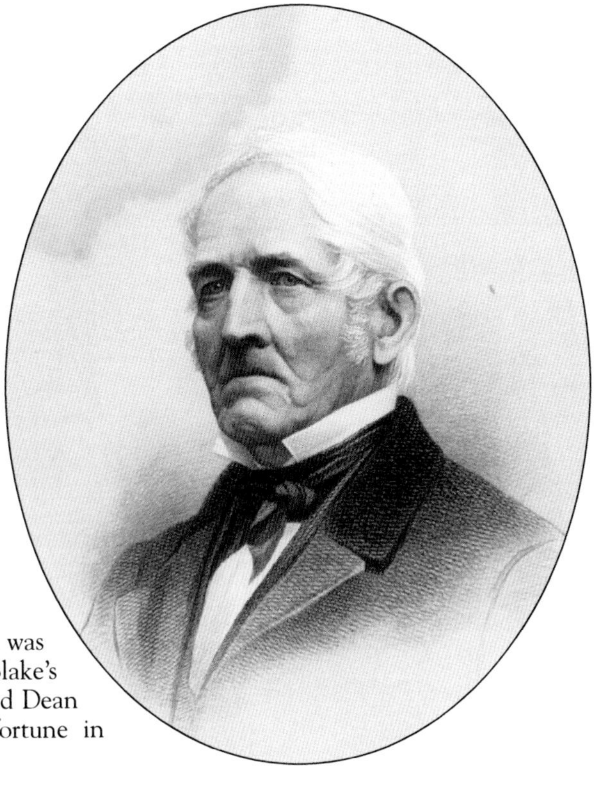

This photograph of Dr. Oliver Dean was turned into a steel engraving for Blake's *History of Franklin* (1878). He founded Dean Academy in 1865, and made his fortune in textile mills, not in medicine.

Mortimer Blake had this photograph taken for his 1878 *History of Franklin*, which is well-written, scholarly, and has stood the test of time as a great historiography.

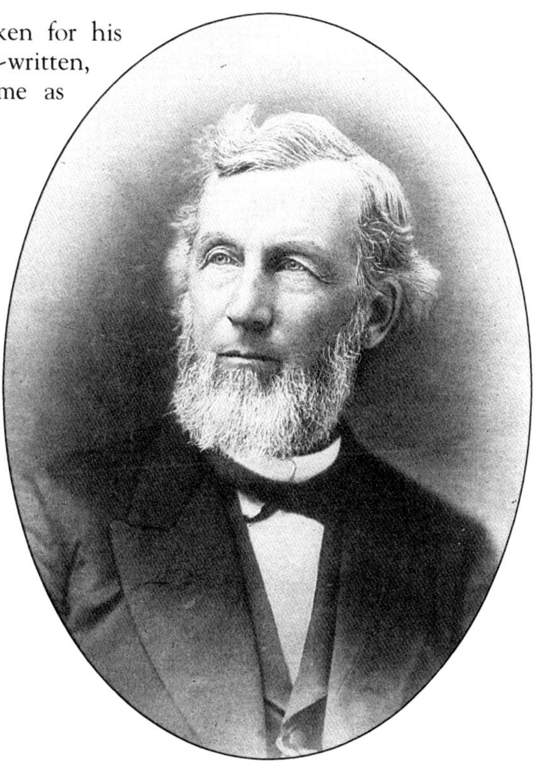

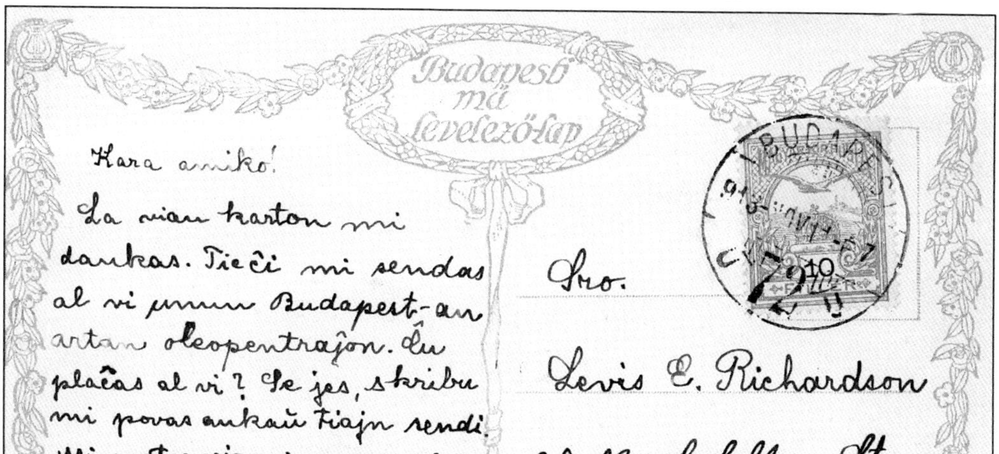


This postcard is included because Lewis E. Richardson was one of the founders of the "Esperanto" movement to promote "International Language." It was sent to him during his student days at Amherst. Richardson was better known outside of the United States than he was locally. He lived his later adult life in Norfolk.

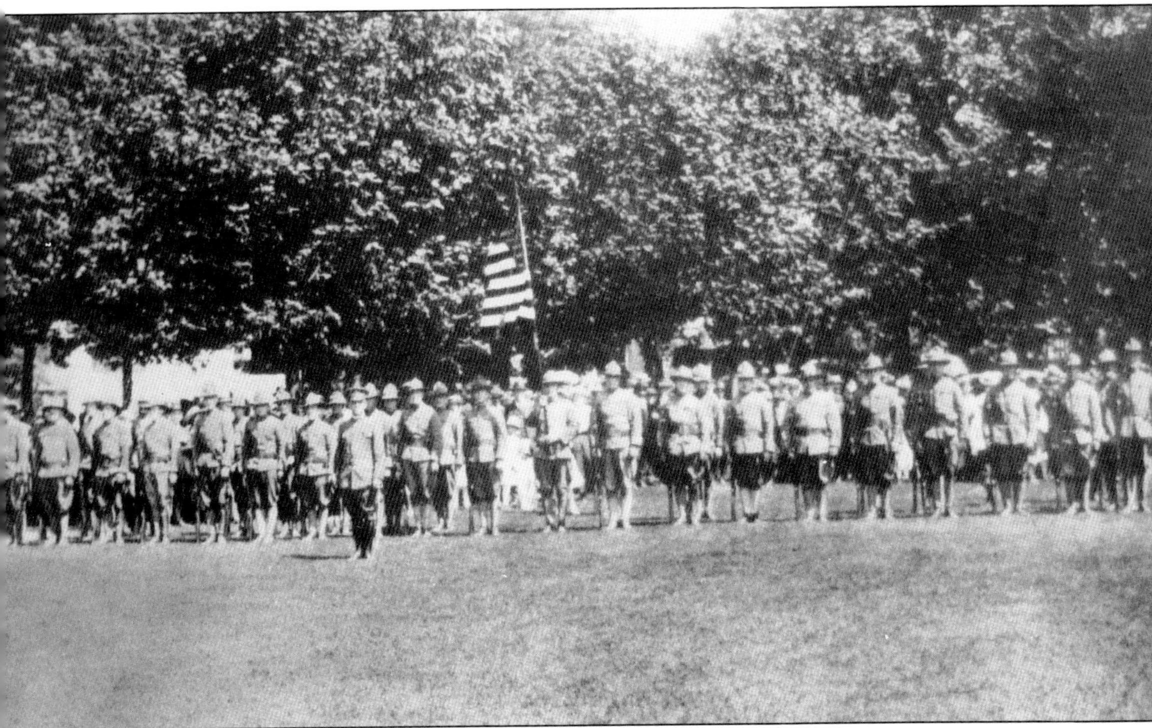

This photograph of Franklin men who enlisted in the United States Army was taken during the World War I period. According to the *1919 Franklin Town Report*, 434 Franklin men participated in the war. Of these, thirteen died in active service, including Eddie Grant.

Little Harold Clark posed in short pants in front of a Federal cottage on Grove Street about 1919.

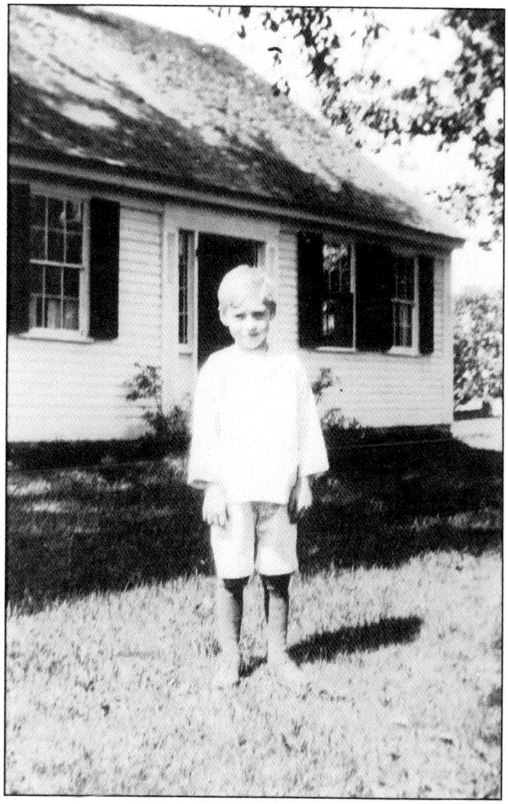

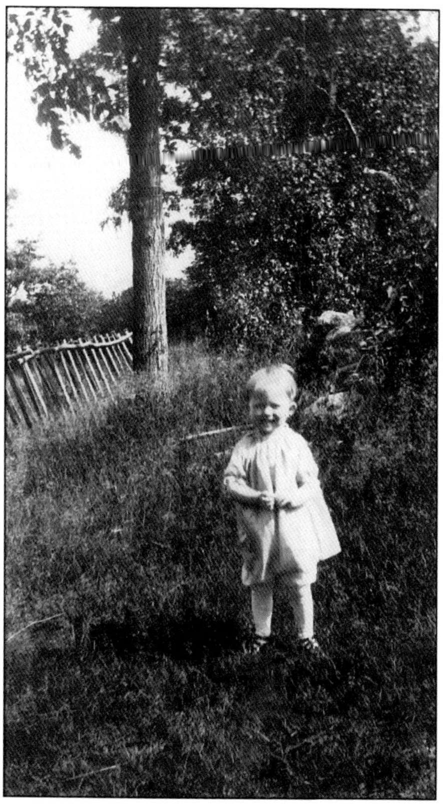

"The Girl Next Door" was twenty months old when this photograph was taken in 1919. She didn't marry Harold.

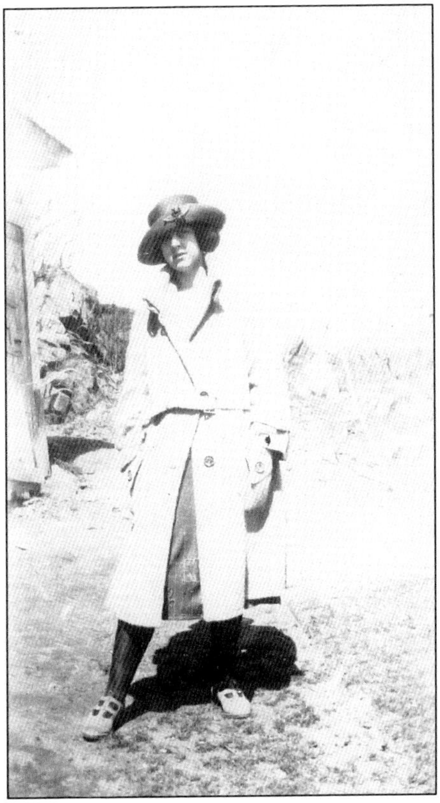

"Franklin Girls" were fashion plates. By 1927, hemlines were on the rise and this casual outfit, sported by Ada Melin of West Central Street, was the very height of fashion.

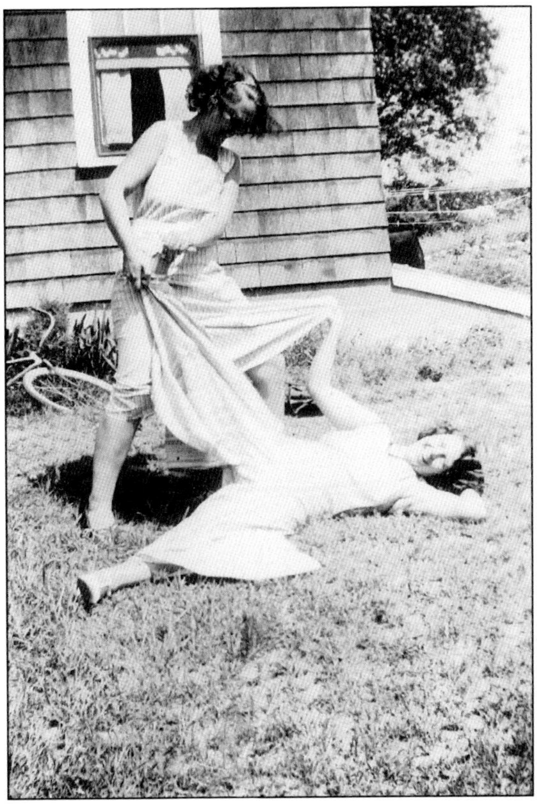

Ada and her sister Maude "horse around" for the camera outside of the Melin home on West Central Street about 1928.

Ruben Melin sports jodhpurs and leather leggings, a sports jacket, tie, and cap. The purpose of this outfit was to ride his motorcycle about 1928.

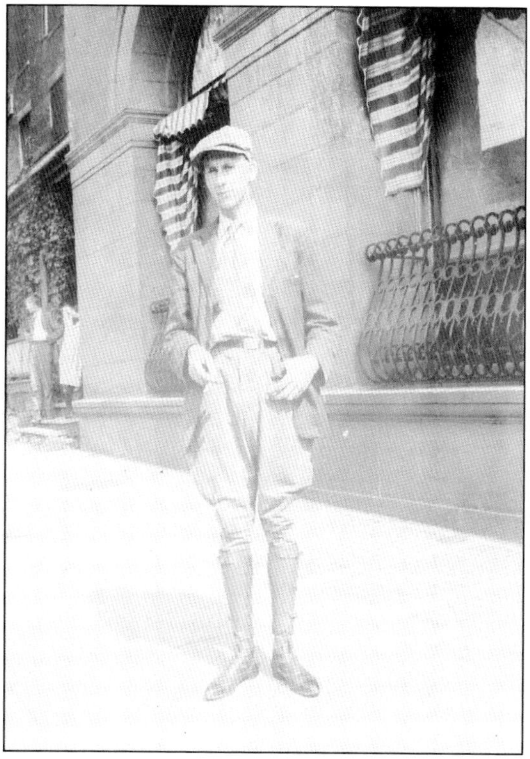

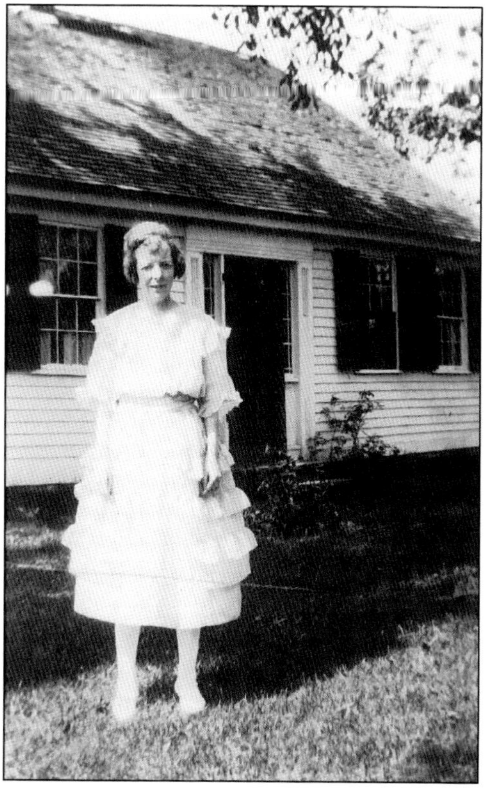

A young guest of the Clark's shows off a party dress about 1922.

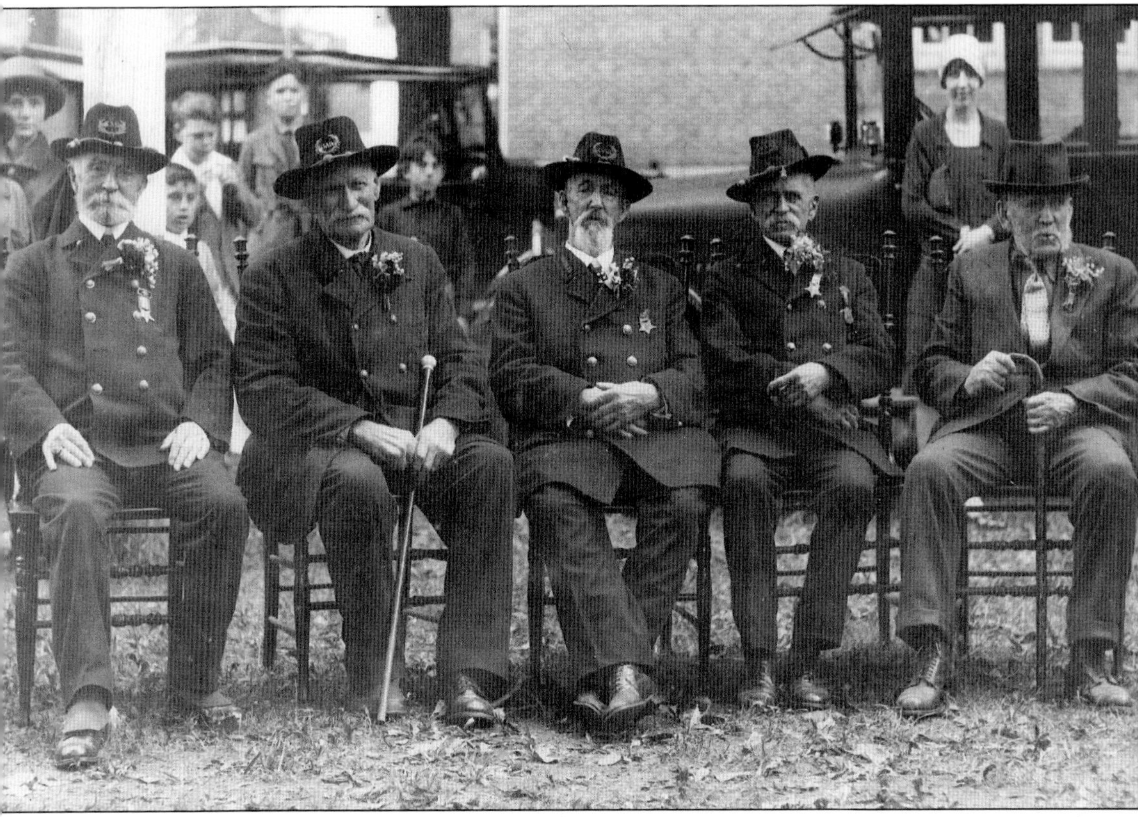

Awe-struck Girl Scouts look on at veterans of the Civil War. Note the flowers pinned on the lapels of, from left to right: Rapert J. Chute, Charles R. Gowen, Albert J. Newell, John C. McWilliams, and Samuel C. Bourne. This photograph was taken by Stanley Chilson in 1928 for the sesquicentennial book edited by Chilson's sister, Grace Buchanan.

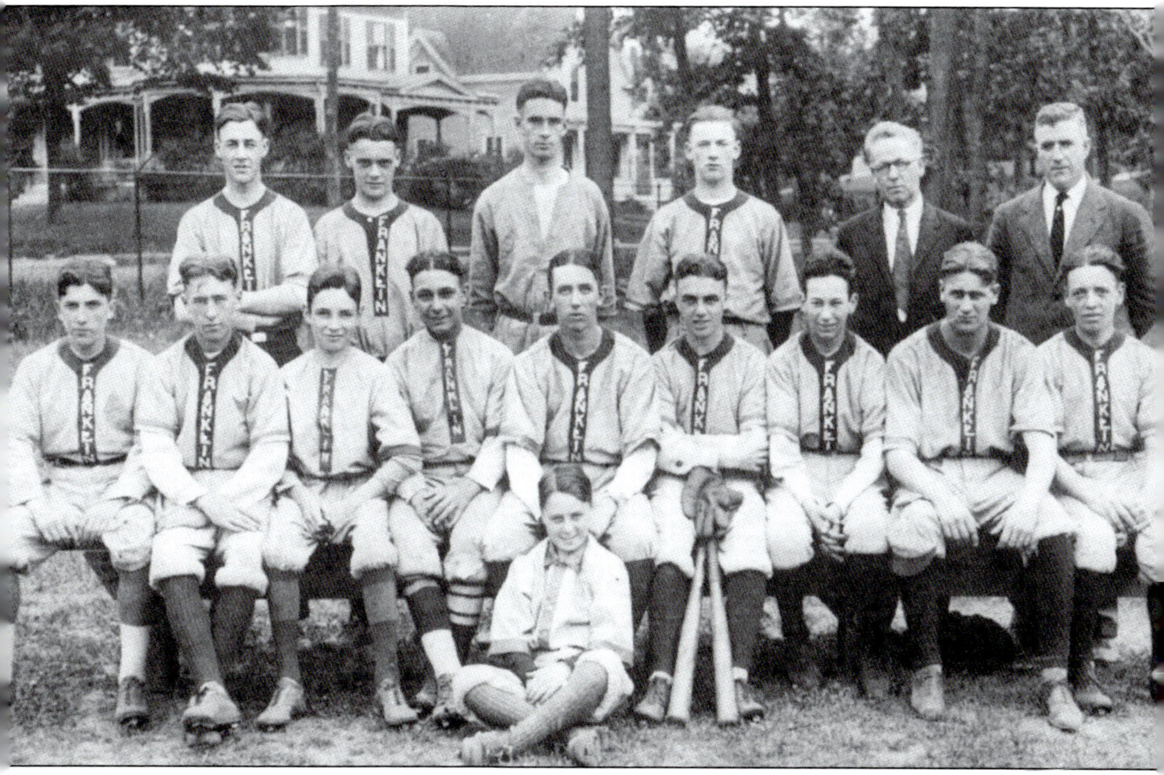

This photograph shows the 1919 Franklin High School baseball team. Coach Dan Sullivan and "Doc" Fraser pose with the team. From left to right are: (front row) Hector Bean, George Brown, "Chug" Costello, Leo Paksarian, Bill Feeley, "Doc" Crowley, Bill McKenna, Arthur Pendelton, and Armand Bourbeau; (back row) Francis Burke, Pat Casey, Normand Costello, Lenny Whalen, "Doc" Fraser, and Coach Dan Sullivan. Mascot Joe Crowley sits on the ground in front of the team. Many of the buildings in the background still stand.

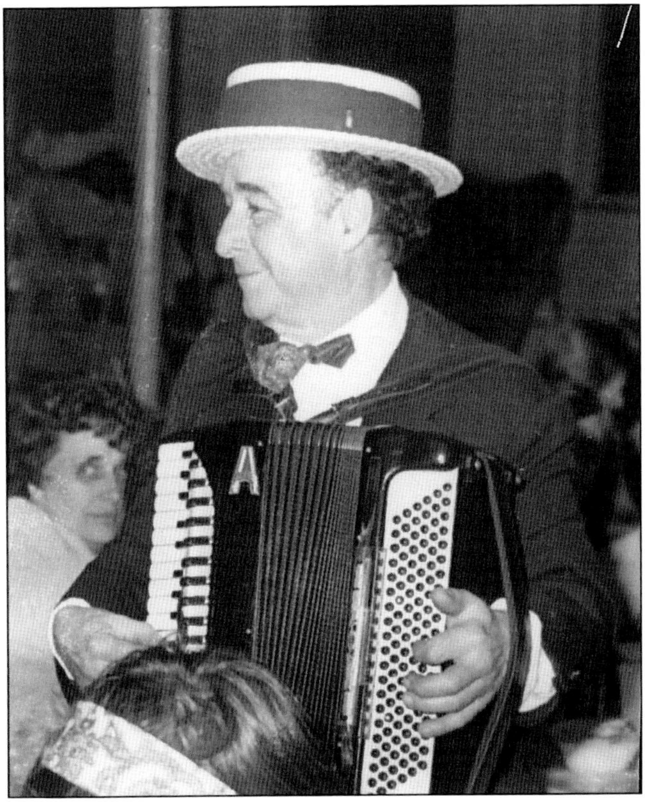

Gigi Raneri has provided entertainment for all sorts of social events for six decades.

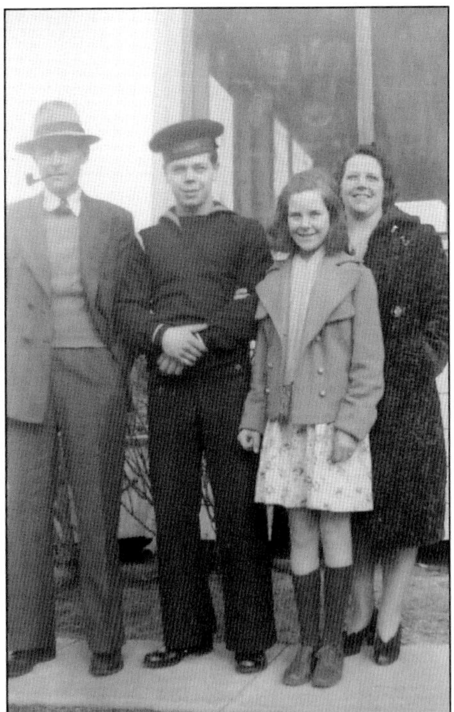

The Cusson family prepares to send their son, Alfred Jr., off to World War II in 1942.

James C. Johnston Sr. went off to war in 1943 as a Seabee. Here he poses for the folks back home while in the Philippines.

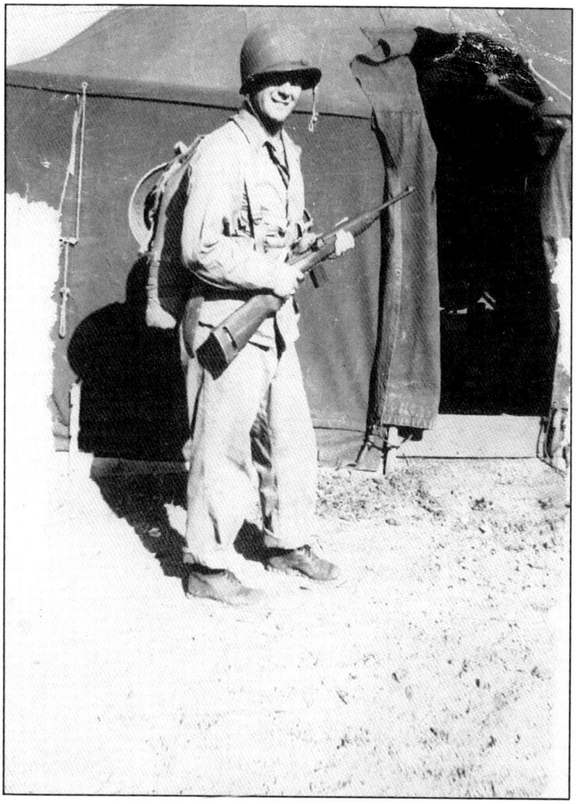

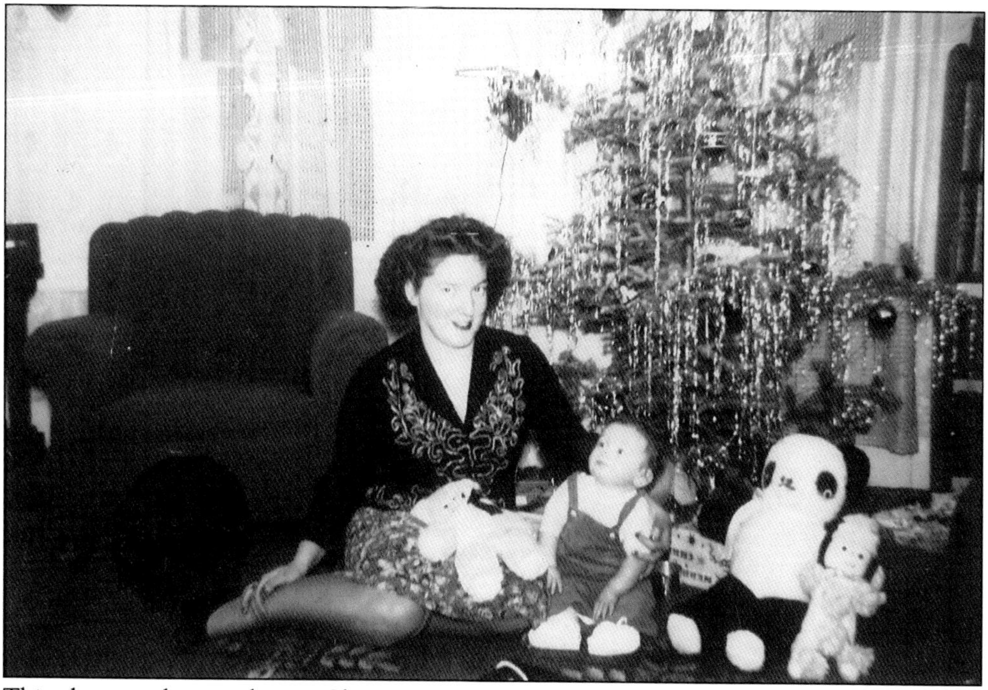

This photograph was taken at Christmas time and sent to Jim Johnston in the Philippines to show him his seven-month-old son and heir. Note the decor of the 1940s living room.

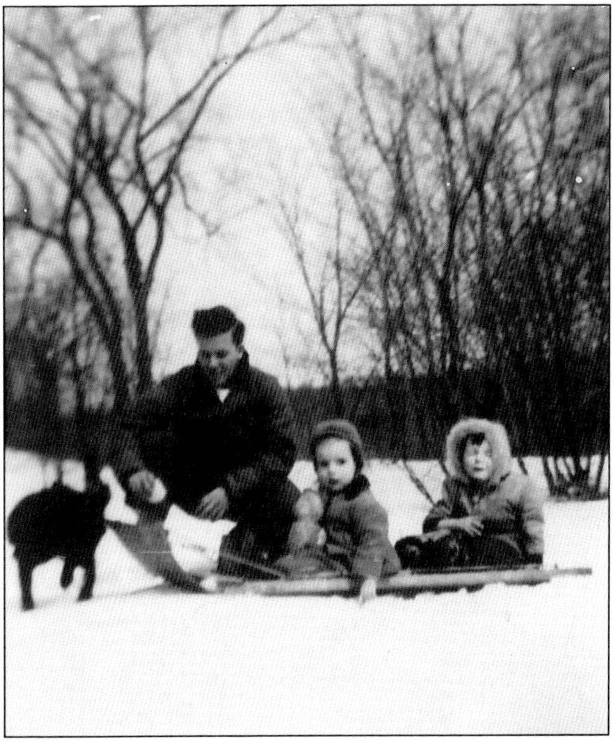

These kids didn't worry about wars, "the bomb," or the Cold War as they prepared to go on a toboggan ride with Uncle Joe Foss down a not-too-steep Franklin drumlin.

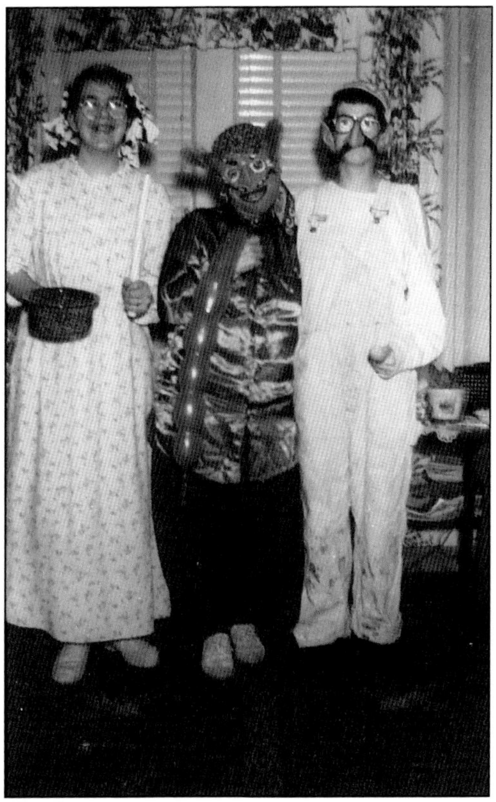

The members of this sewing circle look more like the members of a coven in this photograph, taken on Halloween 1949.

# *Nine*

# Transportation: From Here to There in Old Franklin

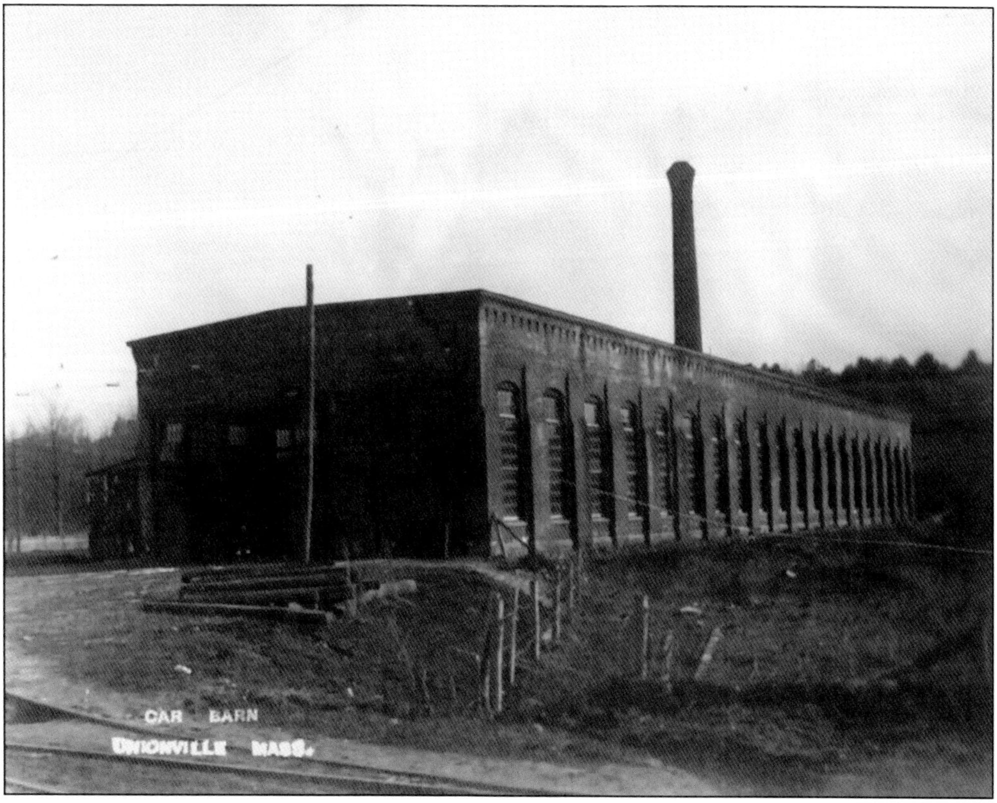


This 1905 photograph shows the old car barn, where trolley cars were once stored, in the Unionville section of Franklin.

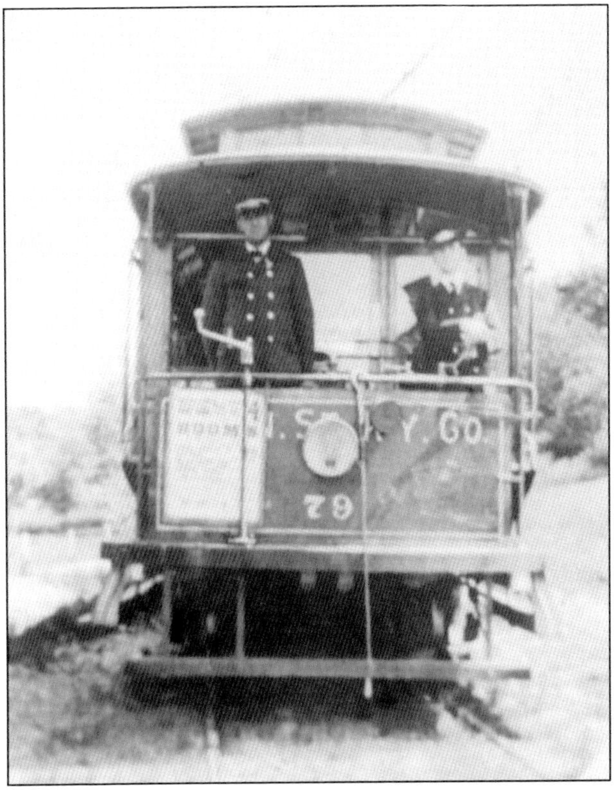


Gordon Ross was the motorman on Franklin's trolley cars during the entire time that they ran in Franklin.

This trolley linked the rural part of Franklin to the downtown area where the shops were. If you didn't keep a horse or own an automobile, the trolley was the way to travel. Five cents took you where you wanted to go and saved shoe leather. One could also make a trip to Wrentham or faraway Milford on the trolley.

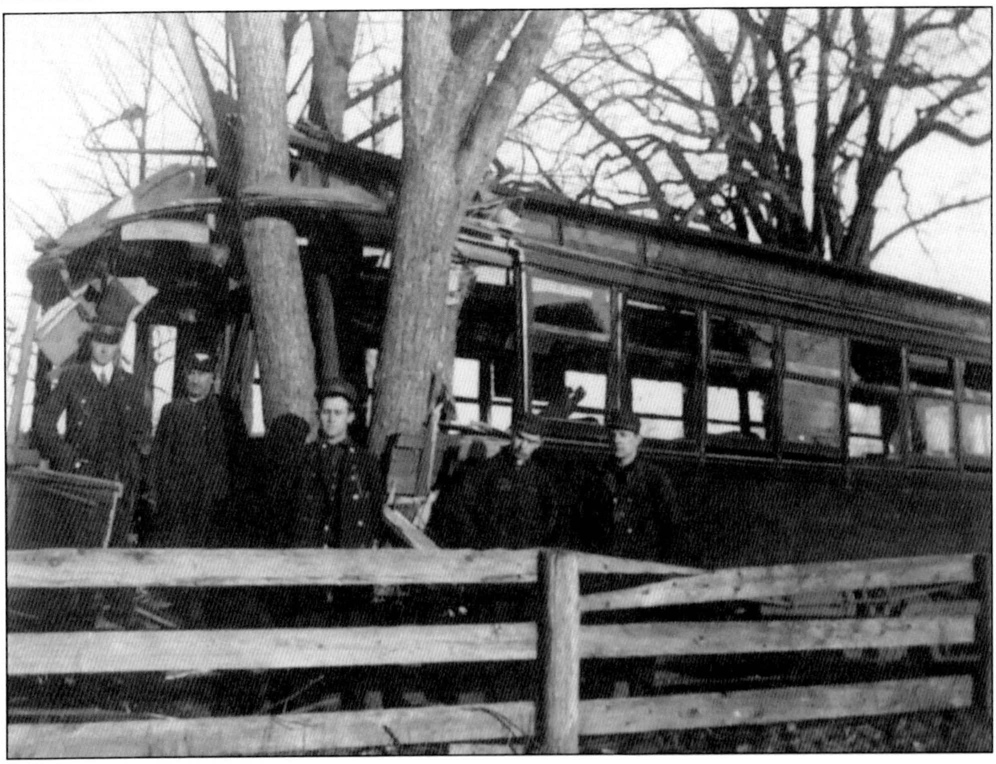

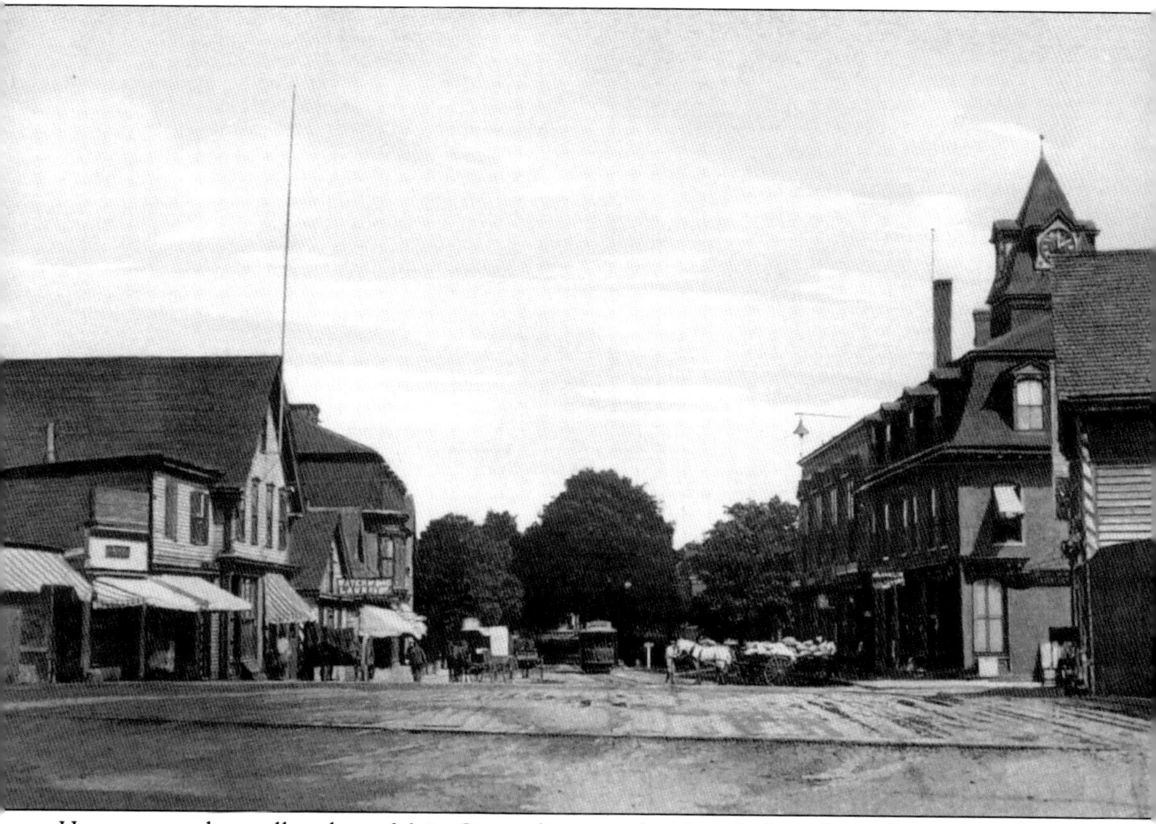

Here comes the trolley down Main Street (incorrectly identified as Central Street in this postcard). Teams of horses and wagons still provided most of the transport around 1905, when the photograph for this postcard was taken. This card was printed in Germany for Albert E. Smith of Franklin.

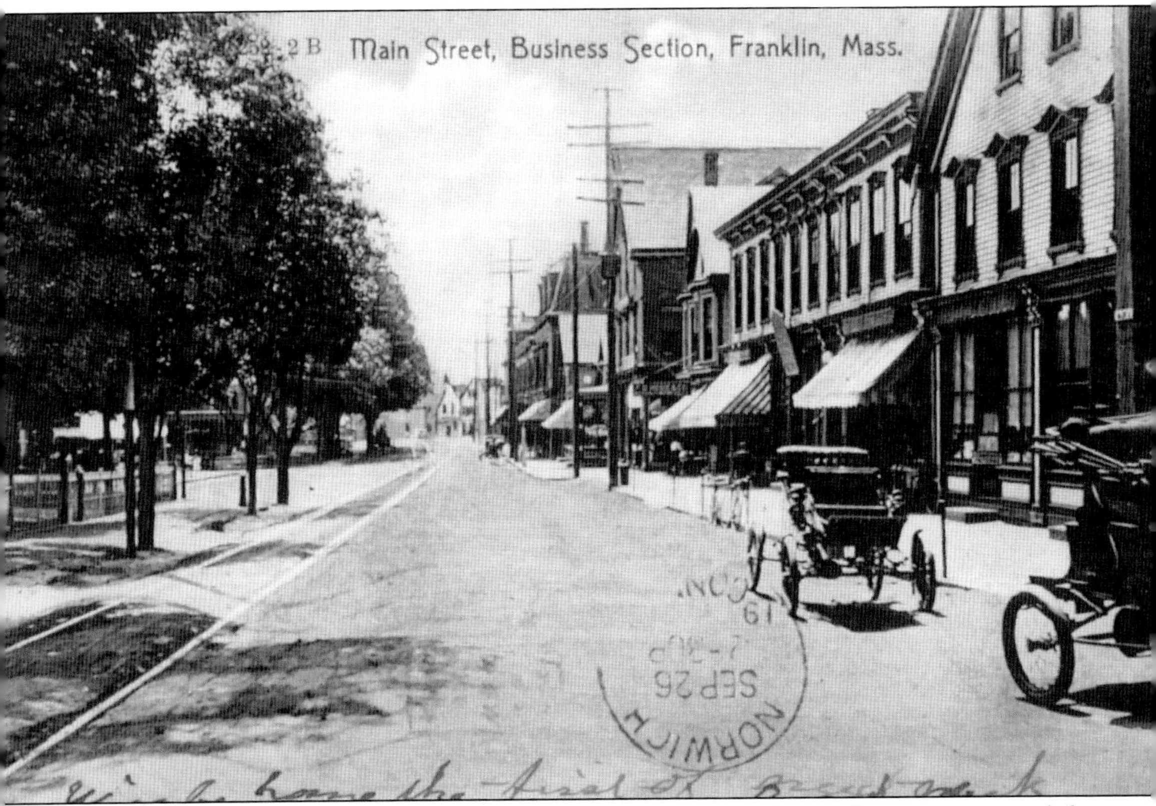


This photograph, correctly identified as Main Street, was also made into a postcard for Arthur E. Smith and shows two horseless carriages parked in the shopping district in 1907. This was two years before Mr. Ford made his Model "T," which put automobiles within the reach of the common man. In 1907, cars were rich men's toys. Note the trolley tracks to the left of the picture.

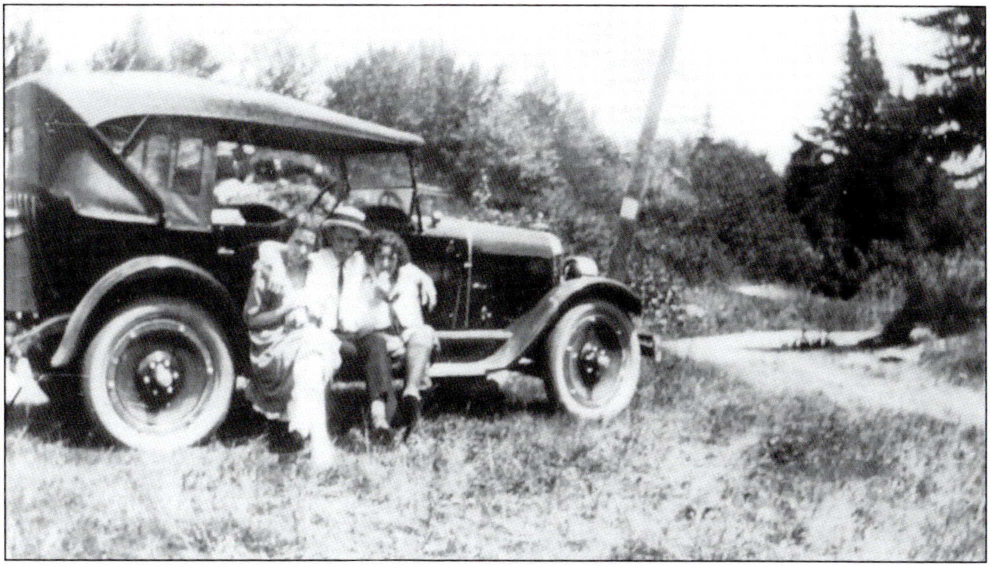

No, this isn't Bonnie and Clyde: it's a family outing in 1929. Mrs. Gertrude Foss and some members of her party were photographed on their way up the Mohawk Trail by her husband, Richmond Foss, owner of the Unionville Woolen Mill of Franklin.

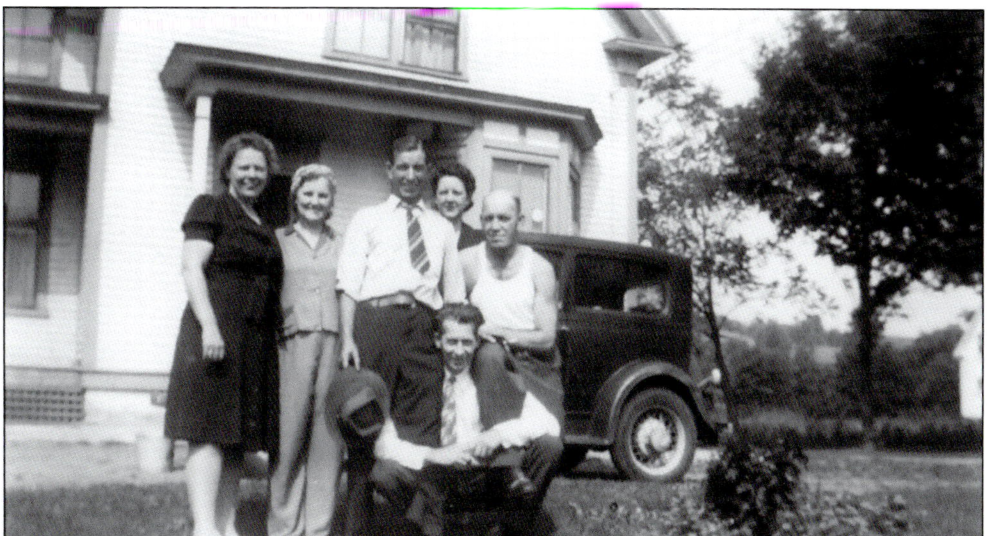

In the 1930s, summer vacations for a lot of people meant a road trip to see relatives. This road trip saw Birger Melin and company on their way to Montpelier, Vermont, and back. During the Depression, Americans spent more money on photographic film than ever before in history. Photography was still an inexpensive hobby.

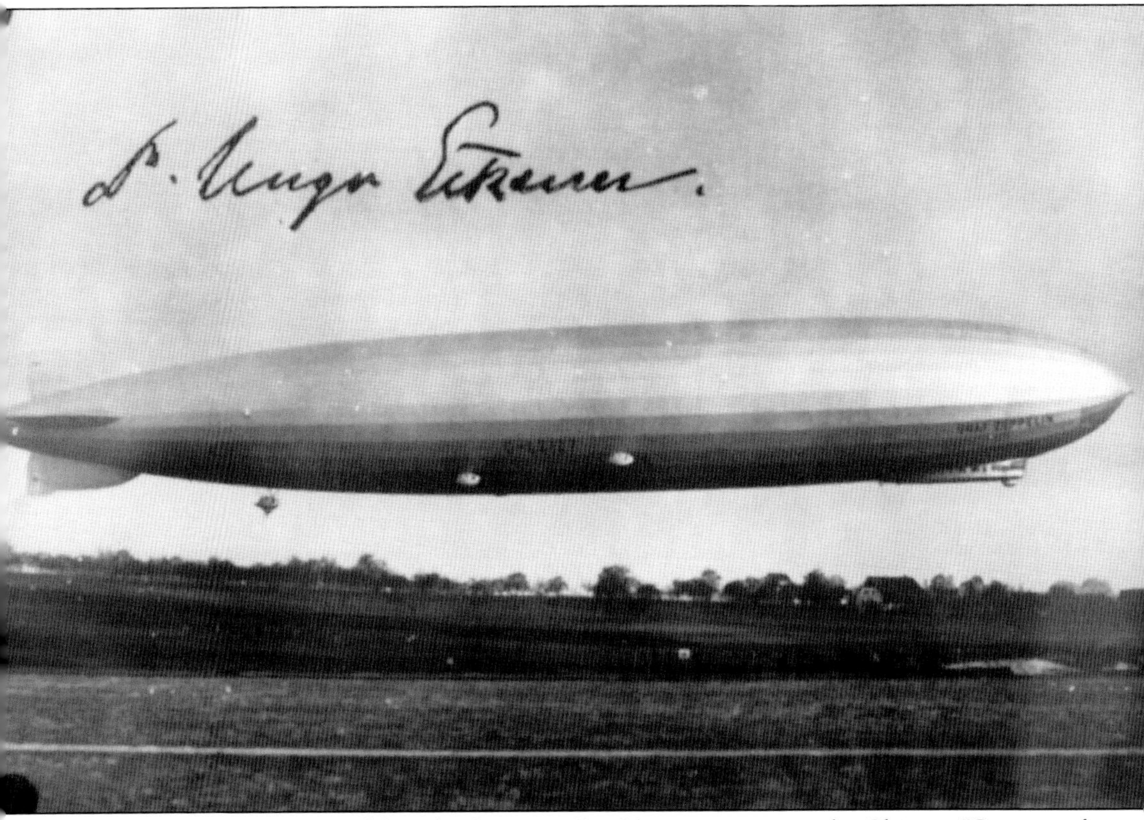

In 1933, Germany's *Graf Zeppelin* flew over Franklin on its way to the Chicago "Century of Progress" World's Fair. The airship was over 800 feet long. All of Franklin's schoolchildren were let out of class to see the fantastic *Graf Zeppelin* as it passed over town. This photograph is signed by Dr. Hugo Eckner, the founder and president of the Zeppelin Company.

# *Ten*

# Franklin at Work

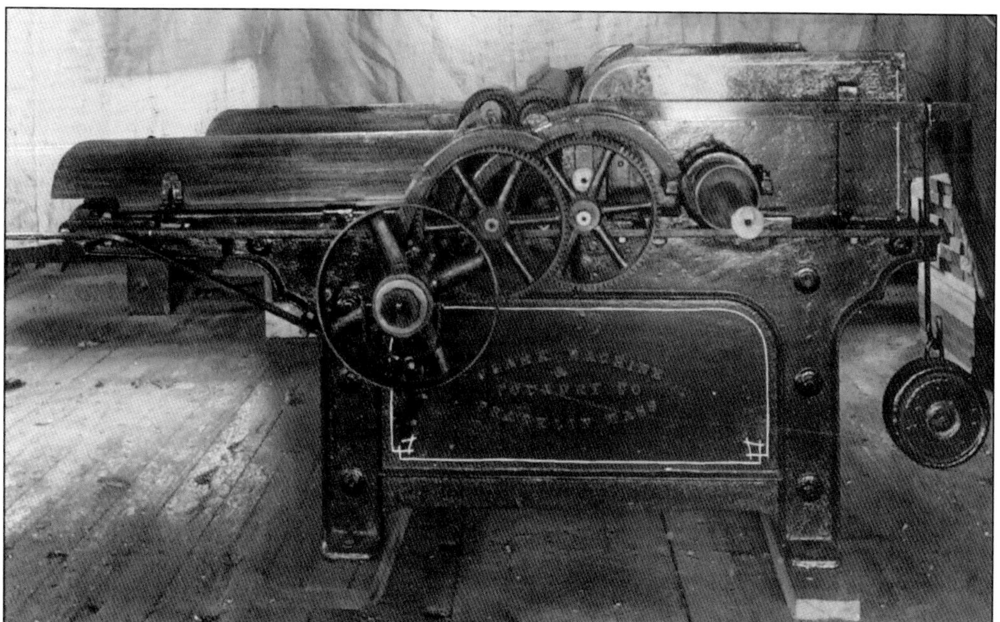

Joseph W. Clark founded the first real factory in Franklin in 1841 at the corner of Union and Cottage Streets. Textile mills all over the United States ordered and used Clark's shredding and carding machines. Joseph W. Clark was a genius and inventor; unfortunately he never applied for or got a single patent, and others made millions on his inventions. This photograph shows a "Picker" about 1860.

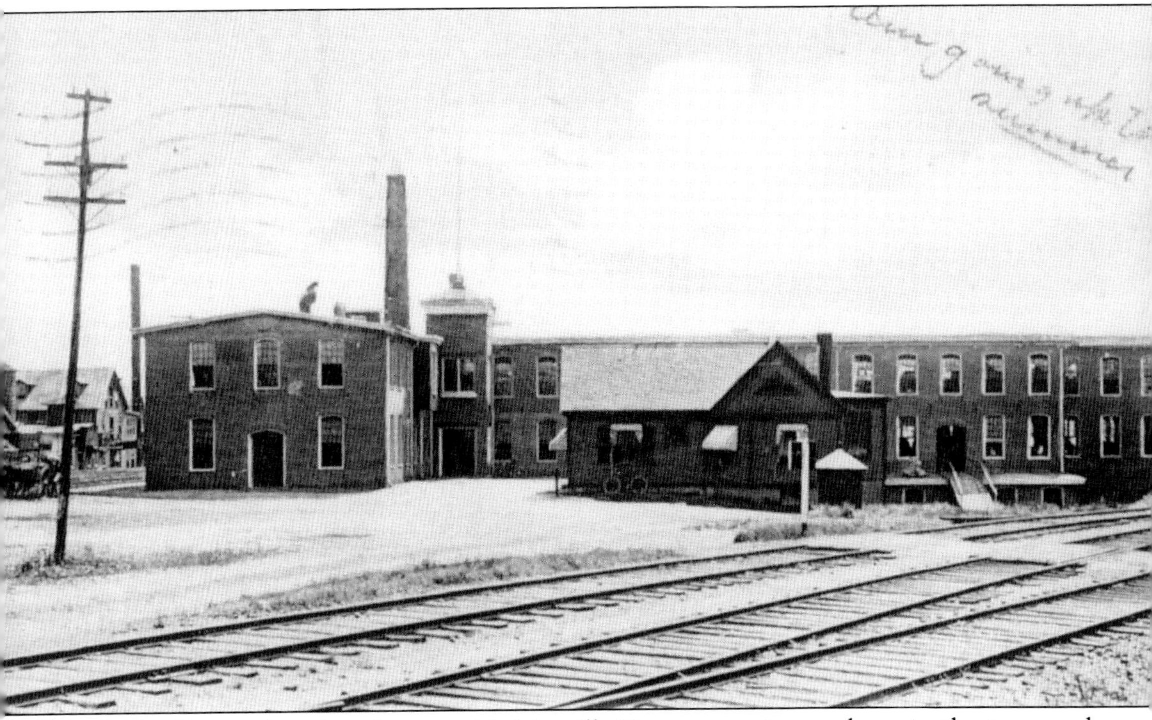

Harry Haywood made a fortune with his mill. He was a major employer in the town and the railroad helped to make his fortune. The Victorian Haywood Mansion was a showplace in Franklin featured on many postcards. Mrs. Haywood disliked the mansion and had it razed (see p. 62).

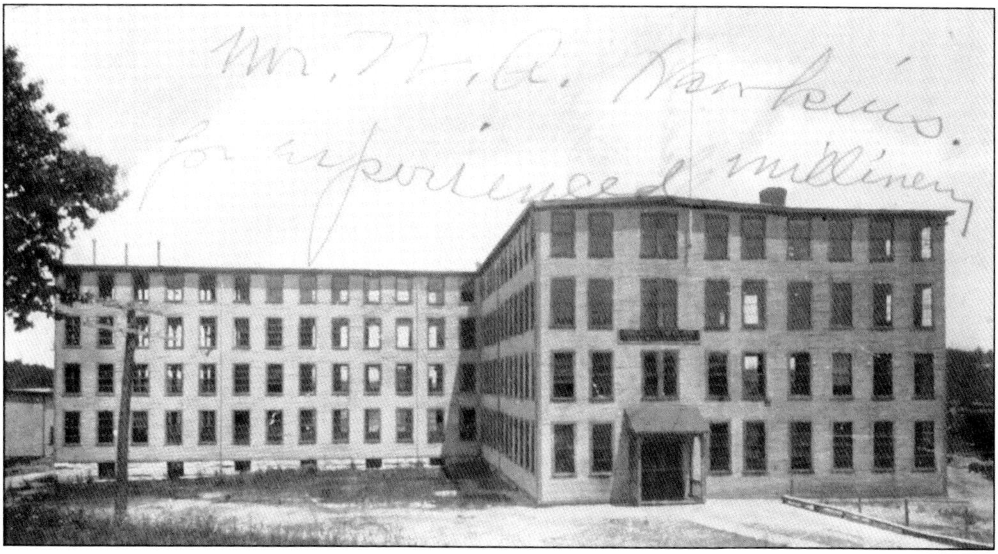

Hat making was the oldest industrial operation in Franklin, going back to the 1790s. This industry remained very important to the local economy well into the 1960s. Hats for the 1939 production of *Gone With the Wind* were made here.

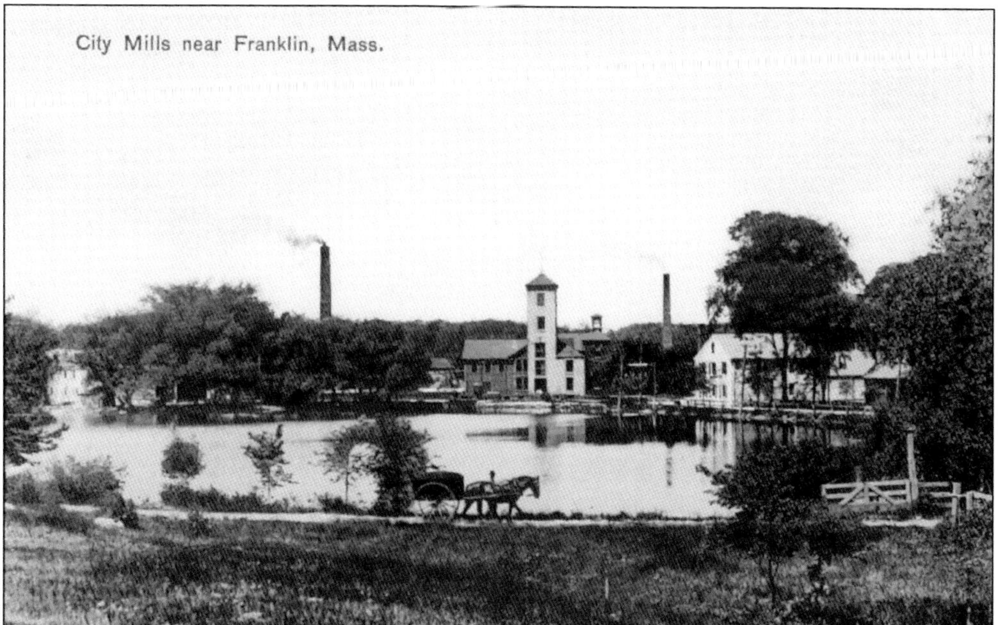


Many Franklin people worked in nearby City Mills. Here a teamster leads his horse and wagon down a Franklin cart lane to City Mills. This 1900 postcard was painted for Albert C. Mason and sold in his Franklin drug store. There are many historic links between Franklin and Norfolk.

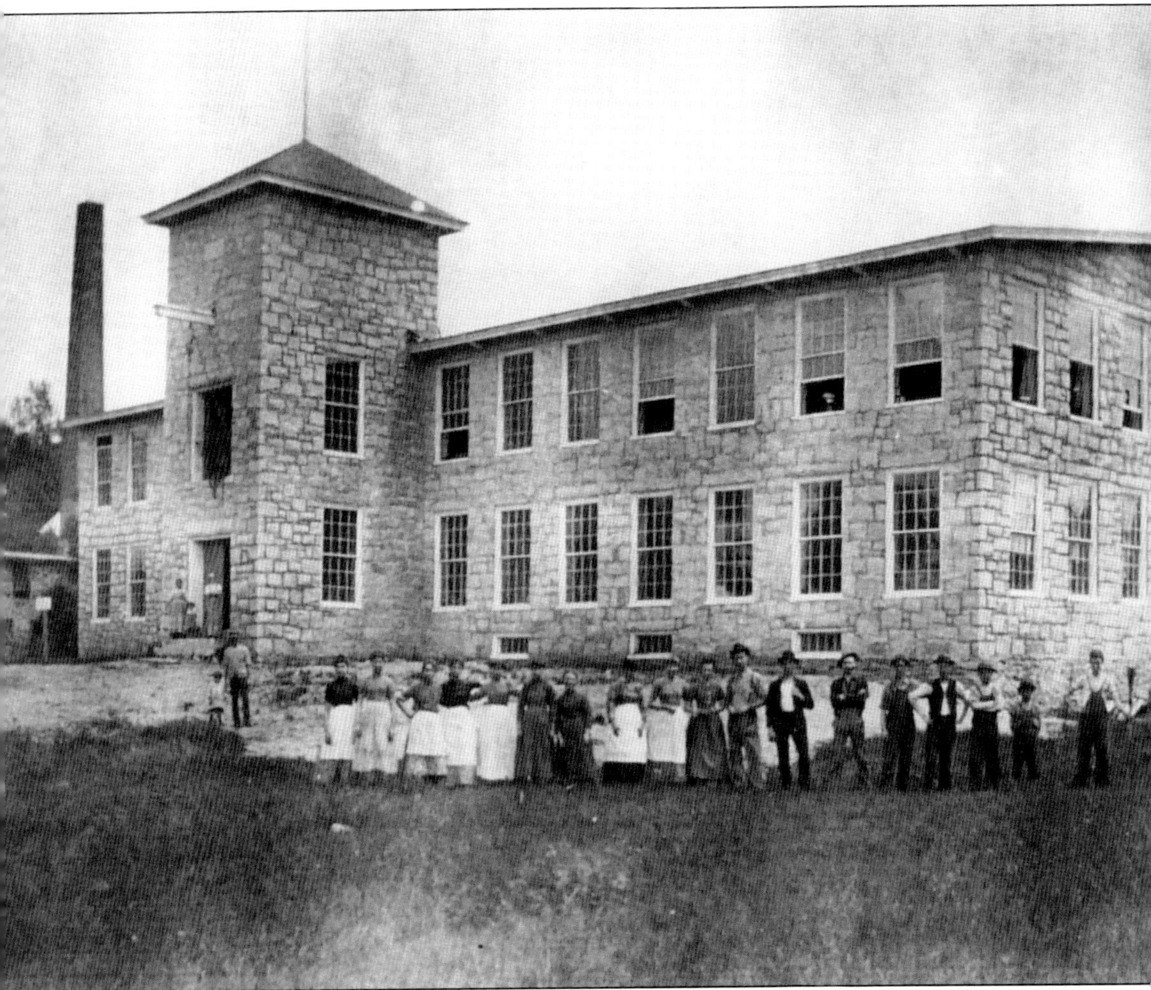

Brookdale Mill, in the Unionville section of Franklin, was built in 1883. It is one of the most beautiful examples of local mill architecture.

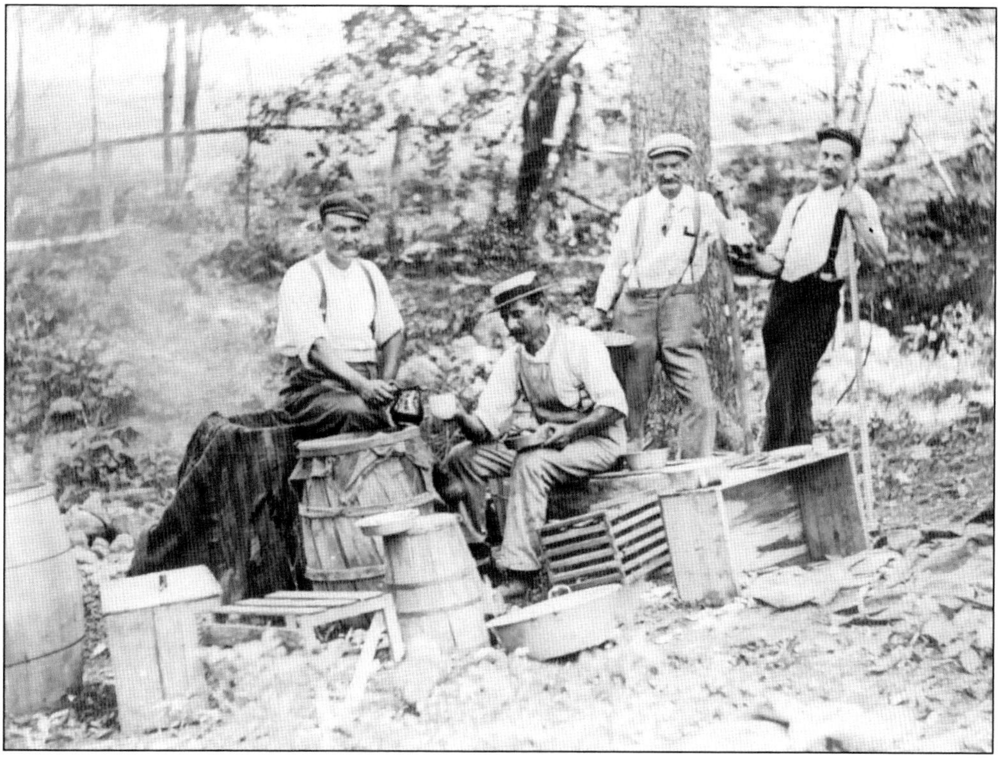

The Clarks didn't dig clams for a living, but when they were not making textile machines, they liked to go off to the Cape for a clambake. Here are Grampa Clark (Joseph W. Clark), Ed Clark, and Mr. Gorham, who was a Clark foreman. The Clarks bought several cottages on the Cape and continued to summer there for the next sixty years at Dennisport.

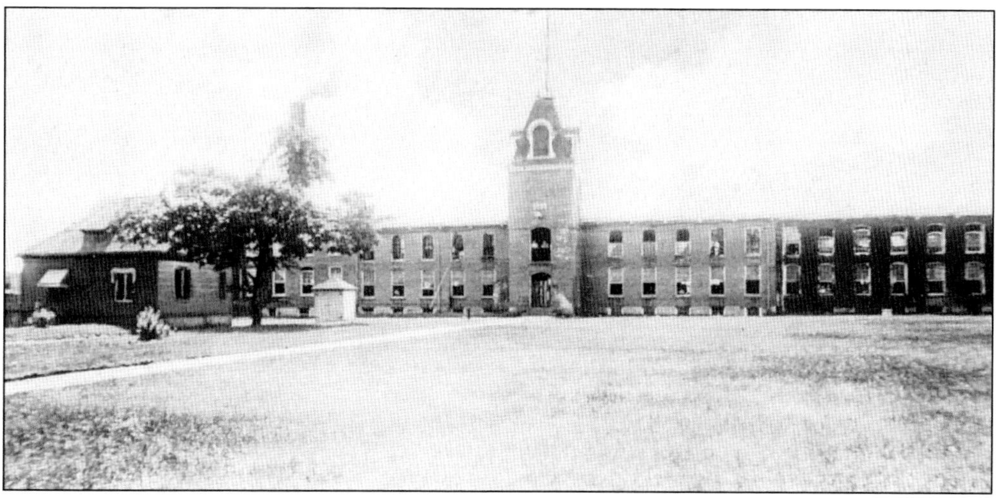

The American Woolen Mills building was located next to the Hayward Mill on Union Street. Today the building has been recycled as an apartment building.

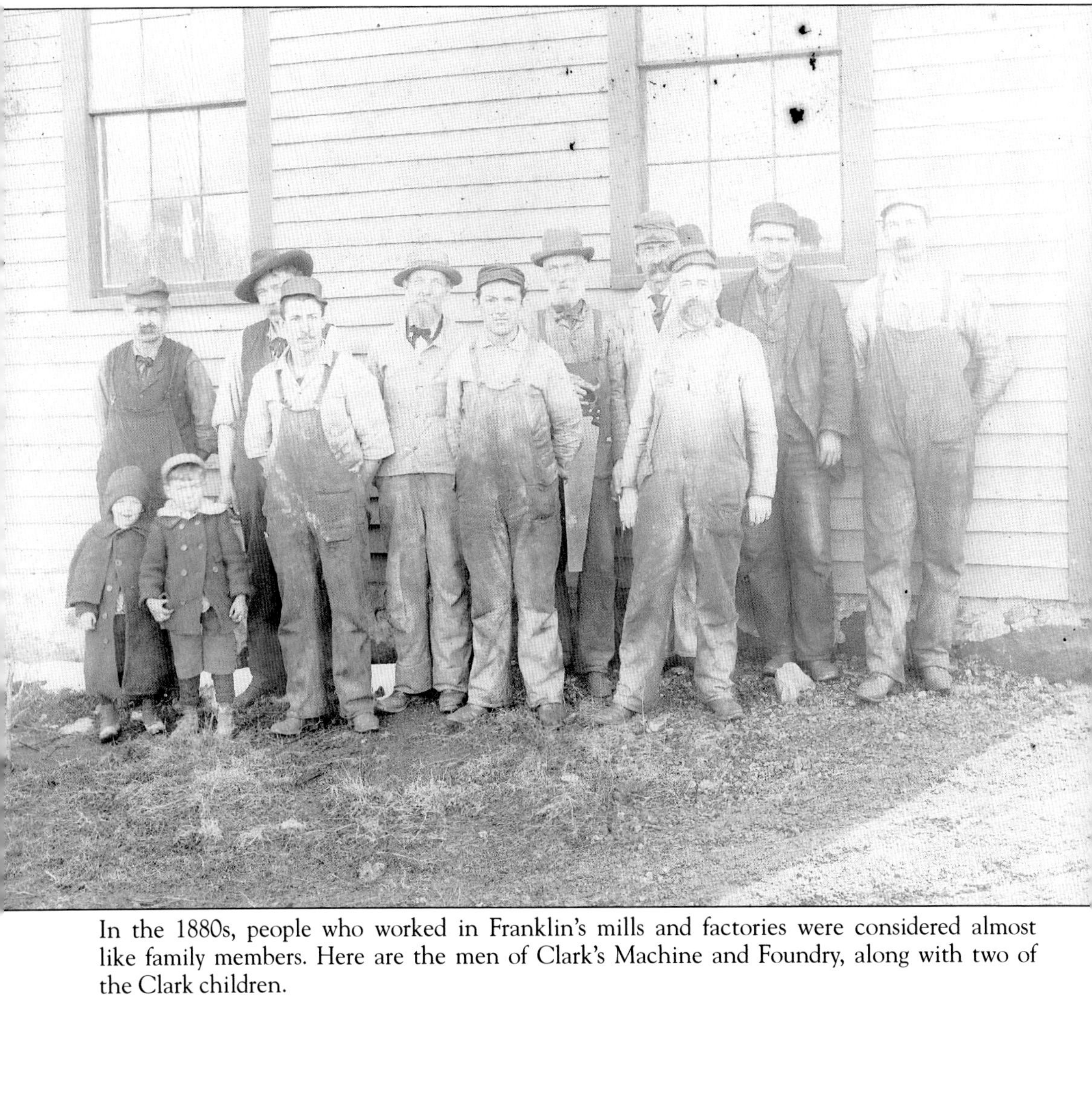

In the 1880s, people who worked in Franklin's mills and factories were considered almost like family members. Here are the men of Clark's Machine and Foundry, along with two of the Clark children.

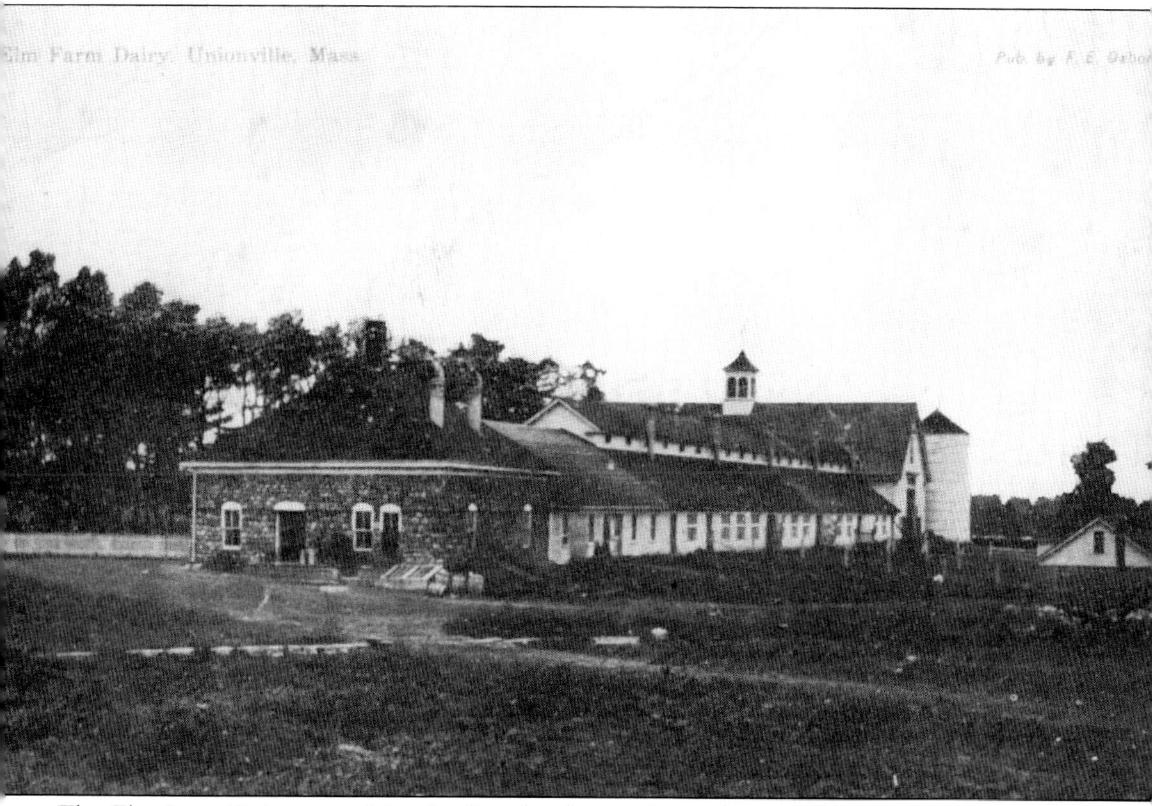


The Elm Farm Dairy, owned by the Ray family, was located in the Unionville section of Franklin. The Ray House was the scene of summer, winter, fall, and spring entertainment. This photograph was taken about 1895 and turned into a postcard for Frank E. Osborne, who ran Osborne's Store and the Unionville Post Office.

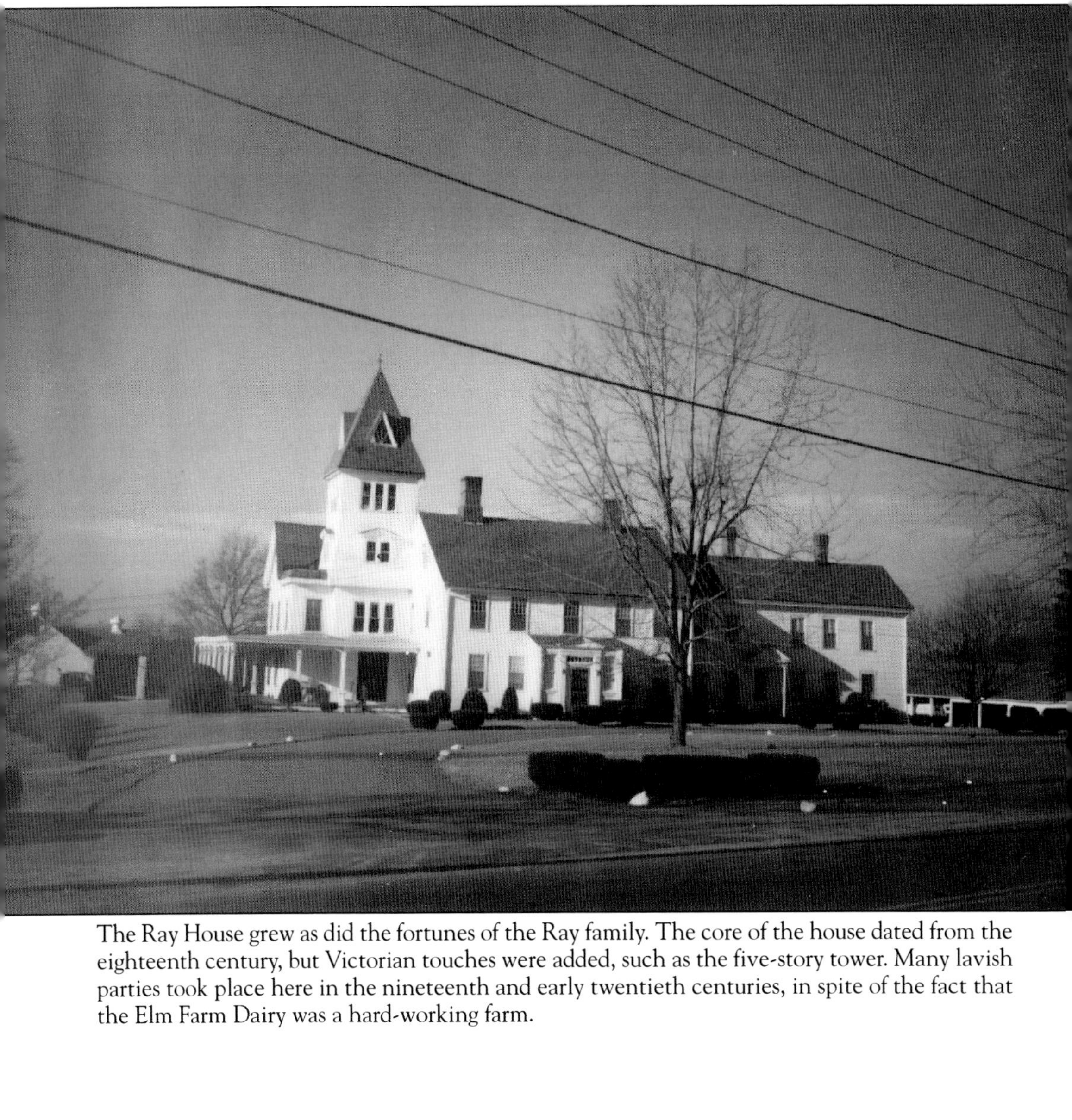

The Ray House grew as did the fortunes of the Ray family. The core of the house dated from the eighteenth century, but Victorian touches were added, such as the five-story tower. Many lavish parties took place here in the nineteenth and early twentieth centuries, in spite of the fact that the Elm Farm Dairy was a hard-working farm.

# *Eleven*

# Franklin Through the Seasons

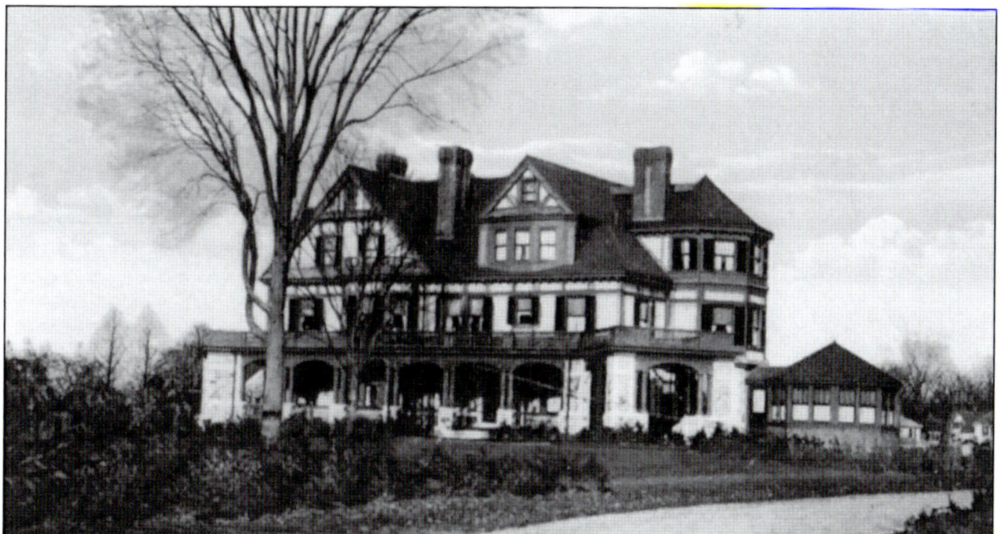

Smith's News Store in Franklin had this postcard of the Hayward Mansion in springtime printed in France. The garage of this house had an interesting feature. An automobile could be driven into it and parked on a huge turntable, which would allow the vehicle to be turned 180 degrees so that it could be driven out in a forward direction.

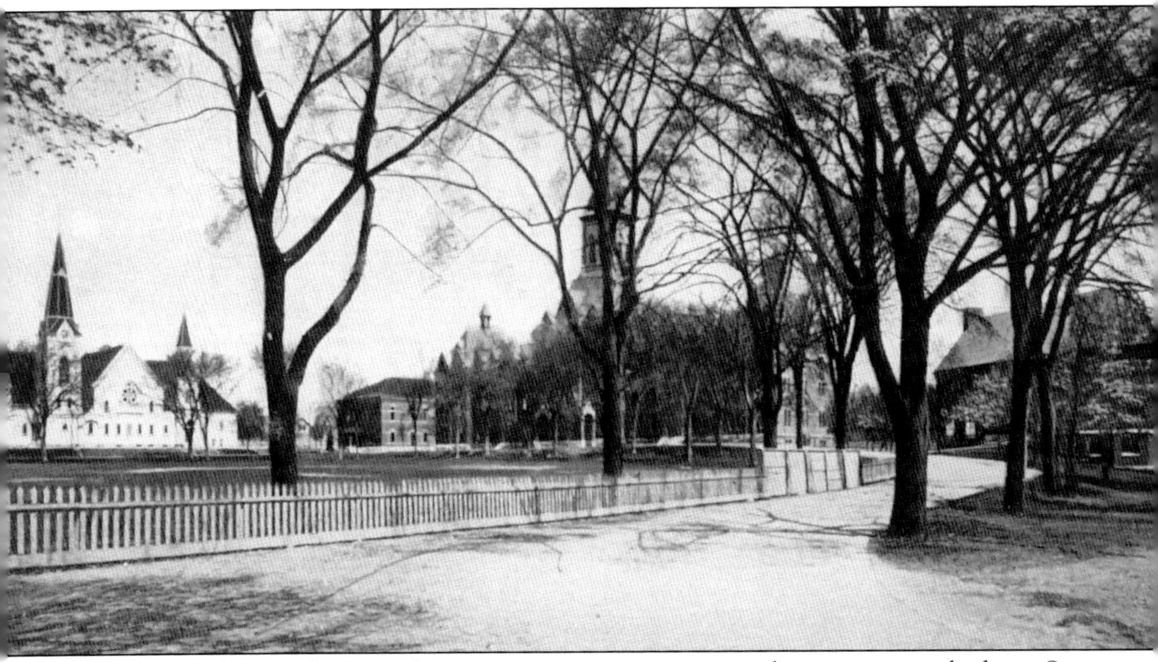

Dean Academy is shown in this sweeping panoramic view as the trees start to leaf out. Seen here, from left to right, are the Grace Universalist Church, Dean Hall, and the Dean Science Building. This photograph was taken in the spring of 1902.

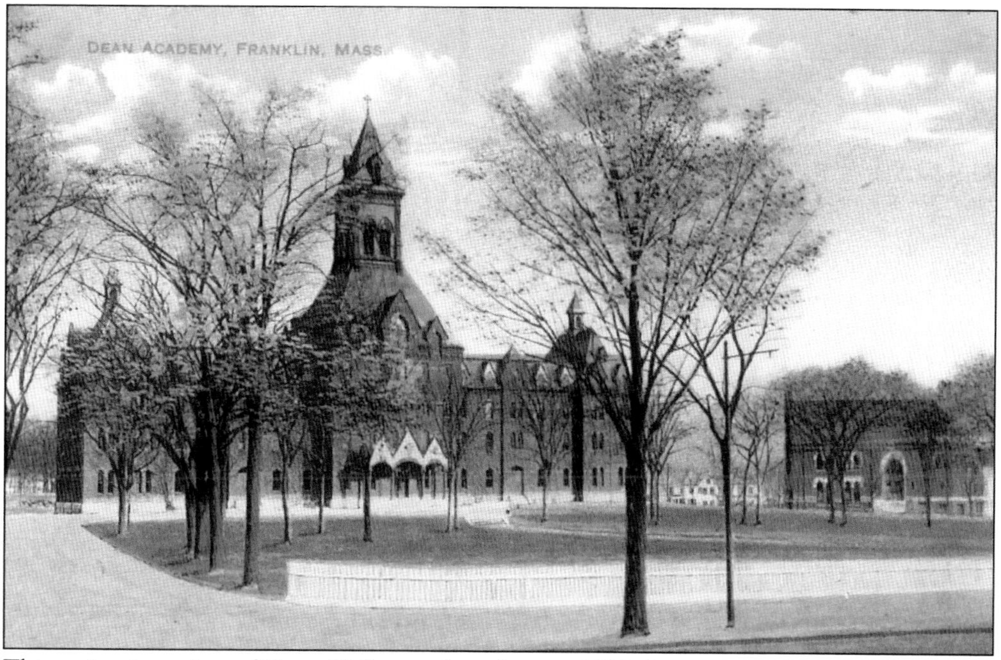


This springtime view of Dean Hall was also taken in 1902. It was turned into a postcard for Albert C. Mason to sell in his store.

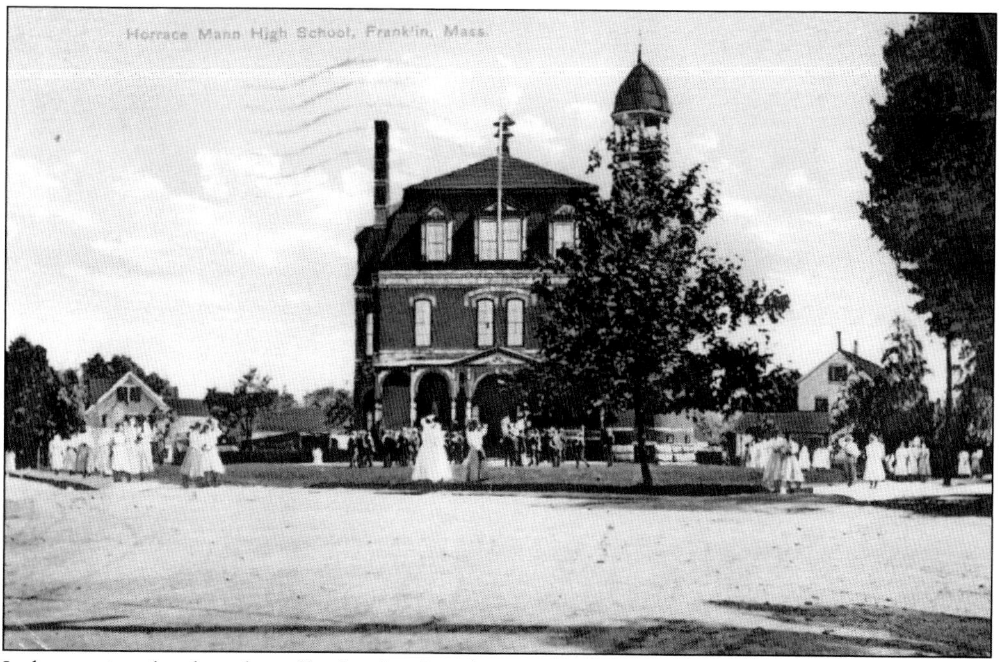


In late spring the thoughts of high school students turn to summer vacation. Here at the Horace Mann High School (now the municipal building), a rehearsal seems to be in progress. This photograph was taken in late May 1905.

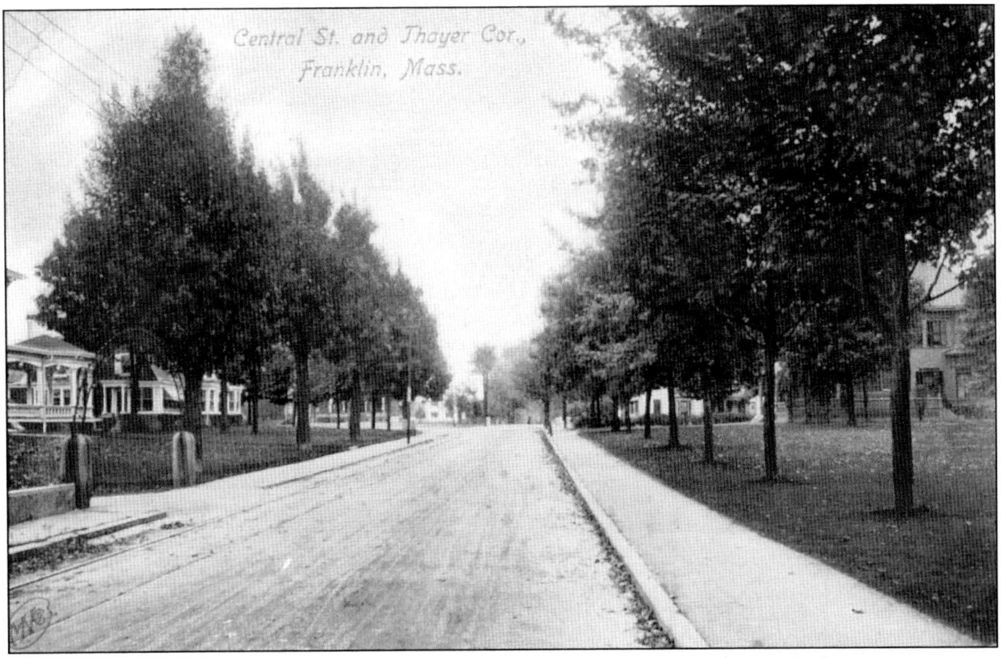


A lazy early summer settled on Central Street and Thayer's Corner about 1905.

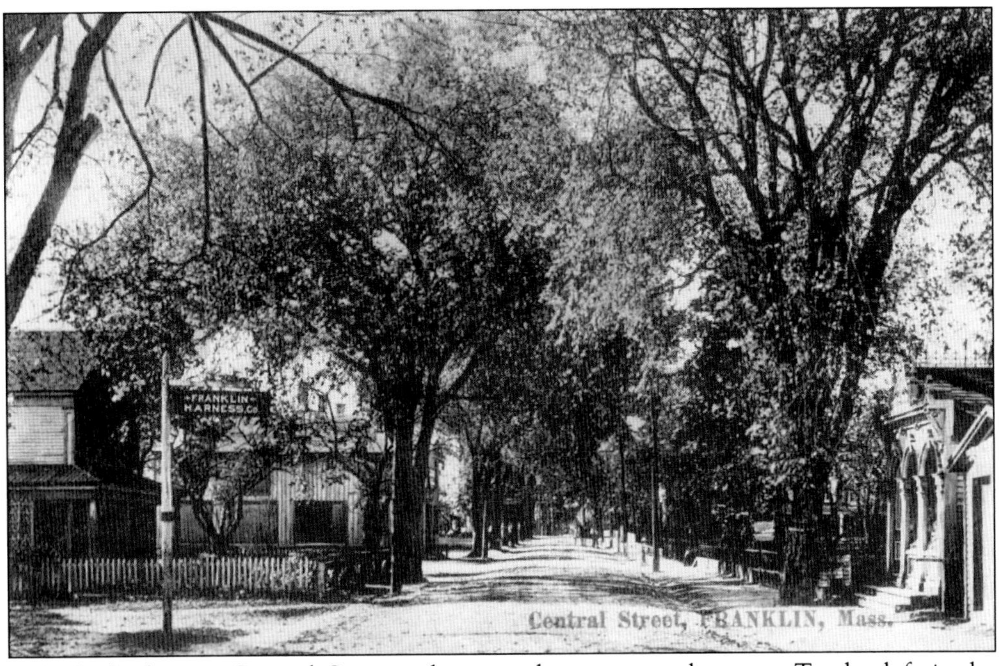


A little further up Central Street a horse and wagon can be seen. To the left is the Franklin Harness Company.

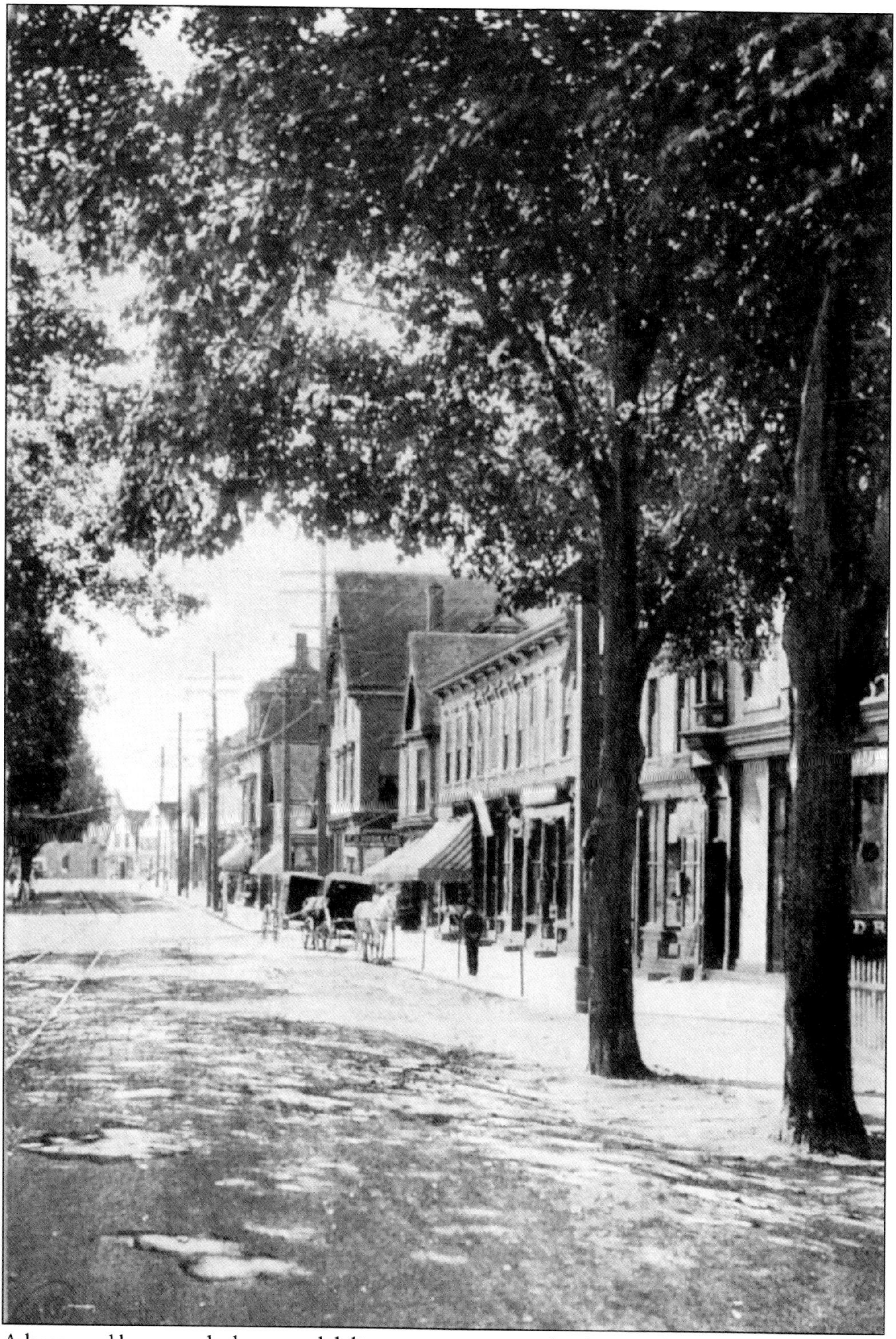

A horse and buggy and a horse and delivery wagon wait in the drowsy afternoon summer sun for their masters to return, about 1905.

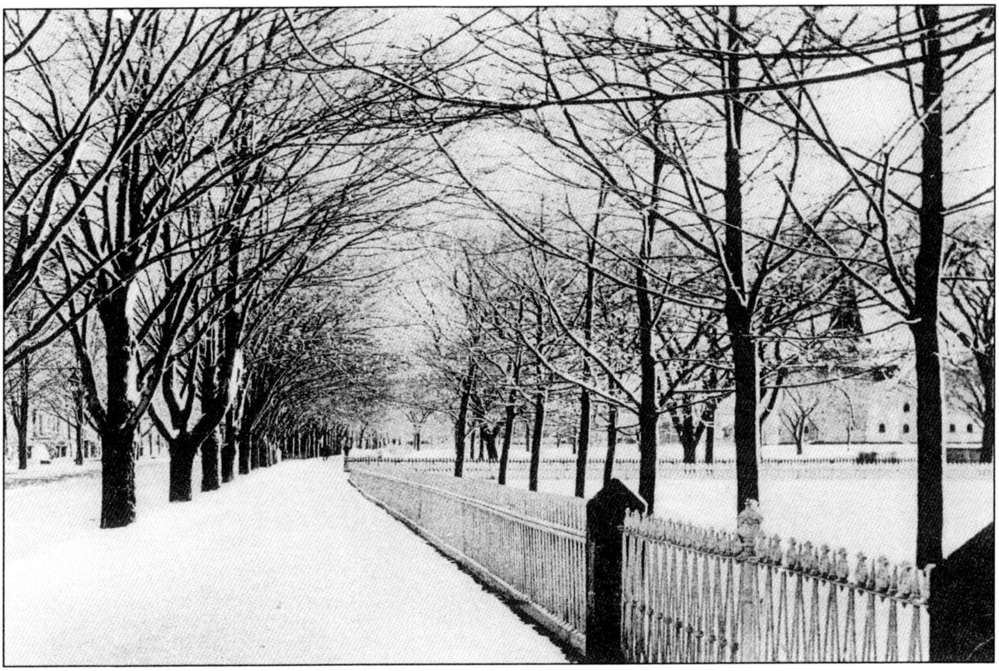

A boy, out of school, crosses Main Street on his bicycle about 1905.

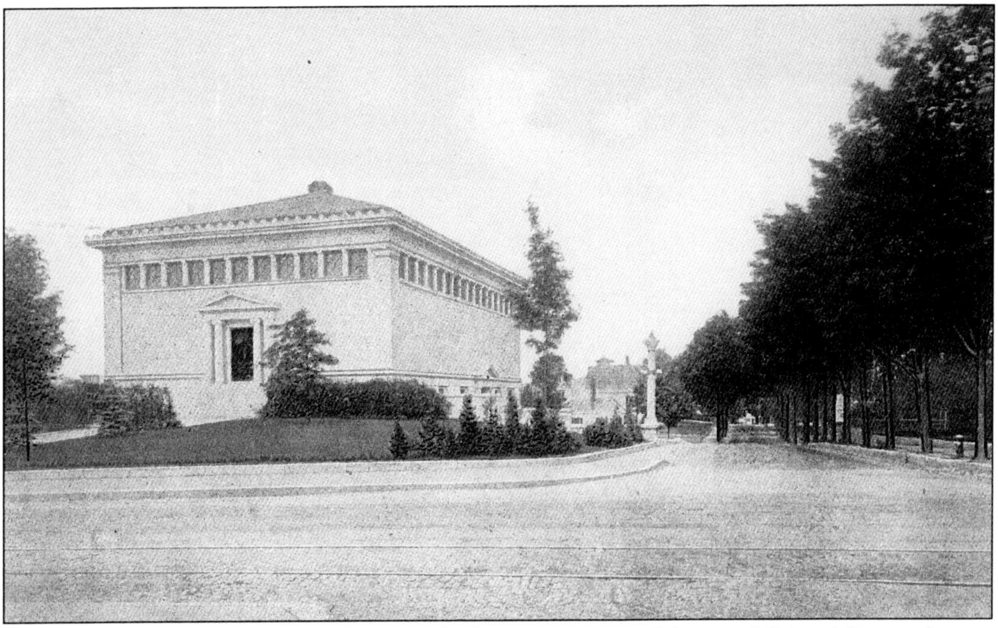

The Ray Memorial Library was photographed on its corner at Main and School Streets late in the summer of 1905.

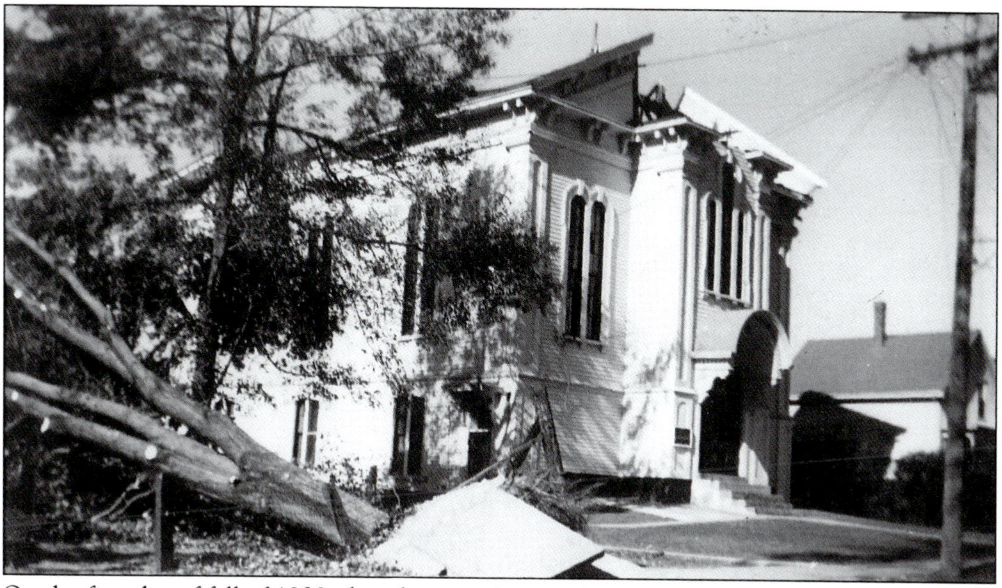

On the first day of fall of 1938, this photograph was taken of the Franklin Baptist Church. Its beautiful tall spire was ripped away by the Hurricane of 1938 (see p. 44).

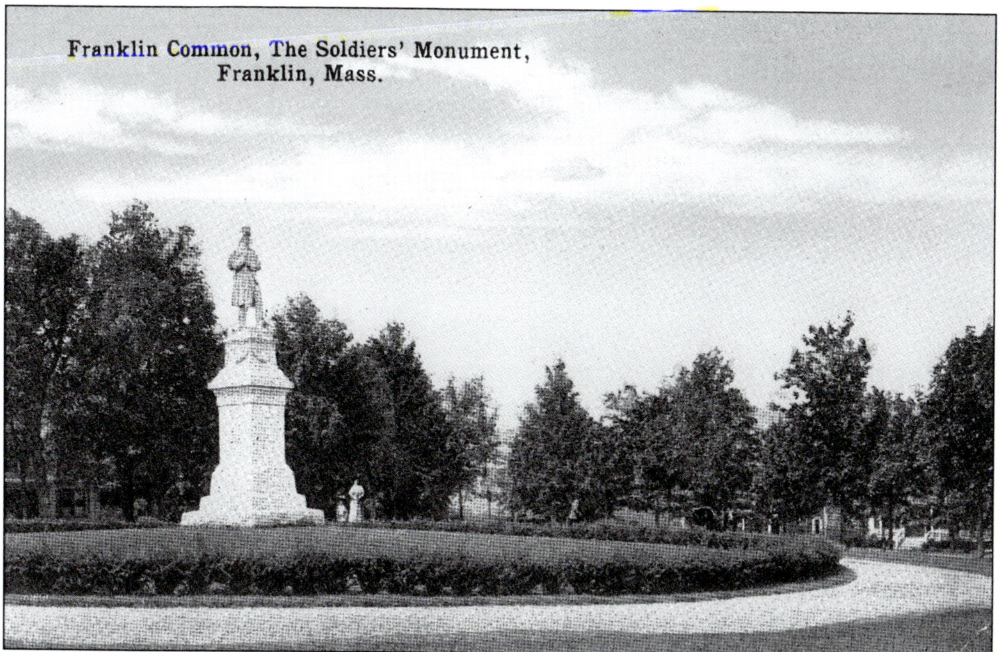


This photograph of the Civil War Soldier's Monument was taken around 1910.

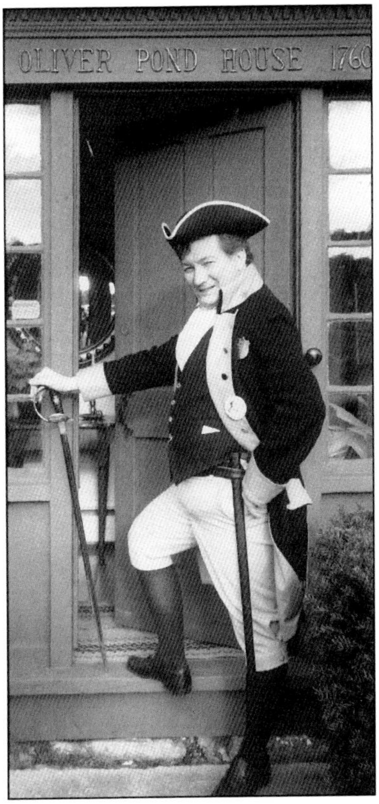


Halloween brings out the child in all of us regardless of our age. Take notice of good old Oliver Pond standing in his doorway. He is a prime example of a ghost caught on camera.

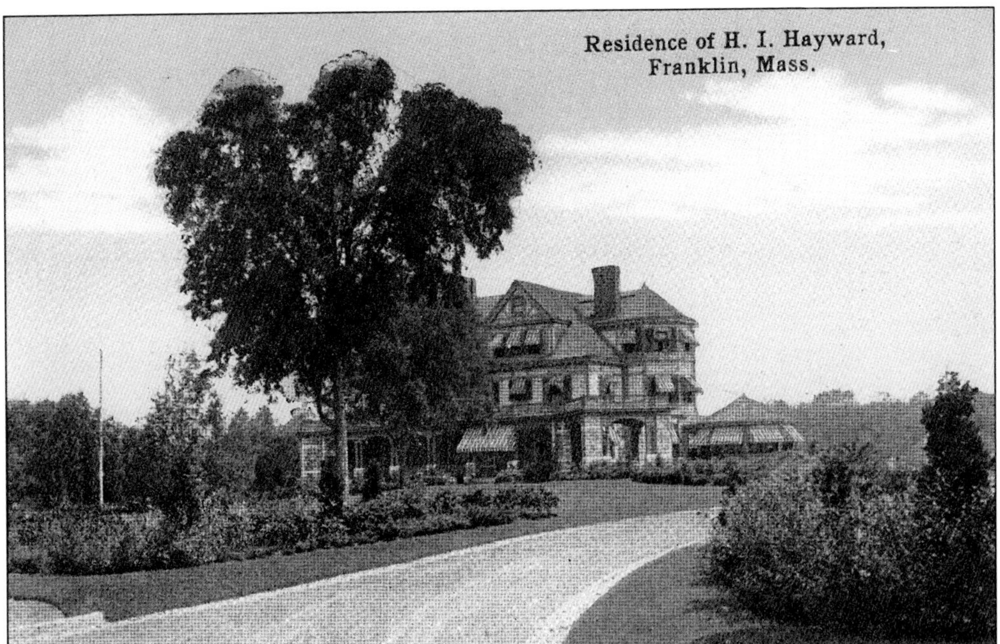


The Haywood Estate is shown here in the fall of 1907.

This photograph is a tribute to Yankee thrift, as the woodsmen and their dog pose before a massive pile of chopped and split wood. During the colonial period, part of a minister's pay was made up of split firewood. This stack was at the rear of the Oliver Pond House.

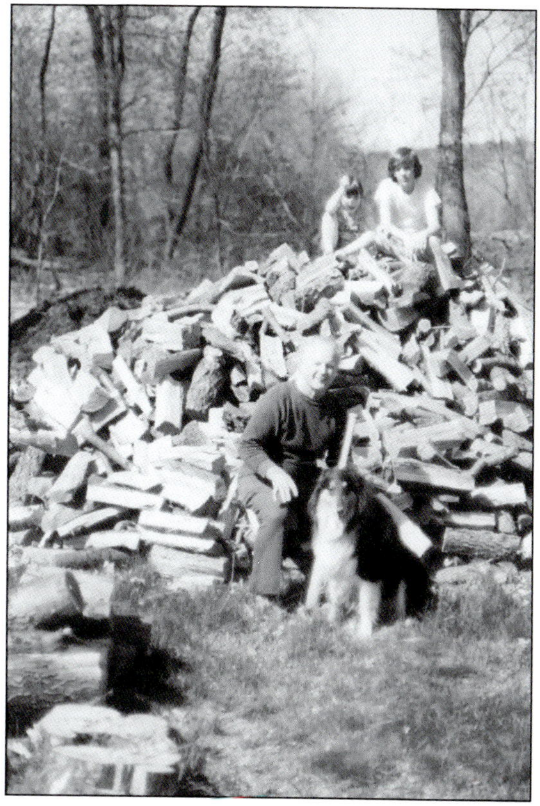

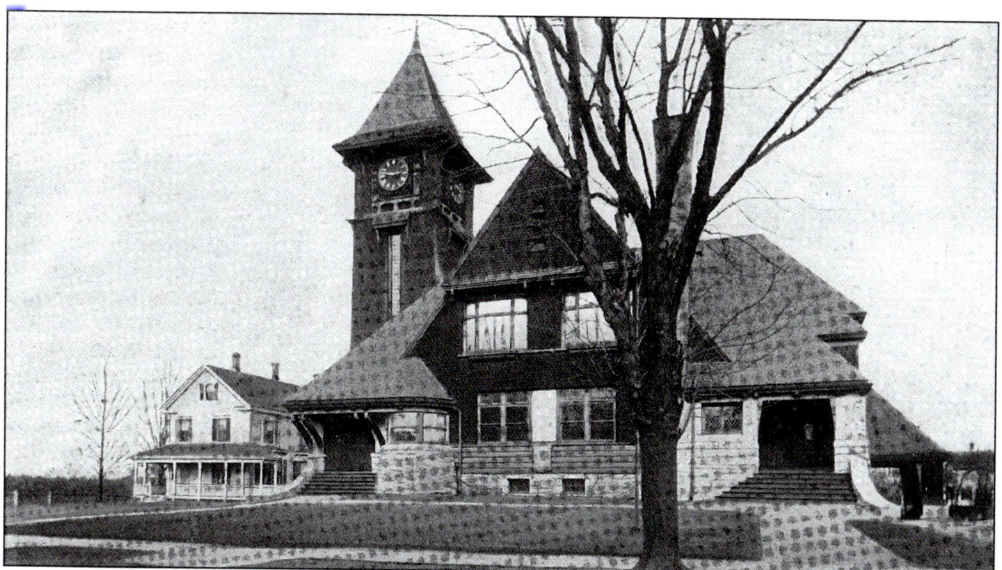

The Congregational church looks bleak as autumn turns into winter. This 1907 photograph shows the tall bell tower to great advantage.

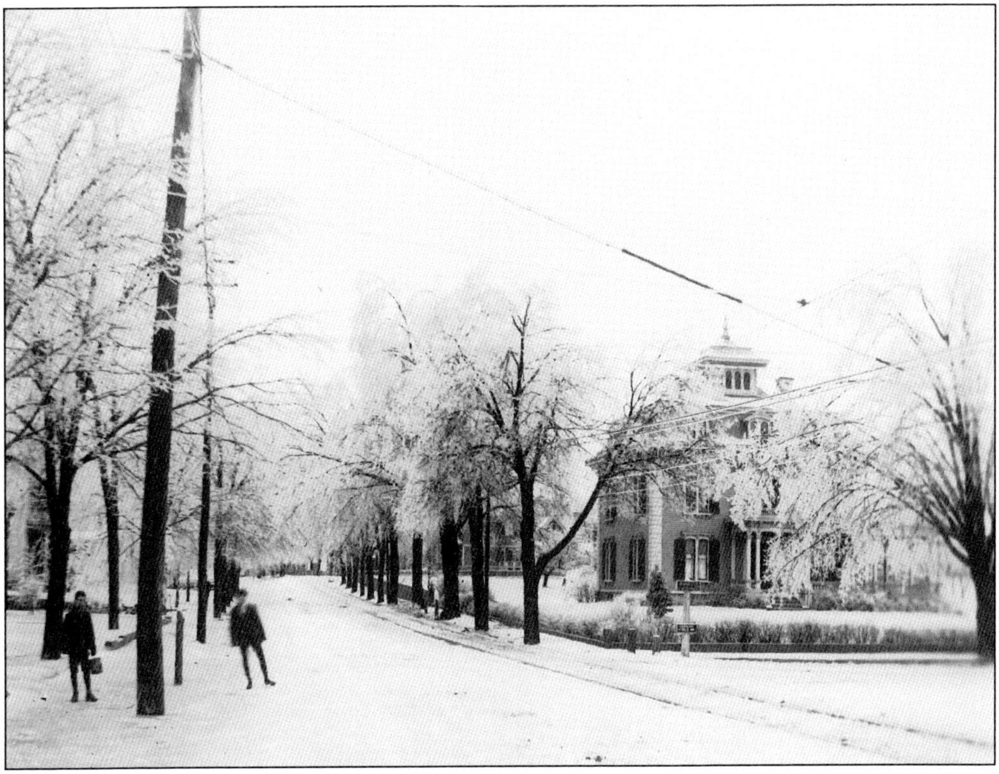

Here is "The Hawthorne," covered in winter white in 1906.

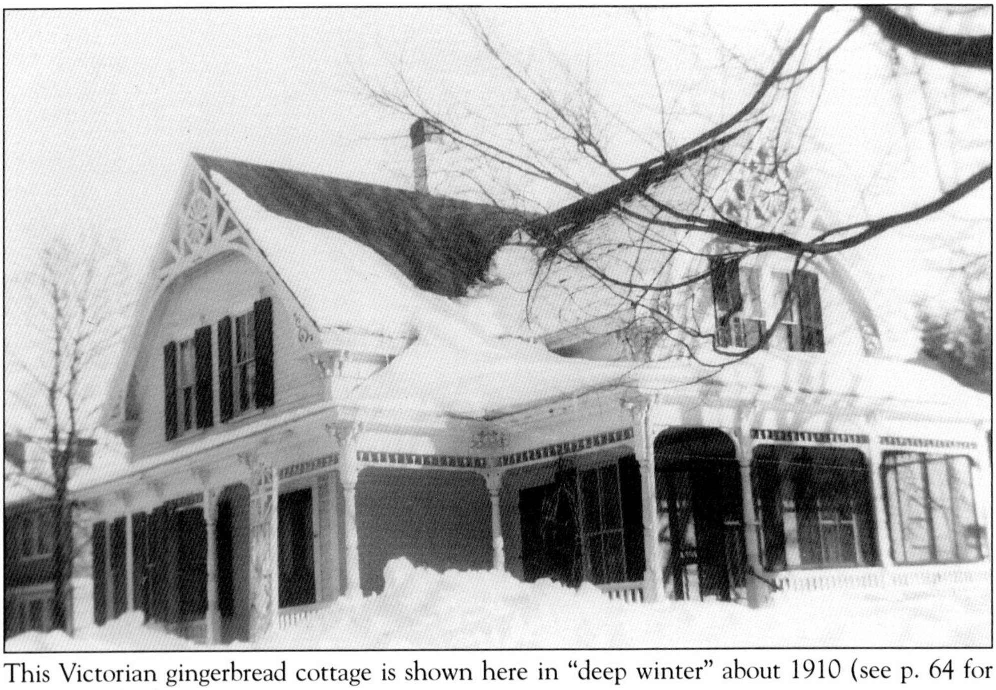

This Victorian gingerbread cottage is shown here in "deep winter" about 1910 (see p. 64 for a warmer view).

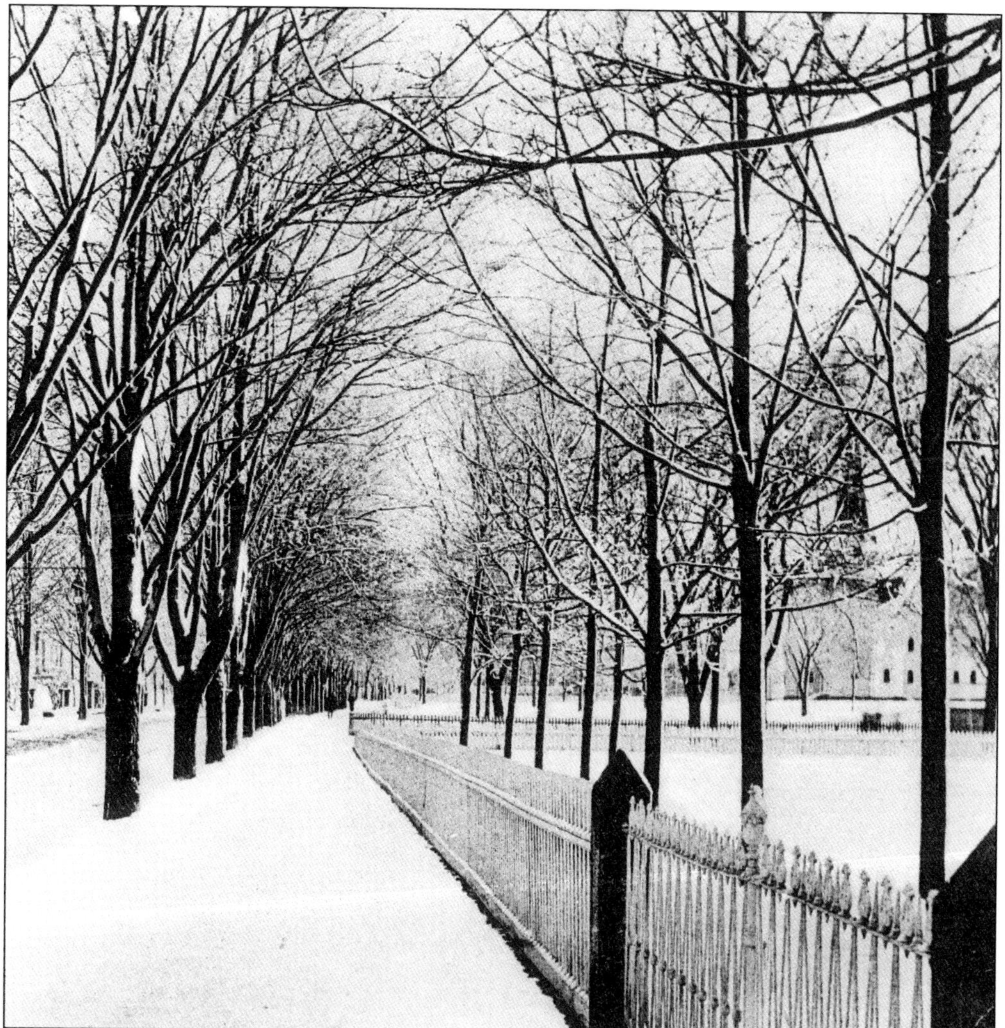

Main Street is shown here deep in the winter of 1913. This postcard picturing the Grace Universalist Church and the fence at Dean Academy was sent to Mr. D.D. Willis in El Paso, Texas. It must have been a chilling reminder of life back home.

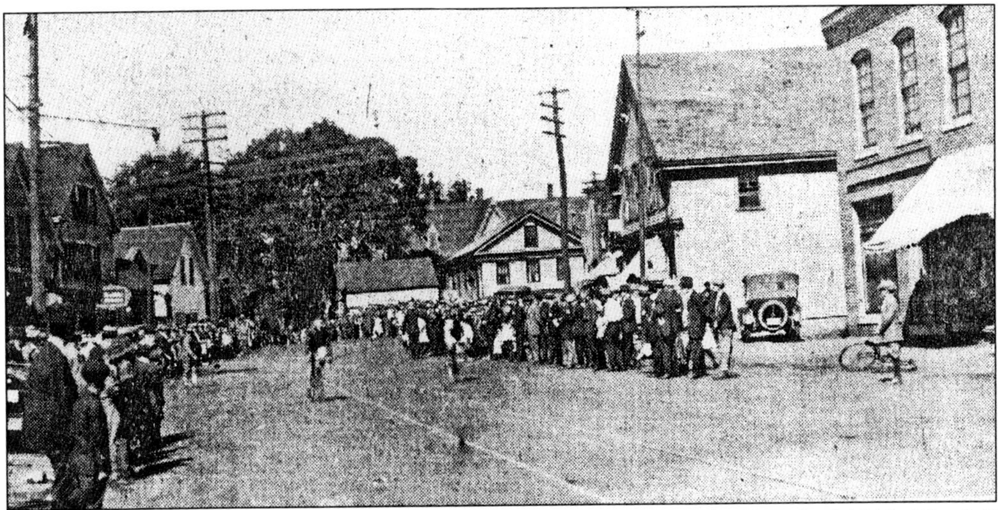

Here we are on Main Street in sweet springtime for the "Great Bike Race" of 1915. The full cycle of the seasons is now complete.

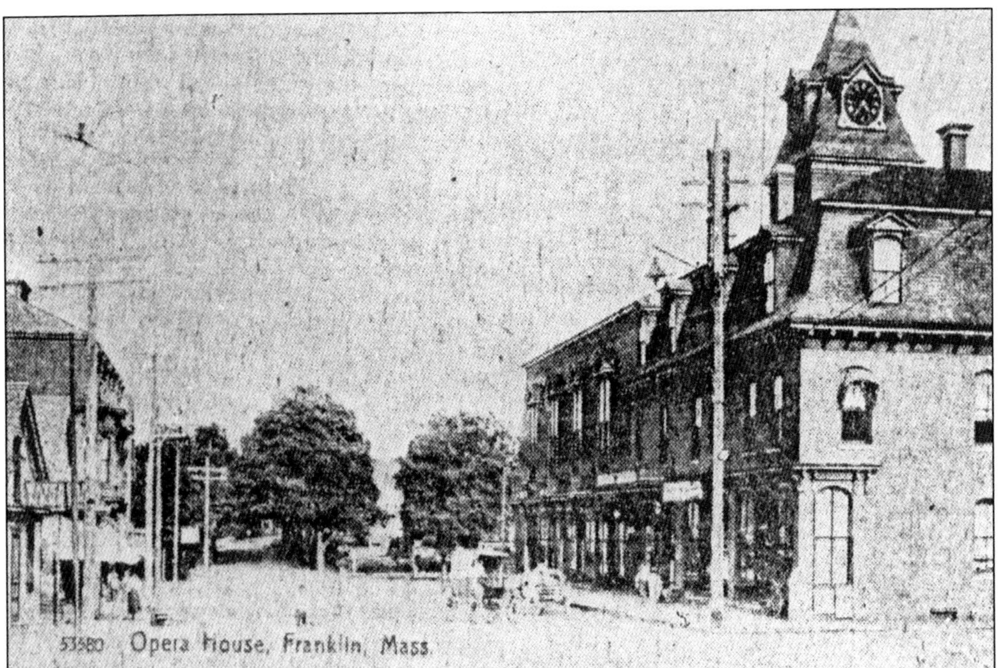


The Franklin Opera House is shown here in the summer of 1907.

# *Twelve*

# The Lost Empire of Wadsworth

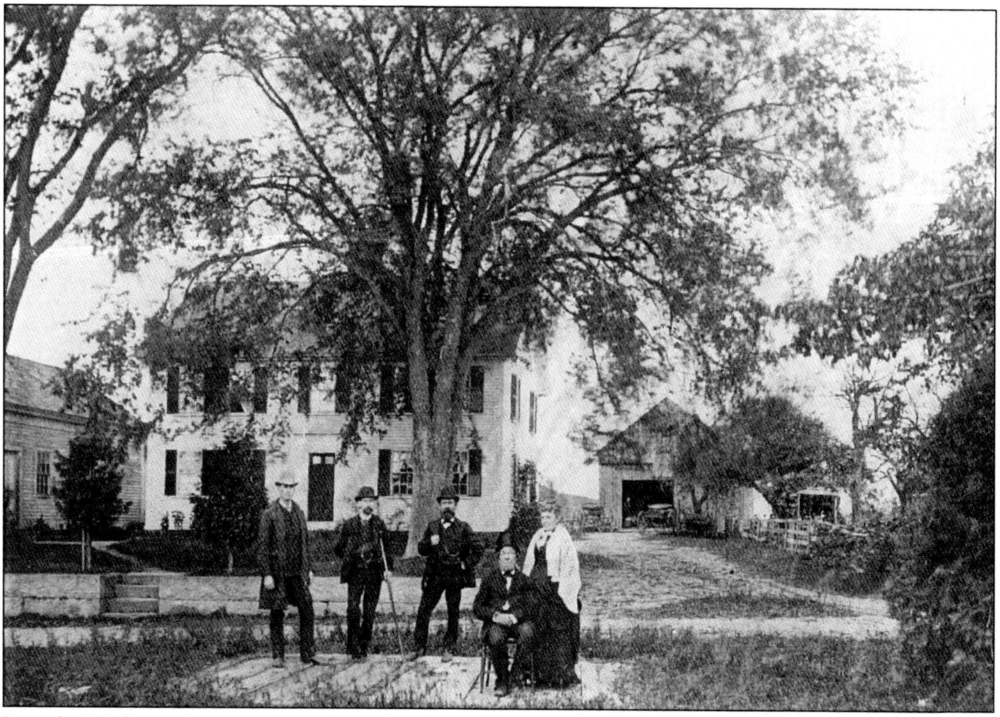

Joseph Wadsworth, seated in the splendor of his top hat and broadcloth suit, ruled over the "Empire of Wadsworth" in the south of Franklin. He held sway over acres of farmland and orchards, the Wadsworth General Store and Railroad Station, the Wadsworth Post Office, and other enterprises, including shipping freight and lodging tourists. In 1906, a disastrous fire wiped everything out. These photographs were provided through the kindness of Mr. Melvin and Alice Root.

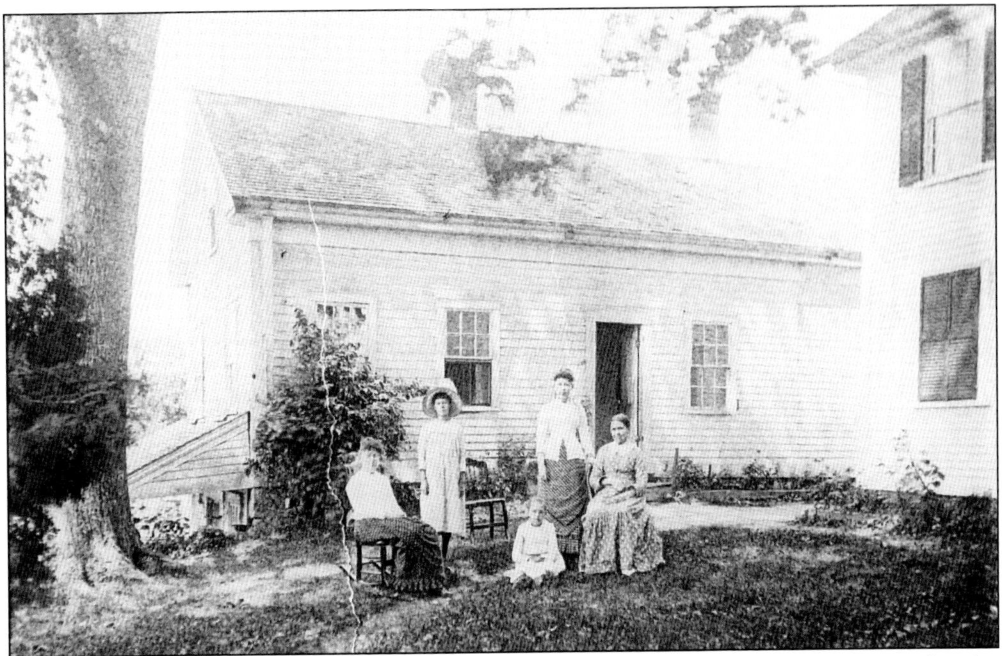

The Wadsworth women take time out from their fourteen-hour workday to pose for the camera about 1902.

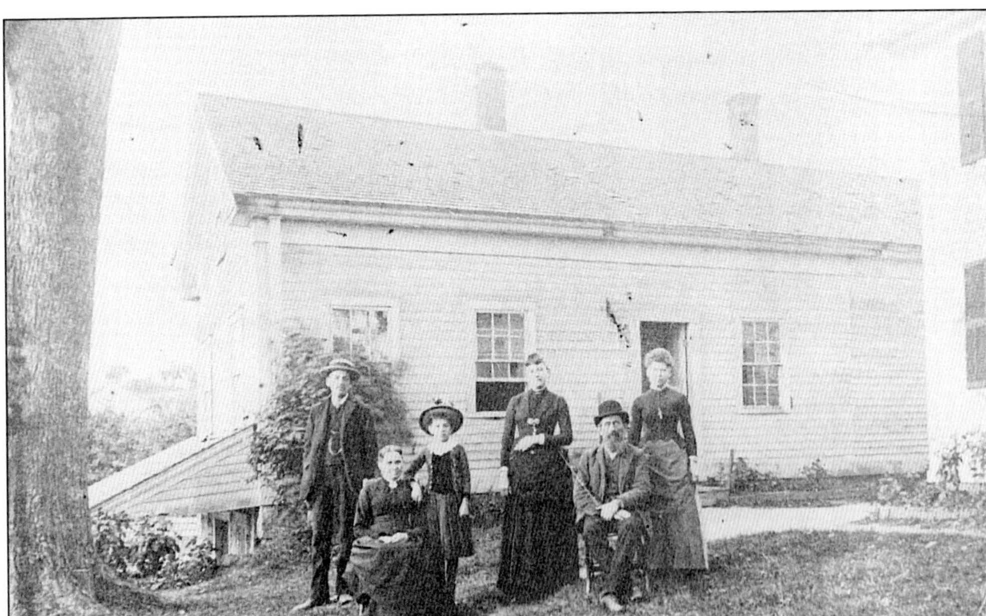

Joseph Wadsworth poses here for the camera, in his derby and the clothes he wore during the work week, about 1902.

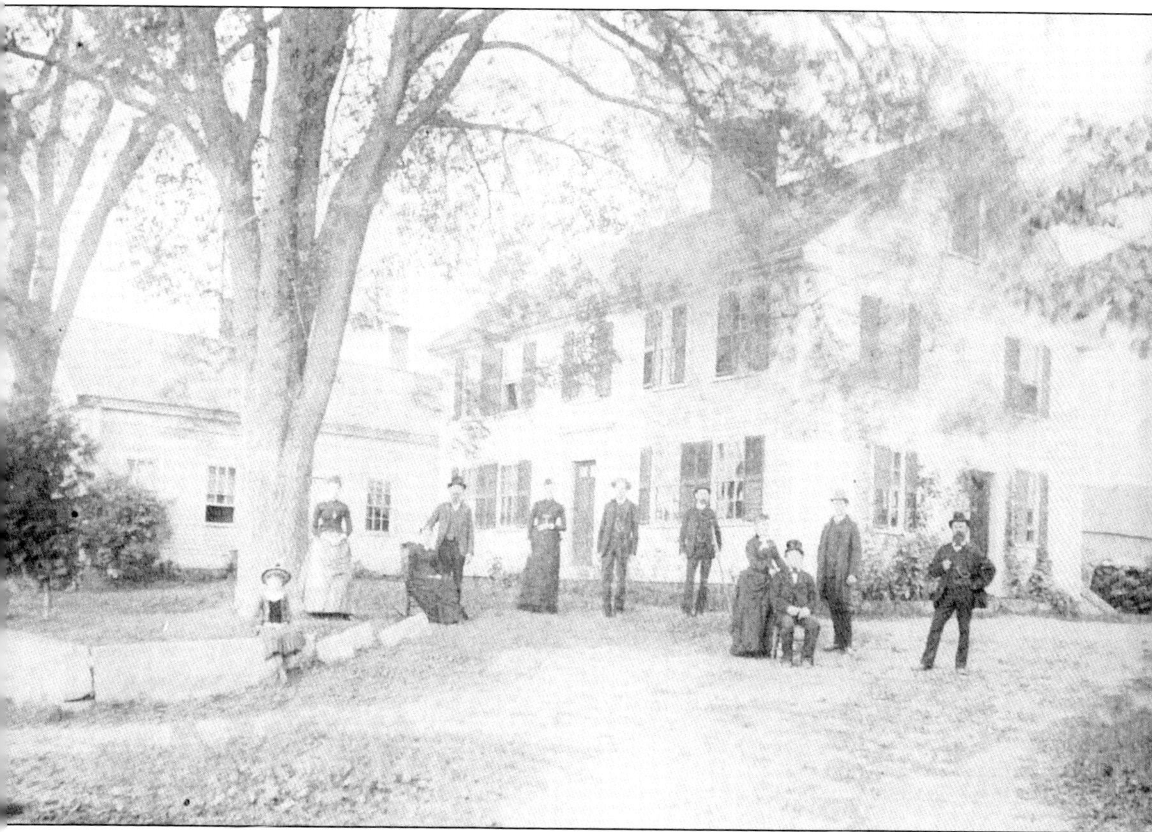

Joseph Wadsworth is shown here with his family in front of his large and comfortable house When a train was held up by misadventure in Norwood, he sent his freight wagons to the stranded passengers loaded with apples to sell them. Joseph never missed the chance to make the odd dollar. Some of the travelers to returned to Franklin on the wagons, for a price, and were boarded at the Wadsworth Estate.

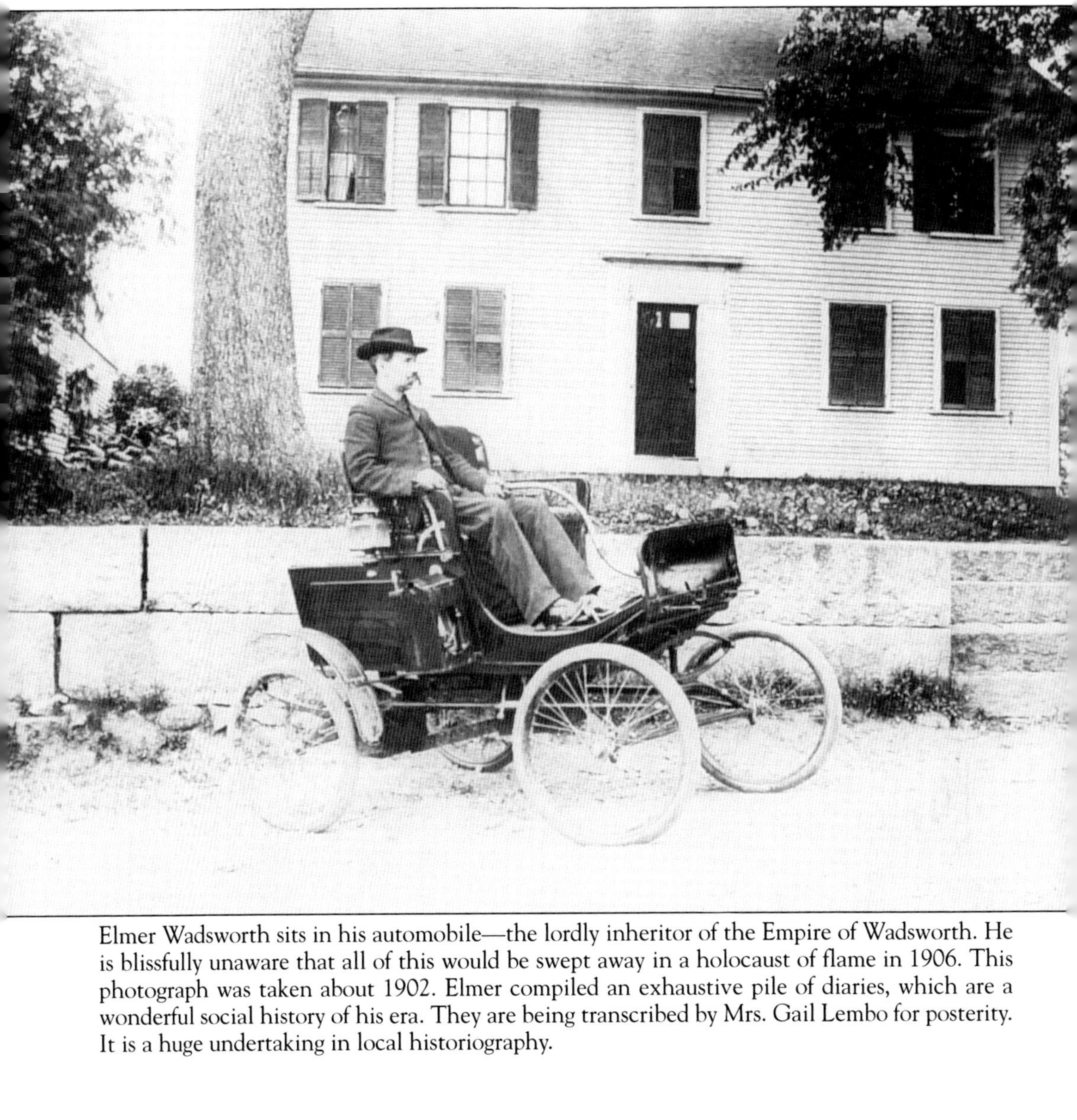

Elmer Wadsworth sits in his automobile—the lordly inheritor of the Empire of Wadsworth. He is blissfully unaware that all of this would be swept away in a holocaust of flame in 1906. This photograph was taken about 1902. Elmer compiled an exhaustive pile of diaries, which are a wonderful social history of his era. They are being transcribed by Mrs. Gail Lembo for posterity. It is a huge undertaking in local historiography.

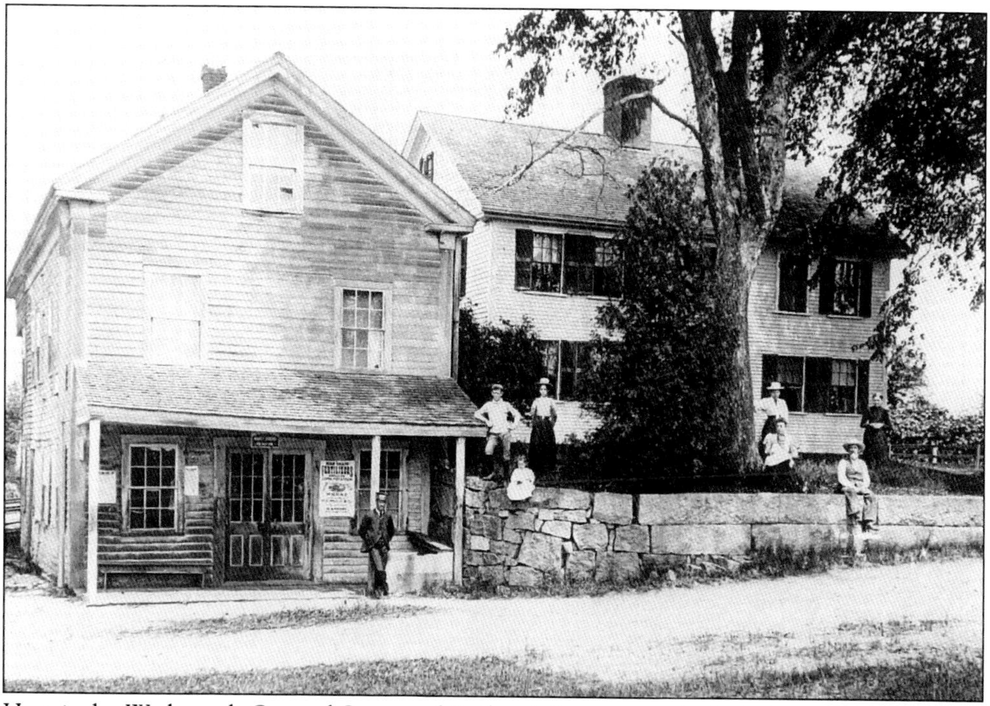

Here is the Wadsworth General Store and Railroad Station as it looked about 1902. Note the station master in his cap leaning against the porch.

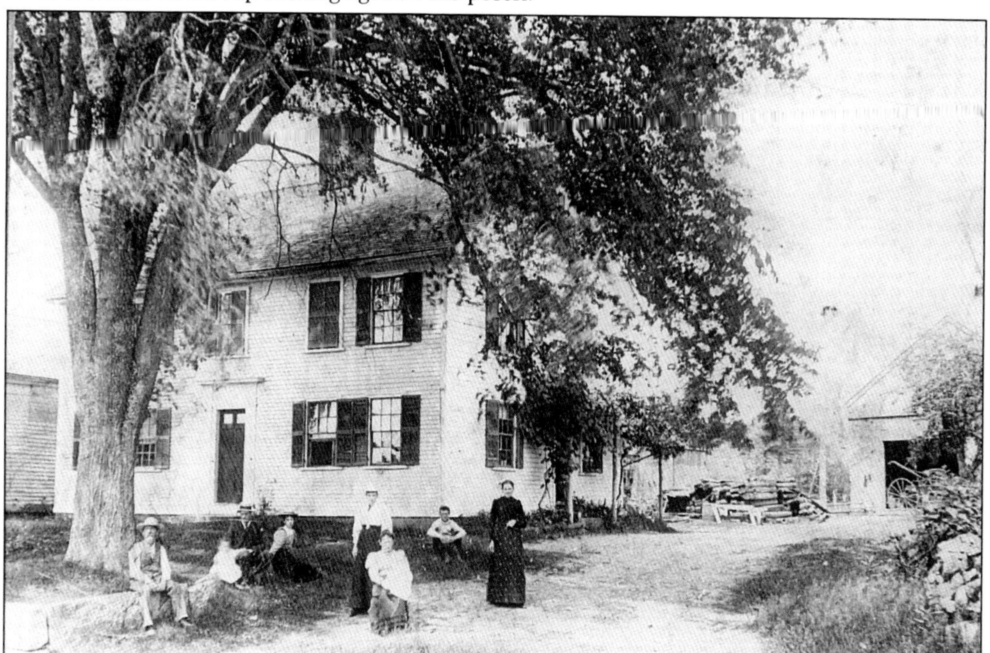

The Wadsworths employed a number of young people as seasonal labor. Local families with such old Franklin names such as Newell and Miller had children who worked their first jobs for wages for the Wadsworths. Joseph (relaxing in his shirtsleeves on a wall of cut granite) is among this group, photographed about 1902.

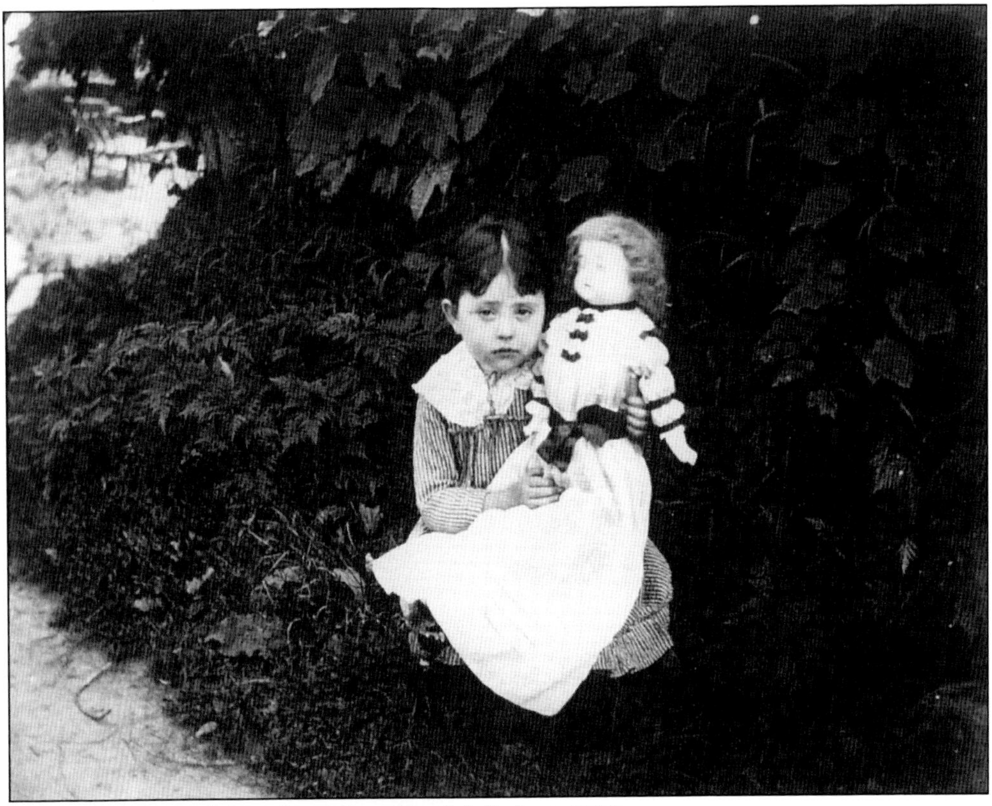

Little Annie Daniels hugs her China Head doll about 1890.

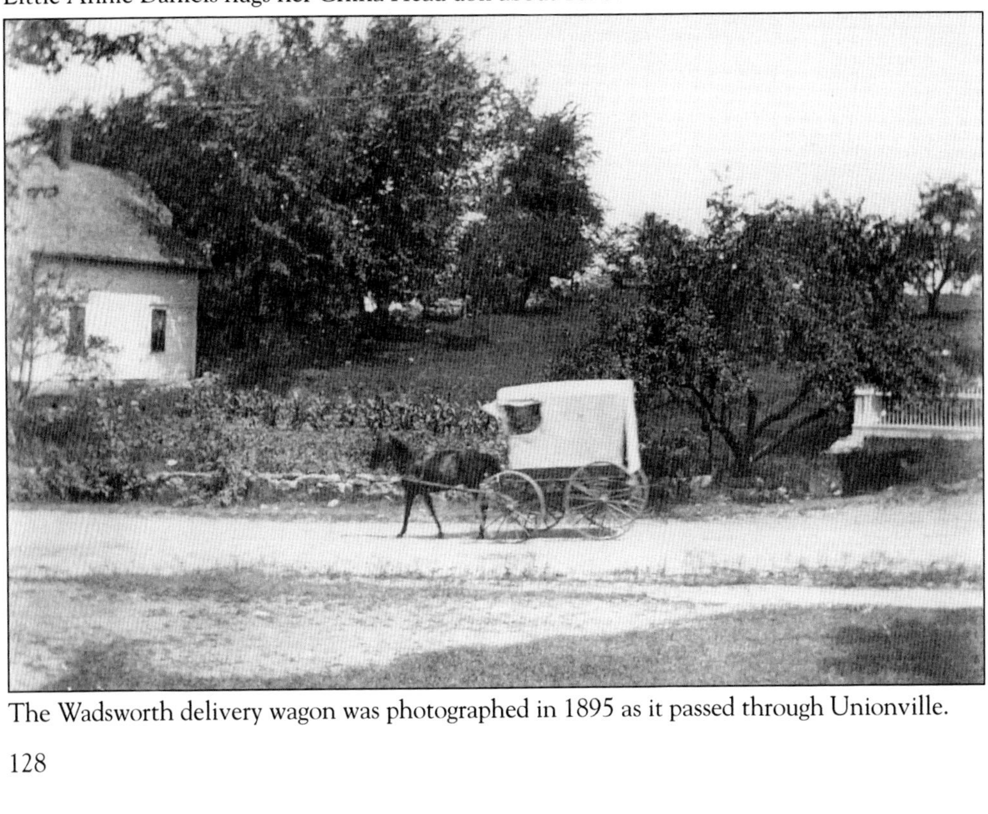

The Wadsworth delivery wagon was photographed in 1895 as it passed through Unionville.